The Best of MasterChef

MASTER
CHEF

The Best of
MasterChef

General Editor: Janet Illsley

EBURY PRESS
LONDON

This book is dedicated with gratitude to all of the MasterChef contestants.

1 3 5 7 9 10 8 6 4 2

First published in the United Kingdom in 1997 by Ebury Press,
Random House, 20 Vauxhall Bridge Road, London SW1V 2SA

Random House Australia (Pty) Limited
20 Alfred Street, Milsons Point, Sydney,
New South Wales 2061, Australia

Random House New Zealand Limited
18 Poland Road, Glenfield
Auckland 10, New Zealand

Random House South Africa (Pty) Limited
Endulini, 5A Jubilee Road, Parktown 2193, South Africa

Random House UK Limited Reg. No. 954009

A CIP catalogue record for this book is available from the British Library

ISBN: 0 09 185306 0

MasterChef
A Union Pictures production for BBC North

Series devised by Franc Roddam
Executive Producers: Bradley Adams and Richard Kalms
Producer and Director: Richard Bryan
Associate Producer: Glynis Robertson
Production Co-ordinator: Julia Park

General Editor: Janet Illsley
Design: Clive Dorman

Typeset in Garamond by Clive Dorman & Co.
Printed and bound in Great Britain by Mackays of Chatham plc, Kent.

Papers used by Ebury Press are natural recyclable products made from wood grown in sustainable forests.

Contents

Cookery Notes

- All recipes serve 4.
- Both metric and imperial measures are given for the recipes. Follow one set of measurements only, not a combination, because they are not interchangeable.
- All spoon measures are level unless otherwise stated.
- Use fresh herbs unless otherwise suggested.
- Ovens must be preheated to the specified temperature. Grills should also be preheated.
- Size 2 eggs should be used except where otherwise specified. Free-range eggs are recommended.
- Stocks should be freshly made if possible. Alternatively buy good quality ready-made stock.

Soups & Starters

Light Crab Bisque

1 cooked crab, weighing about 700 g (1½ lb)
60 ml (4 tbsp) olive oil
1 stick celery, sliced
1 small onion, chopped
1 leek, diced
1 carrot, diced
60 ml (4 tbsp) sherry
450 g (1 lb) tomatoes, chopped
½ bottle medium white wine
300 ml (½ pint) water
pinch of saffron strands
salt and freshly ground white pepper
50 g (2 oz) plain flour
50 g (2 oz) butter, softened
parsley or chervil sprigs, to garnish

1 Scrub the crab thoroughly under cold water to rid it of any remaining grit. Discard the inedible dead man's fingers and stomach sac from the crab (if not already done). Break off the claws and extract all of the white meat. Using a teaspoon, scoop out into separate bowls the white and dark meat from the shell. Break the shell into pieces and reserve.

2 Heat the olive oil in a large pan, add the celery, onion, leek and carrot and sauté until softened. Add the pieces of crab shell and sauté for 2 minutes. Add the sherry and allow it to evaporate. Add the tomatoes, wine, water, brown crabmeat and saffron and bring to the boil. Reduce the heat and simmer for 45 minutes.

3 Strain through a fine sieve into a clean saucepan, pressing hard to extract all of the juices. Bring back to the boil and season with salt and pepper to taste. Blend the flour into the softened butter to make a beurre manie and gradually whisk into the bisque, a piece at a time, until slightly thickened.

4 To serve, divide the white crabmeat between warmed soup plates, then pour on the bisque. Garnish with sprigs of parsley or chervil.

Elaine Bates

Oxtail Soup with Herb Dumplings

15 ml (1 tbsp) butter
900 g (2 lb) oxtail, in 2.5 cm (1 inch) pieces
2 onions, diced
1 small clove garlic, crushed
1 thyme sprig
1 bay leaf
salt and freshly ground black pepper
½ bottle red wine
900 ml (1½ pints) beef stock
30 ml (2 tbsp) Madeira

Herb Dumplings:
110 g (4 oz) shredded suet
225 g (8 oz) self-raising flour
large pinch of salt
1 egg, beaten
60-90 ml (2-3 fl oz) water
300 ml (½ pint) chicken stock

To Garnish:
chopped parsley

1 Heat half of the butter in a large heavy-based saucepan or flameproof casserole. Add the oxtail and fry, turning, until browned on all sides, then remove from the pan. Add the onions and garlic to the fat remaining in the pan and fry until golden brown.

2 Return the oxtail to the pan and add the herbs, seasoning and half of the red wine. Let bubble until the wine has almost totally reduced. Add the meat stock, cover and simmer very gently over a low heat for 1½ hours.

3 Meanwhile, make the dumplings. Mix the shredded suet, flour and salt together in a bowl. Mix in the egg and sufficient water to form a fairly firm dough. Shape into 2.5 cm (1 inch) balls.

4 Add the Madeira to the soup and simmer for a further 15-30 minutes until the meat starts to fall from the bone.

5 Meanwhile, bring the chicken stock to the boil in a saucepan. Add the dumplings, lower the heat, cover and simmer for approximately 20 minutes until they are light and fluffy.

6 About 5 minutes before the end of cooking, transfer the dumplings from the stock to the soup, using a slotted spoon. Ladle the soup and dumplings into warmed bowls. Garnish with chopped parsley to serve.

Amanda Farnese

Wood Pigeon Consommé served in a Gourd

1 wood pigeon, about 225 g (8 oz)
4 small gourds or squash

Consommé:
½ chicken carcass (including wings, neck and legs, but not the breast, heart or liver)
125 g (4 oz) shin of beef, trimmed of fat
1 large carrot, finely chopped
1 leek, finely chopped
2 celery sticks, finely chopped
1.25 ml (¼ tsp) salt
freshly ground black pepper

Caramel:
25 g (1 oz) sugar

Vegetables:
2 white cabbage leaves
1 small courgette

To Garnish:
assorted salad leaves
snipped chives

1 Cut the breasts off the wood pigeon, remove the skin and set aside.

2 To make the consommé, break the wood pigeon and chicken carcasses into pieces and place in a large pan. Chop the beef and add to the pan together with the remaining consommé ingredients and about 1.75 litres (3 pints) cold water. Bring slowly to the boil, cover and simmer for 3 hours, skimming occasionally. Allow to cool and chill until the fat solidifies on the surface; remove the fat. Strain through a muslin-lined sieve to obtain a clear broth.

3 To prepare the gourds, cut a slice from the base of each one so that it will stand flat. Cut off the tops and reserve for the lids. Carefully scoop out the seeds and flesh, leaving a 2 cm (¾ inch) outer shell. Rinse the insides with hot water, drain and set aside.

4 Pour the consommé into a pan and bring to the boil. Cut the wood pigeon breasts into thin strips and add to the consommé. Simmer gently for 10 minutes.

5 Meanwhile prepare the caramel. Put the sugar in a small heavy-based pan and heat gently until dissolved, then cook for 5 minutes without stirring, until caramelised to a dark golden brown colour. Very carefully add 120 ml (4 fl oz) boiling water (the mixture will splutter) and bring to the boil, stirring, to melt the caramel. Add the caramel to the consommé to impart colour.

6 To prepare the vegetables, fold the cabbage leaves and cut the courgette into thin strips retaining the skin. Using a corrugated cutter, cut small decorative shapes from these vegetables. Add to the consommé and simmer for 2 minutes. Check the seasoning.

7 Just before serving, fill the gourds with boiling water and leave to stand for 1 minute to warm through. Arrange the salad leaves on individual serving plates. Drain the gourds and place one on each plate. Fill with the hot consommé, making sure each serving has a portion of meat strips and vegetable slivers. Sprinkle with snipped chives and replace the gourd lids. Serve at once.

Derek Johns

Parsnip and Coriander Soup

45 ml (3 tbsp) olive oil
1 medium onion, finely chopped
2 cloves garlic, finely chopped
700 g (1½ lb) parsnips, peeled, cored and diced
5 ml (1 tsp) turmeric
5 ml (1 tsp) ground cinnamon
30 ml (2 tbsp) chopped fresh coriander leaves
5 ml (1 tsp) ground coriander
1.2 litres (2 pints) vegetable stock
salt and freshly ground black pepper
120 ml (4 fl oz) creamed coconut

To Finish:
desiccated coconut for sprinkling
40 ml (8 tsp) yogurt
coriander leaves

1 Heat the oil in a large saucepan and fry the onion and garlic for a few minutes until tender. Add the parsnips, turmeric, cinnamon, chopped coriander leaves and ground coriander. Cook for 2 minutes, stirring all the time to ensure that the parsnips are thoroughly coated in all the flavourings.

2 Add the vegetable stock and bring to the boil. Lower the heat, cover and simmer for about 10-15 minutes until the parsnips are tender.

3 Remove from the heat and purée in a blender or food processor until smooth. Season generously with salt and pepper.

4 Return the soup to the pan and stir in the creamed coconut over a low heat.

5 Ladle the soup into warmed serving bowls and sprinkle with a little desiccated coconut. Swirl 10 ml (2 tsp) natural yogurt on top of each portion and sprinkle with coriander leaves to serve.

Nicholas Pound

Cauliflower and White Stilton Soup

50 g (2 oz) butter
225 g (8 oz) cauliflower florets
125 g (4 oz) onion, finely chopped
125 g (4 oz) leeks, finely chopped
125 g (4 oz) celery, finely chopped
50 g (2 oz) potatoes, finely chopped
50 g (2 oz) plain flour
1 bouquet garni (bay leaf, thyme and peppercorns)
600 ml (1 pint) vegetable stock
450 ml (¾ pint) milk
175 g (6 oz) white Stilton cheese
150 ml (¼ pint) double cream
freshly ground black pepper
30 ml (2 tbsp) yogurt
15 ml (1 tbsp) chopped parsley

1 Melt the butter in a large heavy-based pan. Add the cauliflower, onion, leeks, celery and potatoes, cover and sweat until transparent but not coloured. Stir in the flour and cook gently for 5 minutes.

2 Add the bouquet garni, stock and milk. Cover and simmer for about 30 minutes. Remove the bouquet garni.

3 Crumble the Stilton cheese and add to the soup, stirring until melted, then stir in the cream. Season with pepper to taste; salt is unnecessary.

4 Divide between warmed soup plates and swirl in the yogurt. Sprinkle with chopped parsley and serve immediately, with hot toast or warm crusty bread.

Juliette Forden

Note: There is no need to add salt to this soup because Stilton cheese is quite salty and therefore provides sufficient.

Marrow and Cumin Soup

2 medium potatoes, about 225 g (8 oz) total weight
salt and freshly ground black pepper
1 small marrow, or 450 g (1 lb) courgettes
10 ml (2 tsp) cumin seeds
150 ml (¼ pint) soured cream
chopped parsley, for sprinkling

1 Peel the potatoes, place in a saucepan and cover with plenty of salted water.

2 Peel and core the marrow or courgettes, cut into pieces and put into a steamer. Tie the cumin seeds in a square of muslin and add to the marrow.

3 Place the steamer on top of the saucepan of potatoes. Bring to the boil and simmer for about 20 minutes until the potatoes are tender and the marrow is softened. Discard the cumin.

4 Transfer the marrow or courgettes and potatoes to a blender or food processor and add 600 ml (1 pint) of the cooking water. Work until smooth, then return the soup to the pan. Reheat gently.

5 Divide between warmed soup bowls and top each serving with a generous swirl of soured cream and a sprinkling of parsley. Serve at once, accompanied by warm crusty bread.

Ann Neale

Cream of Watercress Soup

4 bunches of watercress
50 g (2 oz) butter
1 onion, finely chopped
2 cloves garlic, crushed
50 g (2 oz) plain flour
600 ml (1 pint) chicken stock
600 ml (1 pint) milk
salt and freshly ground black pepper
1.25 ml (¼ tsp) freshly grated nutmeg
juice of ½ lemon
150 ml (¼ pint) single cream
watercress sprigs, to garnish

1 Trim the watercress, discarding the tough stalks, then chop roughly.

2 Melt the butter in a saucepan and gently fry the onion and garlic until soft. Reduce the heat and stir in the flour. Gradually add the stock and milk, stirring all the time.

3 Stir in the chopped watercress, salt, pepper, nutmeg and lemon juice. Simmer gently for 5 minutes. Don't worry if it appears to separate at this point!

4 Purée the soup in a blender or food processor until smooth, then return to the clean pan. Reheat gently; do not allow to boil. Stir in most of the cream and adjust the seasoning.

5 Pour the soup into warmed individual bowls and top each serving with a swirl of cream. Serve immediately, garnished with sprigs of watercress and accompanied by crusty bread or hot croûtons.

Rachel Southall

Note: To make croûtons, shallow-fry cubes of bread in hot oil until crisp and golden. Drain on kitchen paper.

Carrot and Coriander Soup

30 ml (2 tbsp) olive oil
1 small onion, finely chopped
1 clove garlic, crushed
450 g (1 lb) carrots, chopped
5 ml (1 tsp) crushed coriander seeds
5 ml (1 tsp) ground coriander
900 ml (1½ pints) vegetable stock
salt and freshly ground black pepper
15 ml (1 tbsp) chopped coriander leaves
coriander leaves, to garnish

1 Heat the olive oil in a pan, add the onion and garlic and sauté until softened. Add the carrots and cook gently for 10 minutes.

2 Add the crushed coriander seeds and ground coriander and cook for a further 2 minutes.

3 Pour in the vegetable stock, bring to the boil, then cover and simmer for 15 minutes.

4 Purée the soup in a food processor or blender until smooth, then return to the pan. Season with salt and pepper to taste and reheat gently. Stir in the chopped coriander.

5 Pour the soup into warmed individual bowls and garnish with coriander leaves. Serve with warm bread or croûtons.

Tricia Humber

Creamy Lemon Grass and Basil Soup with Seafood

24 large raw prawns
16 green-lipped mussels (thawed if frozen)
40 g (1½ oz) butter
75 g (3 oz) shallot, finely chopped
1 clove garlic, crushed
300 ml (½ pint) dry white wine
3 lemon grass stalks, bruised
1 kaffir lime leaf
15-30 ml (1-2 tbsp) lemon juice, to taste
300 ml (½ pint) single cream
30 ml (2 tbsp) shredded basil leaves
2 rashers sweet-cured back bacon, derinded and chopped
2 egg yolks
salt and freshly ground black pepper

Garlic Croûtes:
50 g (2 oz) butter
1 clove garlic, crushed
4-6 slices French bread
30 ml (2 tbsp) finely chopped basil

1 Shell and de-vein the prawns, reserving the shells.

2 To make the stock, melt 25 g (1 oz) of the butter in a saucepan, add the prawn shells and fry until pink. Add half of the chopped shallot with the garlic and cook until translucent. Add 300 ml (½ pint) water, the wine, lemon grass and kaffir lime leaf. Bring to the boil, reduce the heat and simmer for 30 minutes. Strain the stock and adjust the flavour with lemon juice.

3 Meanwhile prepare the garlic croûtes. Melt the butter in a pan, add the garlic and cook until softened. Add the bread slices and fry until golden on both sides; drain on kitchen paper. Toss in the chopped basil and keep warm.

4 Bring the stock to the boil in a large pan. Add the prawns and cook until just pink, about 2-3 minutes. Remove with a slotted spoon and set aside. Add the mussels to the stock, heat through, then remove and set aside. Add the cream and shredded basil and simmer for 2-3 minutes. Meanwhile, cook the remaining shallot and the bacon in the rest of the butter until tender.

5 To serve, add the onion and bacon to the soup, with the prawns and mussels. Heat through, then transfer the seafood to warmed soup plates. Off the heat, work the egg yolks into the soup. Season with salt and pepper to taste and ladle the soup over the seafood. Serve immediately, with the garlic croûtes.

Gillian Humphrey

Spicy Butternut Squash and Apple Soup

40 g (1½ oz) butter
1 onion, finely chopped
1 large clove garlic, crushed
700 g (1½ lb) butternut squash, peeled, seeded and cut into chunks
3 Granny Smith apples, peeled, cored and cut into chunks
750 ml (1¼ pints) chicken stock
5-10 ml (1-2 tsp) ground cumin
salt and freshly ground black pepper
60 ml (4 tbsp) crème fraîche

To Garnish:
1 red apple, quartered, cored and sliced

1 Melt the butter in a heavy-based saucepan, add the onion and sauté until soft. Add the garlic and sauté for a further 2 minutes.

2 Add the butternut squash, apple and chicken stock. Bring to the boil, lower the heat and simmer for about 15 minutes, until the squash is tender. Stir in the cumin and salt and pepper to taste.

3 Using a blender or food processor, purée the soup in batches until smooth, transfering the puréed soup to a clean saucepan.

4 Heat through, then divide the soup between warmed soup bowls. Add a spoonful of crème fraîche to each portion and garnish with the apple slices.

Holly Schade

Note: If butternut squash is unobtainable, try using pumpkin or another variety of squash instead.

Oysters with Raspberry Sauce

16 oysters
25 g (1 oz) shallots, finely chopped
50 g (2 oz) unsalted butter
15 ml (1 tbsp) raspberry vinegar
15 ml (1 tbsp) raspberry purée
30 ml (2 tbsp) double cream
30 ml (2 tbsp) medium dry white wine
salt and freshly ground white pepper
50 g (2 oz) fine French beans
25 g (1 oz) mushrooms, finely chopped

To Garnish:
coarse sea salt
raspberries

1 Open the oysters over a bowl to collect the juice. Lay the oysters on kitchen paper and set aside. Strain the juice.

2 Gently fry the shallots in a little of the butter until soft, but not coloured. Add the oyster juice, vinegar and raspberry purée. Cook over a high heat until reduced and syrupy. Add the cream and wine. Let the sauce bubble briefly, then remove from the heat and beat in the rest of the butter, a little at a time. Adjust the seasoning.

3 Cut the French beans into 1 cm (½ inch) lengths and boil until tender but still crisp; drain. Refresh under cold water, drain and cut into julienne. Set aside half of the beans for garnish; add the rest to the sauce.

4 Boil the empty deeper halves of the oyster shells to clean and warm them. Set the shells on warmed plates lined with sea salt.

5 Add the chopped mushrooms and oysters to the sauce and place over a medium heat. As soon as the sauce starts to tremble, spoon into the oyster shells. Garnish with the julienne of French beans and raspberries to serve.

Amita Baldock

Oysters au Gratin

12 oysters, scrubbed clean
100 ml (3½ fl oz) dry white wine
1 carrot, sliced
1 stick celery, sliced
15 ml (1 tbsp) lemon juice
100 ml (3½ fl oz) single cream
2 egg yolks
salt and freshly ground black pepper
30 ml (2 tbsp) grated mozzarella cheese

To Serve:
45 ml (3 tbsp) rock salt
lemon wedges
herb sprigs

1 Put the oysters on a baking tray and place in a preheated oven at 180°C (350°F) mark 4 for 1-2 minutes until they open. Remove the oysters from their shells, reserving the juices. Clean out the empty shells.

2 Place the white wine, carrot, celery, lemon juice and reserved oyster juice in a saucepan and cook for 5 minutes until the vegetables are tender and the stock is reduced. Strain the stock, discarding the vegetables (they are simply used to add flavour).

3 Return the oysters to their shells and place in a baking dish. In a bowl, whisk the cream and egg yolks together, then pour on the stock, stirring. Return to the pan and cook gently over a low heat, stirring constantly, until slightly thickened. Season with salt and pepper to taste, then pour the sauce evenly over the oysters.

4 Sprinkle with the grated cheese and place under a preheated grill until melted and lighly browned. Serve the oysters, three per person, on a bed of rock salt. Garnish with lemon wedges and herb sprigs.

Betsy Anderson

Lightly Poached Oysters with Trompettes

1 cucumber
salt and freshly ground black pepper
24 oysters, scrubbed clean
150 g (5 oz) unsalted butter, chilled and diced
2 large shallots, finely chopped
15 ml (1 tbsp) dry white wine
5 ml (1 tsp) white wine vinegar
5 ml (1 tsp) single cream
squeeze of lime juice (optional)
15 ml (1 tbsp) oil
24 horn of plenty mushrooms (trompettes), cleaned
pinch of paprika (optional)

1 Peel the cucumber, reserving about 50 g (2 oz) of the peelings. Prepare a garnish of small lozenges, about 1 cm x 5 mm (¾ x ¼ inch), from the cucumber flesh. Sprinkle these with a little salt and freeze for 1 hour. Finely chop the cucumber peelings. Open the oysters and drain, reserving the juices; clean thoroughly.

2 Melt 5 ml (1 tsp) of the butter in a small saucepan, add the chopped cucumber peelings and shallots and sweat gently until softened. Add the wine and vinegar and allow to reduce until only 5 ml (1 tsp) of liquid remains. Reduce the heat to a minimum, then add the cream and 10 ml (2 tsp) of the reserved oyster juices.

3 Gradually whisk in the butter, a piece at a time, on and off the heat, until it is all incorporated. Purée in a blender or food processor until smooth, then pass through a fine sieve into a small jug. Season with salt and pepper, and add a squeeze of lime juice if desired. Keep warm by placing the jug in a bowl of warm water.

4 Rinse the cucumber garnish and warm gently in a bowl over a pan of hot water.

5 Heat the oil in a sauté pan, add the mushrooms and sauté gently until softened.

6 Heat the rest of the oyster juices in a shallow pan. When the juices are very hot, add the oysters and poach for 3 seconds only. Remove with a slotted spoon and drain.

7 To assemble, place a spoonful of the beurre blanc in the centre of each warmed serving plate and arrange 6 oysters on top. Interleave the oysters with trompettes and garnish with the cucumber lozenges and a pinch of paprika if desired.

Ross Burden

Skewered Oysters and Scallops with a Sweet Pepper Sauce

8 oysters
8 scallops (4 with corals), cleaned
6 rashers of thin-cut back bacon
2 red peppers
1 yellow pepper
1 orange pepper
10 small shallots, blanched for 2 minutes and peeled
5 ml (1 tsp) sugar
75 ml (5 tbsp) Muscadet or other dry white wine
8 cloves garlic, peeled
15-30 ml (1-2 tbsp) olive oil
1 onion, thinly sliced
1 thyme sprig, leaves only

To Garnish:
thyme sprigs

1 Remove the oysters from their shells and carefully roll a piece of bacon round each one. Thread the oysters and scallops alternately onto 4 kebab skewers, allowing 2 oysters and 2 scallops per skewer. Finish each skewer with a scallop coral. Set aside in a cool place until required.

2 Halve, core and deseed the peppers, then cut each one into 1 cm (½ inch) strips. Cut 8 diamond shapes from the yellow pepper, 8 from the orange pepper, and 16 from the red ones. Set aside.

3 To make the sauce, chop the remaining red pepper flesh and two of the shallots. Place in a saucepan with 2.5 ml (½ tsp) sugar and the wine. Cook for 10-15 minutes until tender, then work in a food processor or blender until smooth, and pass through a sieve.

4 Chop the remaining rashers of bacon and fry in a non-stick pan without additional fat until crisp. Remove with a slotted spoon and set aside. Sauté the garlic and the whole shallots in the bacon fat remaining in the pan until golden, adding a little olive oil if needed.

5 Heat 15 ml (1 tbsp) olive oil in another frying pan, add the sliced onion with the thyme and remaining 2.5 ml (½ tsp) sugar; cook until soft. Add the pepper diamonds and cook until softened. Add the bacon strips and keep warm.

6 Cook the kebabs under a preheated hot grill for 5-6 minutes, turning once or twice. Meanwhile, reheat the pepper sauce.

7 To serve, spread a pool of red pepper sauce on each warmed plate. Spoon the onions and pepper diamonds to one side, garnishing with the shallots and garlic. Mark a criss-cross pattern on each scallop with a hot metal skewer and place the kebabs on the sauce. Garnish with thyme and serve at once.

Marion MacFarlane

Mussels in Mildly Spiced Coconut Sauce

1.75 kg (4 lb) mussels
65 g (2½ oz) unsalted butter
175 g (6 oz) shallots, finely chopped
2 cloves garlic, crushed
2.5 cm (1 inch) piece fresh root ginger, grated
1.25 ml (¼ tsp) turmeric
5 ml (1 tsp) ground cumin
250 ml (8 fl oz) coconut milk (fresh or canned)
250 ml (8 fl oz) chicken stock
salt and freshly ground pepper
15 ml (1 tbsp) chopped coriander leaves

1 Scrub the mussels thoroughly in cold water, discarding any that are damaged or open.

2 Heat 15 ml (1 tbsp) butter in a pan, and fry the shallots until they become translucent. Add the garlic, ginger, turmeric and cumin and fry over moderate heat, stirring continuously, for 5 minutes to thoroughly cook the spices. Add the coconut milk, stock and seasoning. Bring to the boil, then simmer until the sauce has reduced by a third.

3 Strain the sauce into a large pan. Add the mussels, cover and cook over moderate heat for 4 minutes or until the shells open; discard any unopened mussels. Remove the mussels from the sauce with a slotted spoon and keep warm.

4 Strain the sauce and reduce over a high heat until it becomes slightly syrupy. Remove from the heat, then whisk in the remaining butter in pieces, a little at a time.

5 Remove the empty upper shell from each mussel and put the mussels into warmed soup bowls. Pour the desired amount of sauce over the mussels and sprinkle with coriander to serve.

Amita Baldock

Mussels with Rouille

24-32 mussels in shells
600 ml (1 pint) dry white wine (approximately)
30 ml (2 tbsp) finely chopped shallots

Rouille:
5 cm (2 inch) piece of French loaf
pinch of saffron threads
4 cloves garlic, crushed
1 egg yolk
90 ml (6 tbsp) olive oil
5 ml (1 tsp) paprika
large pinch of cayenne pepper
salt and freshly ground black pepper

To Serve:
selection of salad leaves (eg frisée, lamb's lettuce, oakleaf lettuce)
herb sprigs (eg coriander, parsley, snipped chives)
a little extra-virgin olive oil

1 Soak the mussels in a large bowl of cold salted water with a tablespoonful of flour or oatmeal added for about 2 hours to help rid them of grit. Scrub the shells clean and pull off each beard. Discard any mussels which remain open on being sharply tapped against a hard surface.

2 Place the mussels in a large pan and pour in enough wine to cover. Add the shallots, cover and bring to the boil. Cook over a high heat for about 5 minutes, just until the shells open. Remove from the heat and discard any mussels which remain closed; drain. Strain and reserve 90 ml (6 tbsp) cooking liquor. Allow the mussels to cool, then cover and chill in the refrigerator.

3 To make the rouille, cut the bread into small cubes and place in a bowl with the saffron threads. Pour on the reserved mussel cooking liquor and leave to soak for 10 minutes.

4 Meanwhile, put the crushed garlic into a blender or food processor with the egg yolk. With the machine running, add the oil, drop by drop, as if you were making mayonnaise. When the mixture thickens, pour onto the soaked bread and mix well. Season with the paprika, cayenne and salt and pepper to taste.

5 To serve, toss the salad leaves and herbs in a little olive oil until glossy, then arrange on individual serving plates. Serve the mussels on the bed of salad leaves topped with a spoonful of the rouille.

Peter Anderson

Mussels au Gratin

24-30 mussels
1 onion, chopped
few parsley sprigs
1 thyme sprig
50 g (2 oz) butter
5 ml (1 tsp) lemon juice
1 clove garlic, crushed
30 ml (2 tbsp) chopped parsley
25 g (1 oz) white breadcrumbs
25 g (1 oz) freshly grated Parmesan cheese

1 Scrub the mussels clean under running cold water and discard any with open or cracked shells.

2 Put the onion, parsley and thyme in a saucepan with 300 ml (½ pint) water and bring to the boil. Simmer, covered, for 5 minutes. Add the mussels and cook quickly, shaking the pan constantly until the shells open. Remove from the heat and discard any mussels which have not opened. Leave to cool slightly.

3 Discard the empty half shells and arrange the mussels in individual gratin dishes.

4 Melt the butter and stir in the lemon juice and garlic. Spoon the flavoured butter over the mussels and scatter over the parsley.

5 Mix the breadcrumbs and Parmesan together and sprinkle over the top. Cook under a preheated grill for about 3 minutes until golden. Serve immediately.

Sarah Giles

Warm Salad of Fragrant Mussels

1-1.4 kg (2-3 lb) mussels
2 shallots, chopped
125 ml (4 fl oz) white wine
freshly ground pepper
lemon juice to taste
2 carrots, cut into matchsticks

Sauce:
pinch of saffron
pinch of curry powder (your own blend, or bought)
90 ml (3 fl oz) double cream
40 g (1½ oz) butter, in pieces

To Finish:
1 small curly endive
45 ml (3 tbsp) finely snipped chives
pinch of garam masala (your own blend, or bought)

1 Scrub the mussels thoroughly under running cold water and remove their beards. Put the mussels on a rack in a large roasting tin. Sprinkle with the shallots and white wine and cover tightly with foil. Bake in a preheated oven at 240°C (475°F) mark 9 for 8-10 minutes, depending on size, until they open.

2 Meanwhile, blanch the carrots in boiling water for 30 seconds. Drain, rinse in cold water and drain.

3 Remove the mussels from their shells, catching the juices in the roasting tin and discarding any that have not opened. Put the mussels in a bowl, sprinkle with pepper and a little lemon juice and keep warm.

4 To make the sauce, carefully strain the mussel cooking liquid through a very fine sieve or a couple of thicknesses of muslin into a pan. Add the saffron and curry powder and reduce by half; strain again. Mix in the cream and simmer until the sauce is thick enough to just coat the back of a spoon. Swirl in the butter to thicken.

5 Roll up the curly endive and cut into fine strips. Add to the sauce with the mussels, carrots, and most of the chives. Check the seasoning and add lemon juice if wished. Keep warm but do not boil. Arrange decoratively on warmed plates, finishing with a few chives and a dusting of garam masala.

Orlando Murrin

Mussels with Blue Vinney Sauce

1.8 kg (4 lb) mussels in shells
125 g (4 oz) blue Vinney cheese, crumbled
125 ml (4 fl oz) single cream
25 g (1 oz) unsalted butter
2 leeks (white and pale green part only), finely chopped
600 ml (1 pint) dry cider
60 ml (4 tbsp) finely chopped parsley

To Serve:
Walnut Bread (see right)

1 Scrub the mussels thoroughly under cold running water, scraping off any barnacles with a sharp knife, and pulling off the 'beards' protruding from the shells. Discard any mussels with cracked shells and any which remain open when sharply tapped with the back of a knife. Set aside in a colander.

2 Put the cheese and cream in a food processor or blender and process or mash together until the cheese is well broken up.

3 Melt the butter in a large pan, add the leeks and cook gently until soft. Add the cider and bring to the boil. Tip in the mussels and cook for 3-5 minutes until the shells are open; discard any that remain closed.

4 Pour the cream and cheese mixture into the pan and stir until well amalgamated and heated through.

5 Tip the mussels and sauce into warmed large soup plates and sprinkle with the chopped parsley. Serve at once, accompanied by the Walnut Bread (see right).

Mandy Ford

Walnut Bread

This is a close-textured bread, which keeps well. Serve with Mussels with Blue Vinney Sauce (left).

300 g (10 oz) strong plain wholemeal flour
175 g (6 oz) rye flour
5 ml (1 tsp) salt
7 g (¼ oz) fresh yeast, or 5 ml (1 tsp) dried yeast
150-300 ml (¼-½ pint) warm water
50 g (2 oz) walnuts, chopped
10 ml (2 tsp) caraway seeds
15 ml (1 tbsp) walnut oil

1 Sift the flours and salt together into a mixing bowl. (If the flour is very cold put the bowl in a warm place for a few minutes.)

2 Cream the yeast with a little of the warm water in a small bowl and leave for 5 minutes in a warm place or until frothy on the surface.

3 Add the walnuts, caraway seeds and walnut oil to the flour. Now add the creamed yeast and incorporate enough warm water to make a stiff dough. Knead the dough for 5 minutes.

4 Put the dough in a bowl, cover with oiled cling film and leave in a warm place for 1½ hours; it will only rise very slightly.

5 Knead the dough again lightly, then shape into a loaf and place in a greased 900 g (2 lb) loaf tin. Leave in a warm place to prove for a further 1 hour.

6 Bake the loaf in a preheated oven at 220°C (425°F) mark 7 for approximately 45 minutes, until the loaf will turn out of the tin easily and sounds hollow when tapped on the bottom. Transfer to a wire rack. Cut into thin slices to serve.

Mandy Ford

Gingery Crab served on a bed of Sweet Pears

1 dressed crab, weighing about 1.1 kg (2½ lb), shells reserved
50 ml (2 fl oz) olive oil
25 g (1 oz) fennel leaves
4 cardamom seeds
1 clove garlic, crushed
1 thyme sprig
1 large Provençal tomato, chopped
150 ml (¼ pint) medium white wine
15 g (½ oz) fresh root ginger, finely chopped
4 ripe pears
15 g (½ oz) butter
15 ml (1 tbsp) light brown sugar
150 ml (¼ pint) whipping cream
50 g (2 oz) Parmesan cheese, freshly grated
salt and freshly ground pepper
snipped chives, to garnish

1 Heat the oil in a large saucepan, add the crab shells and cook on a high heat for 3-4 minutes. Lower the heat and add the fennel, cardamom, garlic, thyme and tomato. Cook gently for a few minutes, then add the wine and 300 ml (½ pint) water. Simmer for 30 minutes.

2 Meanwhile, heat about 150 ml (¼ pint) water in a small pan. Add the ginger and cook for about 20 minutes, until tender. Drain and reserve.

3 Strain the stock and return to a clean pan. Boil steadily to reduce to approximately 90 ml (3 fl oz). Set aside.

4 Carefully peel and core the pears, then cut each one lengthwise into 4 pieces. Place in a casserole dish with the butter, brown sugar and 150 ml (¼ pint) water. Cover and poach gently in a preheated oven at 190°C (375°F) mark 5 for about 1 hour until tender. Keep warm.

5 Place the prepared crab meat in a saucepan and heat through gently over a low heat. Keep warm.

6 Pour the concentrated stock into another pan. Add the reserved ginger, the cream and the cooking juice from the pears. Heat the sauce through over a low heat, stirring.

7 Preheat the grill to high. Arrange 4 pear segments on each of 4 flameproof serving plates. Spoon the crab meat into the middle. Place a spoonful of sauce over the crab and spread the rest around the sides. Sprinkle the Parmesan over the crab. Place under a hot grill until lightly browned. Season with salt and pepper, garnish with chives and serve immediately.

Jill O'Brien

Crab and Ginger Wontons with a Citrus Sauce

12 wonton skins

Filling:
75 g (3 oz) Dover sole fillet, skinned
1 egg
60 ml (2 fl oz) double cream
175 g (6 oz) white crab meat
7.5 ml (1½ tsp) grated fresh root ginger
7.5 ml (1½ tsp) light soy sauce
5 ml (1 tsp) rice wine
15 ml (1 tbsp) finely chopped coriander leaves
2.5 ml (½ tsp) sugar
salt and freshly ground pepper

Citrus Sauce:
300 ml (½ pint) fish stock
1 pink grapefruit, peeled and segmented
juice of 1 lemon
1.25 ml (¼ tsp) Dijon mustard
2 thin slices fresh root ginger
30 ml (2 tbsp) double cream
50 g (2 oz) unsalted butter, chilled

To Garnish:
tomato concassé (see note)
coriander leaves

1 Place the Dover sole, egg and cream in a food processor or blender and process for about 1 minute. Transfer to a bowl, add the remaining filling ingredients and mix thoroughly by hand. Check the seasoning.

2 Place a generous spoonful of the filling in the middle of each wonton skin. Bring up the sides of the wonton skin and press them down over the top of the filling. Tap the wonton on the bottom to make a flat base. The top should be wide open, exposing the filling. Put the wontons on a heatproof plate and cook in a steamer for 20-25 minutes.

3 Meanwhile, make the citrus sauce. Bring the fish stock to the boil, then add the grapefruit segments, lemon juice, mustard and ginger. Boil the sauce until it has reduced and the grapefruit segments have broken up. Press through a sieve, then add the double cream. Whisk in the butter, a little at a time, over a low heat. Adjust the seasoning.

4 To serve, pour a pool of sauce on to each serving plate. Position 3 wontons on each pool of sauce, with a little tomato concassé in the centre. Scatter coriander leaves between the wontons. Serve immediately.

Amita Baldock

Note: To prepare tomato concasseé, simply peel and deseed a few tomatoes, then finely chop the flesh.

Crab Salad with Chilli and Herb Dressing

Dressing:
5 ml (1 tsp) coriander seeds
2 star anise
4 lemon grass stalks
2 green chillis, halved and seeded
2 cloves garlic, peeled
5 cm (2 inch) piece fresh root ginger, peeled
juice of 2 limes
juice of 1 lemon (approximately)
90 ml (6 tbsp) water
90 ml (6 tbsp) olive oil
30 ml (2 tbsp) sunflower oil
90 ml (6 tbsp) Thai fish sauce (approximately)
pinch of sugar

Crab Salad:
½ cucumber
1 large or 2 small dressed crabs (white meat only)
salt and freshly ground black pepper
60 ml (4 tbsp) chopped fresh coriander

To Serve:
French country-style bread

1 To make the dressing, lightly crush the coriander seeds and star anise. Roughly chop the lemon grass, chillis, garlic and ginger and place in a bowl with the coriander seeds and star anise. Add the lime juice, lemon juice, water, olive oil, sunflower oil, fish sauce and sugar. Whisk together until evenly blended, then set aside to infuse for at least 30 minutes.

2 Strain the dressing through a fine sieve, discarding the chopped flavourings. Taste and adjust the flavouring, adding a little more fish sauce or lemon juice as required.

3 Peel the cucumber, halve lengthwise and scoop out the seeds. Cut the flesh into julienne strips. Sprinkle with a little salt and leave to drain in a colander for 15 minutes. Rinse thoroughly under cold running water and pat dry with kitchen paper.

4 Season the white crab meat with salt and pepper to taste.

5 Pile the crab meat in the centre of each serving plate. Surround with the cucumber julienne. Whisk the dressing, then drizzle a little over the crab meat and pool the rest around it. Sprinkle with chopped coriander. Serve with French country-style bread to mop up the dressing.

Chumki Banerjee

Gingered Crab Cakes with Sweet Pepper Sauce

125 g (4 oz) waxy potato (eg Romano)
225 g (8 oz) very fresh crab meat (mixed white and brown meat)
30 ml (2 tbsp) chopped parsley
5 ml (1 tsp) grated fresh root ginger
2.5 ml (½ tsp) freshly ground nutmeg
pinch of cayenne
salt and freshly ground black pepper
30-45 ml (2-3 tbsp) seasoned flour
groundnut oil for shallow-frying

Sweet Pepper Sauce:
15 ml (1 tbsp) olive oil
2 cloves garlic, crushed
1 shallot, finely chopped
2 medium red peppers, seeded and chopped
¼ large red chilli, finely chopped (optional)
4-5 basil leaves
salt and freshly ground black pepper
300 ml (½ pint) light fish stock
60 ml (2 fl oz) double cream

To Serve:
flat-leaved parsley or basil leaves
Roasted Pepper Salad (see right)

1 Cook the potato in boiling water for 10 minutes. Drain and allow to cool a little, then grate coarsely and place in a bowl. Add the crab meat, parsley, ginger, nutmeg, cayenne and seasoning; mix together using a fork, taking care not to damage the potatoes or crab meat.

2 Carefully shape into 8 flat cakes, squashing the mixture together with your hands. Dip the crab cakes in seasoned flour to coat. Place on a tray and chill in the refrigerator for at least 10 minutes.

3 To make the sweet pepper sauce, heat the olive oil in a pan, add the garlic and shallot and sweat until softened. Add the red peppers, chilli if using, basil, seasoning and stock. Bring to the boil, lower the heat and simmer for 20 minutes. Transfer to a food processor or blender and process until smooth. Pass through a sieve into a small pan and add the cream. Set aside. Reheat gently before serving.

4 To cook the crab cakes, heat the groundnut oil in a heavy-based frying pan. Add the crab cakes and fry for about 2-3 minutes each side until crisp and golden brown. Drain on kitchen paper. Garnish with parsley or basil and serve with the red pepper sauce and salad.

Clare Askaroff

Roasted Pepper Salad

1 red pepper
1 yellow pepper
1 orange pepper
extra-virgin olive oil
salt and freshly ground black pepper

1 Halve the peppers and remove the seeds. Place cut-side down in a roasting tin and drizzle with olive oil. Place under a preheated hot grill for about 10 minutes until the skins are blackened and blistered. Immediately place in a bowl, cover tightly and leave to stand for about 15 minutes; the steam created will help to lift the skins.

2 Peel the peppers and finely shred the flesh. Place in a bowl with 15 ml (1 tbsp) olive oil, season liberally with salt and pepper, and toss to mix; do not refrigerate. Serve with the Gingered Crab Cakes.

Clare Askaroff

Maryland Crab Cakes with Tartare Sauce

Crab Cakes:
1 large egg
22 ml (1½ tbsp) double cream
7.5 ml (1½ tsp) Dijon mustard
2.5 ml (½ tsp) Worcestershire sauce
5 ml (1 tsp) Old Bay seasoning
pinch of cayenne pepper
freshly ground pepper
22 ml (1½ tbsp) minced spring onions
15 ml (1 tbsp) minced fresh parsley
60 ml (4 tbsp) mayonnaise
450 g (1 lb) crab meat
22 ml (1½ tbsp) ground almonds
50 g (2 oz) fine breadcrumbs
225 g (8 oz) clarified butter

Tartare Sauce:
15 ml (1 tbsp) Champagne vinegar
7.5 ml (1½ tsp) Dijon mustard
pinch of salt
freshly ground pepper
Tabasco sauce to taste
125 ml (4 fl oz) mayonnaise
½ medium onion, finely chopped
30 ml (2 tbsp) finely chopped dill pickles
30 ml (2 tbsp) finely chopped parsley
7.5 ml (1½ tsp) finely chopped chives
15 ml (1 tbsp) chopped capers

To Garnish:
60 ml (4 tbsp) finely chopped parsley

1 To make the crab cakes, lightly whisk the egg in a large mixing bowl, then add the cream, mustard, Worcestershire sauce, Old Bay seasoning, cayenne and pepper to taste, and continue whisking until well blended. Add the spring onions, minced parsley and mayonnaise and mix until all of the ingredients are well blended. Gently fold in the crab meat and ground almonds, taking care to break up the crab meat as little as possible.

2 Using the hands, form the mixture into 4 equal-sized cakes and coat each cake lightly with breadcrumbs. Place the crab cakes on a baking sheet, cover and chill for 1 hour.

3 Meanwhile, make the tartare sauce. Put the vinegar, mustard, salt, pepper and Tabasco in a bowl and whisk until well blended. Add the mayonnaise, onion, pickles, parsley, chives and capers, and beat thoroughly until the ingredients are well blended. Cover and chill until required.

4 Heat the clarified butter in a large, heavy-based frying pan over a moderate heat. Add the crab cakes and fry for 3-4 minutes on each side until golden brown. Drain on absorbent kitchen paper and keep warm. Sprinkle each cake with chopped parsley and serve accompanied by the tartare sauce and a green salad.

Martha Spencer

Nuggets of Langoustine in Basil Parcels

24 fresh langoustines
20 large basil leaves, with stems
30 ml (2 tbsp) chopped chervil leaves
600 ml (1 pint) vegetable stock

Ginger Sauce:
2 shallots, finely chopped
30 ml (2 tbsp) white wine
45 ml (3 tbsp) white wine vinegar
5 ml (1 tsp) coarsely ground black pepper
40 ml (scant 3 tbsp) double cream
250 g (9 oz) butter (preferably Jersey butter for its rich colour), in pieces
15-30 ml (1-2 tbsp) chopped fresh root ginger
salt

Salad:
4 small bunches of lamb's lettuce
handful of rocket leaves
handful of radicchio leaves
30 ml (2 tbsp) olive oil
1.25 ml (¼ tsp) Dijon mustard
10 ml (2 tsp) white wine vinegar
salt and freshly ground pepper

1 First make the ginger sauce. Place the shallots, wine, vinegar and pepper in a saucepan. Bring to the boil and simmer until the liquid has reduced by two thirds. Gradually whisk in the cream, butter and ginger and allow to simmer very gently for 5-10 minutes. Pass the sauce through a sieve into a basin. Check seasoning and stand the basin over a pan of simmering water until ready to use.

2 Steam 4 whole langoustines for 4 minutes, or until cooked. Meanwhile peel the remaining langoustines, leaving 1 cm (½ inch) shell on the tail ends. Sprinkle with salt, pepper and chervil.

3 To prepare each nugget, lay a peeled langoustine across the width of each basil leaf. Pierce a tiny hole about 1cm (½ inch) from the tip of the leaf, wrap the leaf around the langoustine and tuck the stem end through the hole.

4 Repeat to make 20 nuggets in total. Place the nuggets in the top of a steamer. Bring the vegetable stock to the boil in the bottom of the steamer and steam the nuggets for 3-4 minutes until the langoustines are cooked, adding the whole langoustines for the final 2 minutes to heat through.

5 Meanwhile prepare the salad. Combine the salad leaves. To make the dressing, place the olive oil, mustard, wine vinegar and seasoning in a screw-topped jar and shake thoroughly to combine. Toss the salad leaves in the dressing.

6 To serve, arrange the salad leaves on individual plates. Position the langoustine nuggets in a circle on each plate and spoon over some of the ginger sauce. Place a whole langoustine in the centre of each circle. Serve immediately, accompanied by the remaining sauce.

Jo Eitel

Pan-fried Langoustines, Monkfish and Scallops with a Spaghetti of Vegetables

15 g (½ oz) unsalted butter
8-12 medallions of monkfish
8-12 peeled langoustines
4-6 shelled scallops
salt and freshly ground black pepper
squeeze of lemon juice

Spaghetti of Vegetables:
2 large carrots
3 outer leaves of a fennel bulb
2 medium courgettes
1 leek
a little sugar
knob of butter

Chive Butter:
2.5 ml (½ tsp) ground cinnamon
125 g (4 oz) cold unsalted butter, diced
30 ml (2 tbsp) chopped chives

1 To prepare the spaghetti of vegetables, trim the ends and rounded edges off the carrots. Cut into 3 mm (⅛ inch) slices, then cut into 3 mm (⅛ inch) strips to resemble spaghetti. Place in a saucepan with a little water, a little sugar and a knob of butter. Bring to the boil and simmer for about 4 minutes until cooked but firm. Drain, refresh in cold water and drain on absorbent kitchen paper.

2 Repeat with the fennel and courgettes, cutting into 3 mm (⅛ inch) strips and discarding the seeds of the courgettes, but add salt to the water instead of sugar. Cook the fennel for 5-6 minutes; the courgettes for 2 minutes. Drain, refresh and drain.

3 Trim the leek, halve and cut into julienne strips. Cook in boiling salted water for 1 minute. Drain, refresh and drain on absorbent kitchen paper.

4 To make the chive butter, heat 60 ml (4 tbsp) lightly salted water and the cinnamon in a small heavy pan over gentle heat. Whisk in the cold butter a little at a time until well incorporated. Add the chopped chives.

5 Meanwhile cook the fish. Melt the unsalted butter in a small frying pan until hot. Add the monkfish and toss for 1 minute, then add the langoustines and cook for a further 1 minute. Finally add the scallops, shake the pan and cook for about 30 seconds. Season with salt and pepper. Add a dash of lemon juice. Remove from the heat.

6 Place the prepared vegetables in a bowl and mix carefully with a fork. Add the warm chive butter and toss well. Using a slotted spoon, lift a portion onto each warmed serving plate. Add any remaining chive butter to the fish, shaking the pan. Carefully lift out the fish and arrange around the vegetables. Drizzle the chive butter remaining in the pan over the vegetables and fish. Serve immediately.

Gregory Lewis

Garlic Prawns on a bed of Leeks

1 large leek
12 raw king or tiger prawns
30 ml (2 tbsp) olive oil
1 clove garlic, crushed
15 ml (1 tbsp) Thai fish sauce (nam pla)
5 ml (1 tsp) brown sugar
5 ml (1 tsp) lightly crushed black peppercorns

To Garnish:
chopped coriander leaves

1 Cut the leek into fine strips, about 3 cm (1¼ inches) long. Add to a pan of boiling salted water and cook briefly until just tender; drain well.

2 Shell the prawns, removing the heads but leaving the tails intact. Cut centrally along the back of each prawn and remove the dark intestinal vein. Flatten the prawns out slightly.

3 Heat the oil in a wok, add the prawns and garlic, and stir-fry for 2 minutes. Add the fish sauce, sugar and peppercorns and stir-fry until the prawns are pink and just tender.

4 Arrange the leek julienne to form a nest on each warmed serving plate. Place 3 prawns in each nest, pour over the cooking juices and sprinkle with chopped coriander leaves to serve.

Jenny Rees

Note: If fresh raw prawns are not available, use frozen ones instead. Defrost thoroughly and drain well before use.

Stir-Fried Tiger Prawns with White Cabbage, Coconut and Shrimp Paste

16-20 raw tiger prawns
75 ml (5 tbsp) sunflower oil
1 large shallot, finely chopped
1 clove garlic, finely chopped
5-10 ml (1-2 tsp) shrimp paste
5-10 ml (1-2 tsp) laos
350 g (12 oz) white cabbage, cored and shredded
250 ml (8 fl oz) coconut milk
sea salt and freshly ground black pepper

To Garnish:
2 spring onions, shredded
cayenne or paprika, for sprinkling

1 Remove the heads from the prawns. Heat 15 ml (1 tbsp) of the oil in a pan, add the shallot and garlic and cook over a low heat for 2 minutes without browning. Add the shrimp paste and laos and cook for a further 1 minute. Bring to the boil.

2 Add the cabbage to the pan. Cover and cook for 10 minutes. Remove the lid and allow most of the liquid to evaporate, stirring to prevent sticking. Adjust the seasoning and keep warm.

3 Heat the remaining 60 ml (4 tbsp) sunflower oil in a sauté pan until smoking. Add the prawns and quickly stir-fry for about 3 minutes until bright pink. Drain on kitchen paper.

4 Make shallow mounds of cabbage on 4 warmed serving plates. Arrange the prawns on the cabbage and scatter the spring onion over the plate. Sprinkle lightly with cayenne or paprika. Serve at once.

Derek Morris

Salad of Grilled Scallops and Celery Leaves with Sesame Croûtons

6 large scallops in shells, cleaned (corals reserved)
150 ml (¼ pint) milk
duck fat for deep-frying
30 celery leaves
salt and freshly ground white pepper

Croûtons:
2 slices day-old white bread
30 ml (2 tbsp) sunflower oil
10 ml (2 tsp) sesame oil
15 ml (1 tbsp) sesame seeds

Salad:
4 handfuls of lamb's lettuce
small handful of rocket leaves
few red chicory leaves (optional)
7.5 ml (½ tbsp) walnut oil
45 ml (3 tbsp) sunflower oil
15 ml (1 tbsp) white wine vinegar

1 First prepare the croûtons. Cut the bread into 1 cm (½ inch) dice. Mix the sunflower and sesame oils together and brush all over the bread cubes. Sprinkle evenly with the sesame seeds. Bake in a preheated oven at 180°C (350°F) mark 4 for 20-30 minutes until golden and crunchy.

2 For the salad, wash and thoroughly dry the salad leaves; set aside. For the dressing combine the walnut oil, sunflower oil, wine vinegar and seasoning in a screw-topped jar and shake well to combine.

3 To prepare the scallops, remove the corals from the scallops and pierce each one with a knife. Poach gently in the milk for 30 seconds, then drain and cut into smaller pieces.

4 Heat the duck fat in a suitable pan and deep-fry the celery leaves for a few seconds until golden; drain on kitchen paper.

5 Slice each scallop horizontally to make thin discs. Preheat a cast-iron griddle or heavy-based pan until very hot, add the scallop discs and cook briefly until seared and golden.

6 To serve, toss the salad leaves with the dressing and divide between 4 serving plates. Arrange the scallop slices on top and sprinkle with the hot croûtons and scallop corals. Serve at once.

Sophie Buchmann

Warm Salad of Scallops in a Herb Butter Sauce

8 large shelled scallops with corals

Herb Butter Sauce:
125 g (4 oz) unsalted butter
1 egg yolk
1 small bunch each of fresh tarragon, parsley, chervil and chives, chopped
4 basil leaves, chopped
juice of ½ lemon
salt and freshly ground black pepper

To Serve:
4 handfuls of mixed salad leaves, (eg, frisée, lamb's lettuce, radicchio, rocket, watercress)

1 Clean and trim the whole scallops, then cut in half horizontally, retaining the coral. Place on a piece of kitchen paper in the refrigerator to firm up.

2 For the sauce, put the butter, egg yolk, herbs, lemon juice and a little seasoning in a food processor and process until the mixture becomes light in texture and colour.

3 Place the scallops in a single layer in a shallow ovenproof dish. Season with salt and pepper, then cover with the buttery herb mixture. Cook under a preheated grill for about 5 minutes until the sauce is bubbling and browned – by which time the scallops will be cooked. Check the seasoning.

4 Arrange 4 scallop halves in a circular pattern on each warmed serving plate with some of the sauce. Place a mound of mixed leaves in the centre of each plate. Drizzle a little more of the sauce over the top and serve at once.

Gill Tunkle

Seared Scallop and Pancetta Salad with an Orange Saffron Dressing

100 g (3½ oz) pancetta, derinded and cut into strips
a little olive oil, for cooking
3 bunches watercress, stalks removed
12 medium-large scallops, cleaned and halved
sea salt and freshly ground black pepper

Orange Saffron Dressing:
pinch of saffron threads
20 ml (4 tsp) olive oil
2.5 ml (½ tsp) sherry vinegar
15 ml (1 tbsp) orange juice
15 ml (1 tbsp) finely chopped orange zest
½ clove garlic, finely chopped
pinch of cayenne pepper
pinch of caster sugar

1 For the dressing, put the saffron threads in a cup with 5 ml (1 tsp) hot water and leave to infuse for 15 minutes. In a bowl, whisk together the oil, vinegar and orange juice, then mix in the saffron and all the other ingredients, seasoning with salt and pepper to taste. Place in a screw-topped jar and leave to stand for at least 30 minutes.

2 Meanwhile, gently fry the pancetta in a little oil until crisp. Divide the watercress between 4 individual serving plates.

3 Preheat a skillet or heavy-based frying pan. Brush the scallops with olive oil and season with salt and pepper. Add to the hot pan and cook over a moderately high heat for 1 minute each side.

4 Arrange the scallops on top of the watercress, and sprinkle over the crisp pancetta. Shake the dressing to emulsify, then pour over the salad. Serve immediately.

James Hurd

Seared Scallops with Spring Greens and Red Pepper Sauce

12 medium scallops, cleaned
salt and freshly ground black pepper
15 ml (1 tbsp) olive oil

Red Pepper Sauce:
15 ml (1 tbsp) olive oil
1 celery stick, finely chopped
1 shallot, finely chopped
2 medium red peppers, cored, seeded and finely chopped
1 clove garlic, finely chopped
small bunch of parsley, stalks only (flat-leaf if possible)
600 ml (1 pint) fish stock
1 glass dry white wine
100 ml (3½ fl oz) double cream
salt and freshly ground white pepper

Spring Greens:
15 ml (1 tbsp) olive oil
1 small clove garlic, finely chopped
400 g (14 oz) spring greens, shredded
squeeze of lemon juice, to taste

1 First make the sauce. Heat the olive oil in a heavy-based saucepan and add the vegetables, garlic and parsley stalks. Add the fish stock and wine and bring to the boil. Lower the heat and simmer for 15 minutes until the vegetables are tender. Transfer the mixture to a blender or food processor and work to a purée. Pass through a sieve and return to the clean pan. Bring to the boil and reduce by two thirds, then adjust the seasoning. Stir in the cream, reheat and keep warm.

2 Prepare the spring greens. Heat the olive oil in a large pan, add the garlic and fry for a few seconds, then add the spring greens with just the water clinging to the leaves after washing. Cover and cook for 3-4 minutes until wilted. Season with salt and pepper, and add lemon juice to taste; keep warm.

3 Put the scallops in a bowl and season with salt and pepper. Add the 15 ml (1 tbsp) olive oil and toss to coat the scallops lightly with oil. Heat a heavy-based non-stick frying pan or griddle over a high heat until smoking. Add the scallops in one layer and sear for 30-45 seconds on each side, depending on size.

4 Place a mound of greens in the centre of each warmed serving plate. Arrange the scallops on top and pour the red pepper sauce around. Serve immediately.

Neil Haidar

Salad of Queen Scallops and Crispy Smoked Bacon with Walnut and Sesame Oil Dressing

125 g (4 oz) lean smoked bacon
125 g (4 oz) salad leaves (eg baby spinach, frisée, oakleaf lettuce)
175 g (6 oz) queen scallops, cleaned
knob of butter
10 ml (2 tsp) light olive oil

Dressing:
15 ml (1 tbsp) walnut oil
15 ml (1 tbsp) sesame oil
45 ml (1 tbsp) light olive oil
30 ml (2 tbsp) sherry vinegar
15 ml (1 tbsp) finely chopped parsley
salt and freshly ground black pepper

1 Cut each bacon rasher into 3 or 4 lengths and twist around a chopstick to form coils. Remove the bacon twists from the chopstick and place on a grill rack. Cook under a preheated grill, turning occasionally, until crisp; keep warm.

2 Meanwhile, tear the salad leaves into bite-sized pieces and place in a large bowl. Put the ingredients for the dressing in a screw-topped jar and shake vigorously until well blended. Pour the dressing over the salad leaves and toss until lightly coated. Arrange a bed of salad leaves on each serving plate.

3 Heat the butter and oil in a heavy-based frying pan, add the scallops and cook over a moderate heat for 2-3 minutes until just tender.

4 Arrange the scallops and bacon twists on the salad leaves and serve at once, while the scallops are still warm.

Simon Jackson

Scallop Mousseline inlaid with Crab

50-75 g (2-3 oz) white crabmeat (including small pieces of coral roe – if available)
210 g (7½ oz) cleaned scallops with corals (see note)
5 ml (1 tsp) salt
freshly ground white pepper
1 egg (size 3)
150 ml (¼ pint) double cream
90 ml (3 fl oz) soured cream

To Serve:
Tartlets of Artichoke Purée (see right)
crab claw tips (optional)
red lumpfish roe (optional)
herb sprigs, to garnish

1 Put the scallops into a food processor, add the salt and pepper and work until smooth. Add the egg and process for 1 minute. Transfer to a bowl, cover and chill for at least 30 minutes. Gradually fold in the cream and soured cream.

2 Butter 4 dariole moulds or ramekins and divide half of the scallop mousseline between them. Spoon the white crab meat in a layer on top, placing a small piece of coral in the centre (if available). Top with the rest of the scallop mousseline. Settle the mixture by bumping the moulds gently on the work surface. Cover each with a circle of greaseproof paper.

3 Put a folded newspaper in the bottom of a roasting tin and stand the moulds on top. Add enough hot water to come halfway up the sides of the moulds. Bake in a preheated oven at 180°C (350°F) mark 4 for 25 minutes.

4 To serve, allow the mousselines to stand for a few minutes. Carefully unmould onto one side of each serving plate and decorate with the small tips of crab claw. Arrange the warm artichoke tartlet on the other side and decorate the plate with small pieces of crab coral or fish roe and herbs.

Marion MacFarlane

Note: If you prepare the scallops yourself, use the scallop frills to make the stock for the tartlet filling.

Tartlets of Artichoke Purée

Serve with Scallop Mousseline (left).

Pastry:
50 g (2 oz) plain flour
pinch of salt
25 g (1 oz) butter
10 ml (2 tsp) water (approximately)

Artichoke Purée:
225 g (8 oz) Jerusalem artichokes, peeled
150 ml (¼ pint) light fish stock
salt and freshly ground black pepper
dash of lemon juice

1 To make the pastry, sift the flour and salt into a bowl. Rub in the butter until the mixture resembles fine breadcrumbs. Add sufficient water to bind the dough. Wrap in cling film and place in refrigerator for 30 minutes.

2 For the filling, simmer the Jerusalem artichokes in the fish stock for about 15 minutes until tender. Drain the artichokes and place in a blender or food processor with a little of the stock. Work to a smooth purée. Add seasoning and lemon juice to taste.

3 Roll out the pastry thinly and use to line barquettes or other small decorative moulds. Prick the bases with a fork. Line with baking beans and bake blind in a preheated oven at 190°C (375°F) mark 5 for 10 minutes. Remove the beans.

4 Just before serving, spoon in the warm artichoke purée. Serve at once.

Marion MacFarlane

Squid Ink Risotto with Monkfish and Prawns

30 ml (2 tbsp) olive oil
1 small onion, finely chopped
2 cloves garlic, finely chopped
225 g (8 oz) fennel, cored and finely chopped
225 g (8 oz) Arborio rice
750 ml (1¼ pints) fish stock
2 sachets of squid ink
225 g (8 oz) monkfish fillet, skinned and cubed
125 g (4 oz) Parmesan cheese, freshly grated
freshly ground black pepper
25 g (1 oz) butter
12 large prawns, or 4 medium langoustines

To Garnish:
parsley or chives

1 Heat the olive oil in a heavy-based pan, add the onion and sweat gently until softened. Add the garlic and fennel and cook, stirring occasionally, for 3 minutes. Add the rice and cook, stirring, for 2 minutes.

2 Meanwhile, heat the stock in another saucepan. Add about 250 ml (8 fl oz) of the hot stock to the rice and cook, stirring, until absorbed. Add the squid ink and monkfish. Continue adding the stock a ladleful at a time, as each addition is absorbed. Continue until the rice is plump and tender yet still has some bite. (You may not need to add all of the stock.) Stir in the Parmesan, pepper and butter.

3 Meanwhile cook the prawns or langoustines in a large pan of boiling water for 4 minutes, or until pink.

4 To serve, divide the risotto between warmed bowls and garnish with the prawns or langoustines and parsley or chives.

Holly Schade

Seafood Parcels with a Chive and Lemon Sauce

50 g (2 oz) bean sprouts
50 g (2 oz) shelled queen scallops
50 g (2 oz) cooked peeled prawns
5 ml (1 tsp) grated fresh root ginger
30 ml (2 tbsp) chopped coriander leaves
salt and freshly ground black pepper
8 sheets filo pastry (maximum – less if very large)
about 50 g (2 oz) butter, melted

Chive and Lemon Sauce:
50 g (2 oz) butter
15 ml (1 tbsp) lemon juice
15 ml (1 tbsp) chopped chives

1 Blanch the bean sprouts for 30 seconds in boiling water; drain. Blanch the scallops in boiling water for 30 seconds; drain.

2 In a bowl, combine the prawns, scallops, bean sprouts, grated ginger and chopped coriander leaves. Season with salt and pepper to taste.

3 To make the parcels, take one sheet of filo pastry and brush it with melted butter. Top with a second sheet of filo and brush again with melted butter. Cut out a 15 x 10 cm (6 x 4 inch) 'double' rectangle. With the long side towards you, place an eighth of the filling in a sausage shape across the centre. Fold in the short sides over the filling, brushing them with a little melted butter, then roll up the parcel to completely enclose the filling.

4 Repeat with the remaining filo and filling to make 8 parcels in total.

5 Place the parcels seam-side down on a greased baking sheet and brush with melted butter. Bake in a preheated oven at 230°C (450°F) mark 8 for 8-10 minutes, or until golden brown and crisp.

6 To make the sauce, melt the butter, then whisk in the lemon juice and chives. Drizzle the sauce over the parcels to serve.

Alison Fiander

Seafood Pastry Chests with Red Pepper Sauce

250 g (9 oz) ready-made puff pastry
beaten egg, mixed with a little milk, to glaze

Sauce:
10 ml (2 tsp) butter
25 g (1 oz) shallots, chopped
100 g (4 oz) red pepper, skinned, seeded and chopped
100 g (4 oz) tomatoes, skinned, seeded and chopped
40 ml (3 tbsp) double cream
salt and freshly ground black pepper

Filling:
10 ml (2 tsp) butter
3-4 shallots, finely chopped
30 ml (2 tbsp) chopped parsley
1 clove garlic, chopped
100 ml (3½ fl oz) fish stock
50 ml (2 fl oz) dry white wine
60 g (2 oz) salmon fillet, skinned
60 g (2 oz) cleaned squid pouches, cut into rings
60 g (2 oz) small cleaned scallops
50 ml (2 fl oz) double cream
pinch of cayenne pepper
60 g (2 oz) cooked peeled prawns

To Garnish:
dill sprigs
8 asparagus tips, cooked

1 Roll out the pastry on a lightly floured surface to a 5 mm (¼ inch) thickness. Cut 4 rectangles, measuring about 6 x 10 cm (2½ x 4 inches). Round off the corners.

2 Leaving a 5 mm (¼ inch) margin, score a cross-cross on each rectangle, cutting about halfway through the depth. Finally, cut around the margin, to the same depth. Chill for at least 30 minutes.

3 Meanwhile, make the sauce. Melt the butter in a pan, and gently sweat the shallots until soft. Add the red pepper and cook for 4 minutes, then add the tomatoes and cook for a further 3 minutes. Stir in the cream and season with salt and pepper to taste. Transfer to a blender or food processor and work until smooth, then pass through a sieve into a clean pan.

4 Brush the pastry with the egg wash. Bake in a preheated oven at 190°C (375°F) mark 5 for about 10 minutes until golden brown. Carefully cut around the rim and lift off the lids; set aside. Remove the loose inner pastry to create space for the filling.

5 For the filling, melt the butter in a pan, add the chopped shallots, parsley and garlic, and sweat over a low heat for a few minutes. Increase the heat and add the fish stock and white wine. Bring to a simmer, then add the salmon fillets, together with the squid and scallops. Poach gently until the salmon is firm to touch, then remove with a slotted spoon and flake into a warm bowl. Poach the squid and scallops for a further 10 minutes, then remove with a slotted spoon; add to the flaked fish.

6 Increase the heat and reduce the cooking liquid by a third, then add the cream, cayenne pepper and salt and pepper to taste.

7 Carefully fold the prawns, salmon, squid and scallops into the reduced cooking liquid. Heat through gently, then spoon the filling into the pastry case.

8 To serve, gently reheat the sauce and pool on warmed serving plates. Position a seafood pastry chest in the centre. Pop the asparagus tips into the pastry chests and replace the lids, setting them slightly off centre. Garnish with dill and serve at once.

Glen Tabor

Buckwheat Pancakes with Smoked Salmon and Horseradish Cream

Pancakes:
150 ml (¼ pint) milk
75 ml (5 tbsp) water
2.5 ml (½tsp) caster sugar
15 g (½ oz) butter
125 g (4 oz) plain flour
50 g (2 oz) buckwheat flour
1.25 ml (¼ tsp) salt
1 egg, separated
butter or oil, for frying

Topping:
50-75 g (2-3 oz) piece smoked salmon fillet, diagonally sliced
5-10 ml (1-2 tsp) freshly grated horseradish (or creamed horseradish)
150 ml (¼ pint) soured cream

To Garnish:
snipped chives

1 To make the pancakes, put the milk, water, sugar and butter in a saucepan and heat gently until melted. Pour into a food processor and add the plain and buckwheat flours, salt and egg yolk. Blend to a smooth batter. Transfer to a bowl, cover and leave in a warm place for 1-1½ hours until frothy.

2 Whisk the egg white until soft peaks form and fold into the batter.

3 To cook the pancakes, heat a griddle or heavy-based frying pan until very hot. Grease with butter or oil and drop dessertspoonfuls of batter into the pan, spacing well apart. Cook for 1-2 minutes, then place a piece of smoked salmon in the centre of each one. Flip over and cook until the underside is golden brown.

4 Wrap the pancakes loosely in a greased foil parcel and keep warm in a low oven, while cooking the remainder.

5 Mix the horseradish with the soured cream. Serve the pancakes immediately garnished with chives and accompanied by the horseradish cream.

Sue Lawrence

Note: You need to buy a piece of smoked salmon which can be sliced obliquely, rather than pre-packed thin slices.

Hot Smoked Wild Salmon Sauce on a Green Salad

50 g (1¾ oz) can anchovies in oil
300 ml (½ pint) double cream
5 ml (1 tsp) tomato purée
freshly ground black pepper
a little finely chopped parsley
125 g (4 oz) smoked wild salmon, cut into ribbons

Salad:
assorted salad leaves 'with bite', eg chicory, watercress, frisée
few spring onions
handful of mangetout, finely sliced
few tarragon leaves
lime juice, to taste
small handful each of green and pink peppercorns in brine, drained

1 Drain the anchovies, reserving the oil. Place half of them in a heavy-based saucepan with the anchovy oil. Cook over a low heat, stirring with a wooden spoon, to make a smooth paste. Add the cream and tomato purée, stirring until the mixture bubbles. Continue cooking over a low heat, stirring occasionally, until a thick sauce is formed.

2 Add pepper to taste and a tiny amount of finely chopped parsley. Set aside a few of the smoked salmon ribbons for garnish; add the rest to the sauce.

3 Combine the salad leaves, spring onions, mangetout and tarragon leaves in a bowl. Sprinkle with lime juice and pepper to taste. Arrange the salad in individual bowls and dot with green and pink peppercorns. Sprinkle with the reserved ribbons of salmon.

4 Pour the hot sauce over the salad and serve immediately.

Linda Yewdall

Millefeuilles of Salmon and Savoy Cabbage with a Sabayon of Sherry

1 medium Savoy cabbage
salt and freshly ground black pepper
12 cm (5 inch) piece of salmon tail, about 225 g (8 oz)
125 g (4 oz) butter, melted
250 ml (8 fl oz) dry white wine
lemon juice, to taste

Sabayon Sauce:
2 egg yolks
15 ml (1 tbsp) dry sherry

1 Remove the 4 outer leaves from the cabbage and discard. Carefully remove the next 16 leaves, cutting through the stalks at the base and peeling off without tearing. Wash and pat dry with kitchen paper.

2 Using a 6 cm (2½ inch) pastry cutter, carefully cut out a round from each leaf. Reserve the rest of the cabbage. Add the cabbage rounds to a pan of boiling salted water and boil for 8 minutes. Drain and pat dry with kitchen paper. Put the leaves on a plate, cover and leave in the refrigerator for 10 minutes to firm up.

3 Meanwhile, prepare the salmon. Remove the skin and bones, then slice the flesh as thinly as possible.

4 Finely shred half of the remaining cabbage leaves, discarding the centre ribs. Put the shredded cabbage in a pan with 75 g (3 oz) of the melted butter and cook, stirring, for 2 minutes. Add the white wine and cook gently for 10 minutes.

5 Remove from the heat and leave until cold, then press the mixture in a fine sieve over a bowl squeezing to extract the cabbage juices; reserve for the sauce. Keep the shredded cabbage for the millefeuilles filling.

6 To prepare the millefeuilles, set aside four dark green cabbage rounds for the top layer. To assemble each millefeuilles, brush a cabbage round with a little melted butter, cover with a fine layer of salmon, then add a squeeze of lemon juice and salt and pepper. Add a thin layer of cold shredded cabbage. Repeat these layers twice, then cover with a reserved dark green cabbage round, leaving the top cabbage round unbuttered. Assemble another 3 millefeuilles, in the same way.

7 To make the Sabayon sauce, put the egg yolks, sherry and 15 ml (1 tbsp) water in the top of a double boiler or in a heatproof bowl over a pan of hot water placed over a medium heat. Whisk constantly until the mixture thickens. Reheat the reserved cabbage juices and whisk into the sabayon, a little at a time. Season with salt and pepper to taste and keep warm.

8 Place the 4 millefeuilles in a steamer basket over a pan of boiling water and steam for 8 minutes. Carefully transfer to warmed serving plates and spoon on the sabayon sauce. Serve immediately.

Derek Johns

Salmon and Dill Paupiettes with a Preserved Lemon Relish

Salmon and Dill Paupiettes:
200 g (7 oz) salmon fillet, skinned
1 egg white
100 ml (3½ oz) double cream
large bunch of dill sprigs, stalks removed, finely chopped
salt and freshly ground white pepper
4 slices smoked salmon, about 15 cm (6 inches) square

Lemon Relish:
4 shallots, finely sliced
60 ml (4 tbsp) white wine vinegar
60 ml (4 tbsp) water
12 green beans, cut into 2 cm (¾ inch) lengths
rind of 1 preserved lemon, finely sliced
10-15 ml (2-3 tsp) caster sugar, to taste
salt and freshly ground black pepper

To Garnish:
dill sprigs

1 Put the salmon fillet in a food processor and work until smooth, then press through a sieve into a large bowl. Mix in the egg white, using a wooden spoon. Slowly mix in the cream, a spoonful at a time. Add the chopped dill and season with salt and pepper to taste. Cover and refrigerate for 20 minutes.

2 Meanwhile, make the lemon relish. Put the shallots, wine vinegar and water in a small pan and simmer for about 10 minutes until the liquid is reduced to 30 ml (2 tbsp). Cook the green beans in a large pan of boiling salted water for 2 minutes; drain and refresh in cold water. Add the beans to the vinegar mixture with the preserved lemon rind and sugar. Cook for a further 3 minutes, or until the mixture is the consistency of a relish. Check the seasoning.

3 Half-fill a large shallow pan with water and bring to the boil. Reduce the heat until the water is just below simmering.

4 Lay each smoked salmon slice on a sheet of greaseproof paper and divide the cooled salmon mousseline between the slices. Spread evenly, leaving a margin at the edges. Roll up the salmon paupiettes and wrap tightly in the greaseproof paper, twisting the ends to seal.

5 Carefully lower the paupiettes into the water and poach for about 6 minutes until firm to the touch.

6 Remove the paupiettes, unwrap and cut into 1 cm (¾ inch) slices. Put a spoonful of the lemon relish on each serving plate and surround with the paupiette slices. Garnish with dill and serve at once.

Andrew Whiteley

Salmon Tartare with Crème Fraîche and Dill Vinaigrette

225 g (8 oz) skinned salmon fillets
125 g (4 oz) gravad lax
125 g (4 oz) clarified butter
1 shallot, finely diced
1 clove garlic, halved
5 ml (1 tsp) chopped dill
lemon juice, to taste
salt and freshly ground black pepper

Dill Vinaigrette:
60 ml (4 tbsp) olive oil
15 ml (1 tbsp) white wine vinegar
2.5 ml (½ tsp) chopped dill
30 ml (2 tbsp) finely diced tomato flesh

To Serve:
60 ml (4 tbsp) crème fraîche

1 Finely dice the salmon and gravad lax and mix well.

2 Heat the clarified butter in a pan and sauté the shallot and garlic for 1 minute, then discard the garlic. Add the butter mixture to the salmon together with the dill and lemon juice to taste. Season with salt and pepper to taste. Mix well and chill in the refrigerator until required.

3 Whisk together the ingredients for the vinaigrette, or shake vigorously in a screw-topped jar, adding salt and pepper to taste.

4 To serve, spoon the dill vinaigrette on to individual serving plates. Form the salmon tartare into quenelles, using two moistened tablespoons to shape the ovals. Position 3 quenelles on each plate and spoon some crème fraîche into the middle. Serve at once.

Michael Baxter

Note: Gravad Lax is lightly salted salmon flavoured with dill; a Swedish speciality, it is widely available in this country. You will find it easier to dice and mix the fish if it is first partially frozen.

Cotswold Trout on a Compote of Roasted Tomatoes with Pesto

4 trout fillets, each about 200 g (7 oz)
120 ml (4 fl oz) extra-virgin olive oil
1 clove garlic, chopped
100 g (3½ oz) red onion, chopped
juice of 1 lemon
30 ml (2 tbsp) white wine
50 g (2 oz) stoned black olives, chopped
6 plum tomatoes
sea salt and freshly ground black pepper
10 ml (2 tsp) oil
20 g (¾ oz) basil leaves, shredded
12 coriander seeds
pinch of sugar

Pesto:
50 g (2 oz) basil leaves
150 ml (¼ pint) extra-virgin olive oil
1 clove garlic
25 g (1 oz) pine nuts
20 g (¾ oz) Parmesan cheese, freshly grated
sea salt and freshly ground black pepper

1 First make the pesto: put all of the ingredients in a blender or food processor and work until smooth; set aside.

2 Heat the olive oil in a pan, add the garlic and onion and fry gently for 3 minutes. Add the lemon juice, wine and olives and cook for 4 minutes. Dice two of the plum tomatoes and add to the pan. Season with salt and pepper to taste, remove from the heat and allow to cool.

3 Halve the other 4 tomatoes and remove their seeds. Place in a pan with the 10 ml (2 tsp) oil and cook on a high heat for 1-2 minutes until lightly coloured. Transfer to a shallow baking tin, sprinkle with the shredded basil, coriander seeds, salt, pepper and sugar.

4 Spoon about a third of the onion and olive mixture into another baking tin and place the trout on top. Season with salt and pepper and spoon on the rest of the onion and olive mixture.

5 Place the tomatoes and trout in a preheated oven at 230°C (450°F) mark 8 for 4 minutes. Arrange the tomatoes on warmed serving plates and place the trout on top. Add the pan juices from the tomatoes to the onion and olive mixture. Sprinkle this over and around the trout and drizzle with the pesto. Sprinkle with sea salt and pepper. Serve at once.

John Thornburn

Pan-fried Red Mullet with Braised Fennel

140 ml (4½ fl oz) olive oil
4 small fennel bulbs, fronds intact
1 clove garlic, peeled and quartered
salt and freshly ground black pepper
juice of ½ orange
juice of ½ lemon
finely pared zest of 1 orange, in strips
8 red mullet fillets
plain flour, for coating
few drops of balsamic vinegar

1 Heat 45 ml (3 tbsp) olive oil in a heavy-based saucepan. Quarter the fennel bulbs, (setting aside the fronds for the dressing). Add to the hot oil and fry, turning, until beginning to brown. Add the garlic and continue to fry until both fennel and garlic are browned. Add just enough water to come two-thirds of the way up the fennel. Season with salt and pepper. Bring to the boil and simmer, uncovered, until tender.

2 Meanwhile, prepare the dressing. Place 50 ml (2 fl oz) olive oil in a blender or food processor with the orange juice, lemon juice and fennel fronds. Blend until evenly amalgamated. Season to taste, and add a little more oil or lemon juice if necessary to achieve the correct balance. Mix in the orange zest.

3 Heat the remaining 45 ml (3 tbsp) olive oil in a large frying pan over a medium heat. Dust the fish fillets with seasoned flour, add to the pan, skin-side down, and fry for 3-4 minutes until crisp underneath. Turn the fillets over and fry for a further 1 minute.

4 Place the red mullet fillets on warmed serving plates with the fennel. Pour over the dressing and drizzle a little balsamic vinegar into the dressing.

Neil Haidar

Grilled Red Mullet on Stir-fried Vegetables with a Cream Sauce

4 red mullet, each 200-225 g (7-8 oz)

Stir Fry:
30 ml (2 tbsp) sesame oil
2 cloves garlic, finely chopped
25 g (1 oz) fresh root ginger, peeled and cut into julienne
50 g (2 oz) carrot, cut into julienne
50 g (2 oz) red pepper, cored, seeded and cut into julienne
50 g (2 oz) yellow pepper, cored, seeded and cut into julienne
50 g (2 oz) spring onions, sliced
50 g (2 oz) radish, sliced
50 g (2 oz) mooli, peeled and cut into julienne
50 g (2 oz) Chinese leaves or cabbage, shredded
125 g (4 oz) bean sprouts

Sauce:
150 ml (¼ pint) dry white wine
150 ml (¼ pint) fish stock
150 ml (¼ pint) double cream
25 g (1 oz) butter, diced
salt and freshly ground black pepper

1 Cut the head and fins off the red mullet, leaving on the tails. Using a knife, remove the scales working from the tail towards the head. Take the fillets off the bone leaving the skin on. Carefully remove any remaining bones from the centre of the fillets. Rinse the fish and set aside in a cool place.

2 To make the fish stock for the sauce, put the head and bones from the mullet into a pan and cover with 300 ml (½ pint) water. Bring to the boil and skim the surface. Simmer gently for 15-20 minutes, skimming as necessary, until reduced to approximately 150 ml (¼ pint). Strain the stock through a fine sieve and set aside.

3 Preheat the grill to high. Meanwhile, heat the sesame oil in a wok or large pan until hot. Add the garlic and ginger and stir for a few seconds, then add the remaining vegetables and stir-fry for 2-3 minutes. Remove from the wok and keep warm.

4 To make the sauce, add the wine to the wok and reduce by two thirds, then add the fish stock and boil until reduced by half. Add the double cream, bring to the boil then simmer for 2 minutes.

5 Meanwhile, grill the mullet skin-side up for 2-3 minutes until the skins begin to turn golden; this is sufficient to cook the fillets through without turning them.

6 To finish the sauce, remove from the heat and add the butter a little at a time, swirling it into the sauce until it is incorporated and the sauce is shiny. Check the seasoning.

7 To serve, pile the stir-fried vegetables in the centre of warmed serving plates. Arrange the mullet skin-side up and slightly overlapping on top. Surround with the sauce and serve at once.

Michael Deacon

Grilled Haddock Fillet with a Cheese and Dill Topping

280 g (10 oz) haddock fillet, skinned

Cheese and Dill Topping:
100 g (3½ oz) Philadelphia cream cheese
5 ml (1 tsp) lemon juice
large bunch of dill, chopped
5 ml (1 tsp) caster sugar
salt and freshly ground white pepper

Cranberry and Red Pepper Marmalade:
100 g (3½ oz) fresh or frozen cranberries
1 small red pepper, cored, seeded and finely sliced
15 ml (1 tbsp) olive oil
40 g (1½ oz) caster sugar (approximately)
5 ml (1 tsp) lemon juice
few drops of Thai fish sauce, or to taste

To Garnish:
dill sprigs

1 For the topping, put the cream cheese in a bowl and mix in the lemon juice, dill, sugar and seasoning to taste, until evenly blended.

2 Cut the haddock into four even-sized pieces and cover with the cheese mixture. Place on a baking sheet in the refrigerator for approximately 10 minutes until the cheese mixture is firm.

3 Meanwhile, make the cranberry and red pepper marmalade. Put the cranberries into a heavy-based saucepan. Cover and place over a low heat until the cranberries begin to pop, then remove the lid. Add the sliced red pepper and olive oil. Cook for 2 minutes, stirring occasionally, then add the sugar, lemon juice and fish sauce. Cook for 5 minutes, adding a little water if the mixture is too dry; it should be the consistency of a chutney. Add a little more sugar to taste if the marmalade is too sharp. Allow to cool slightly.

4 Preheat the grill to high. Place the fish on the grill rack and cook under the grill for 2-3 minutes without turning, or until it is cooked through. Transfer to warmed serving plates and put a spoonful of the warm marmalade to one side. Garnish with dill and serve immediately.

Andrew Whiteley

Monkfish with Lemon and Caperberry Vinaigrette

450 g (1 lb) filleted monkfish, skinned
grated zest and juice of 1 lemon
30 ml (2 tbsp) mixed black and pink peppercorns
30 ml (2 tbsp) plain flour
5 ml (1 tsp) salt
60 ml (4 tbsp) olive oil

Lemon and Caperberry Vinaigrette:
90 ml (3 fl oz) olive oil
grated zest of 1 large lemon
45 ml (3 tbsp) lemon juice
30 ml (2 tbsp) caper berries
1 shallot, finely chopped

To Garnish:
lemon slices

1 Cut the fish into 2 cm (¾ inch) thick rounds. Lay in a shallow dish, sprinkle with the lemon juice and leave to marinate for 10 minutes, or longer if possible.

2 Crush the mixed peppercorns, using a pestle and mortar. Mix with the flour, salt and lemon zest. Spread the seasoned flour on a plate.

3 Pat the fish dry with kitchen paper, then coat with the seasoned flour.

4 Heat the oil in a heavy-based frying pan until hot. Fry the fish in two batches. Add to the hot oil and cook for 2-3 minutes on each side; keep the first batch warm while cooking the second.

5 Meanwhile make the vinaigrette. Put the oil, lemon zest and juice in a screw-topped jar and shake well to combine. Add the caper berries, and a little salt if needed.

6 Add the second batch of cooked fish to the first; keep warm. Add the shallot to the pan with a little more oil if necessary and fry quickly over a high heat for 30 seconds. Pour the dressing into the pan and let it bubble to reduce slightly, whisking briefly.

7 Arrange the fish on warmed serving plates. Garnish with lemon slices and surround with the hot vinaigrette.

Judith Elliott

Note: Jars of caper berries are available from delicatessens and some larger supermarkets.

Quail Terrine with Morello Cherries and Madeira

450 g (1 lb) streaky bacon
6 quail breasts
salt and freshly ground black pepper
15 ml (1 tbsp) walnut oil
345 g (12 oz) chicken livers
1 shallot, finely chopped
30 ml (2 tbsp) chopped tarragon
45 ml (3 tbsp) Madeira
1 egg
60 ml (4 tbsp) French Morello cherries, preserved in syrup
salt and freshly ground black pepper

To Serve:
salad leaves
cherry or cranberry sauce (optional)

1 Line the base and sides of a greased 450 g (1 lb) loaf tin with the bacon rashers, leaving sufficient overhanging the sides to cover the top of the finished terrine. Set aside. Season the quail breasts with salt and pepper and sprinkle with the walnut oil; set aside.

2 Put the chicken livers, shallot, tarragon, 15 ml (1 tbsp) Madeira and the egg in a food processor and work until smooth.

3 Meanwhile place the cherries and remaining 30 ml (2 tbsp) Madeira in a saucepan and heat gently for 3 minutes.

4 Pour half of the chicken liver mixture into the prepared tin and layer half of the cherry mixture on top. Arrange the quail breasts on top and cover with the rest of the cherries. Pour the rest of the chicken liver mixture over the cherries. Fold over the bacon, then cover with foil.

5 Stand the loaf tin in a roasting tin, containing a 5 cm (2 inch) depth of water. Bake in a preheated oven at 180°C (350°F) mark 4 for 1-1½ hours, until cooked through. Leave to cool in the tin, then unmould and slice.

6 Serve the terrine slices on a bed of salad leaves, accompanied by a warmed cherry or cranberry sauce if desired.

Carolyn Dyer

Quails Baked in Red Peppers

4 small boned quail, preferably free-range
a little basil oil, or extra-virgin olive oil, for marinating
30 ml (2 tbsp) pine nuts
salt and freshly ground black pepper
a little ground coriander
freshly ground nutmeg
handful of basil leaves
2 large cloves garlic
4 small red peppers
60 ml (4 tbsp) extra-virgin olive oil

To Serve:
herbs (chives, chervil, basil), to garnish
Corn Muffins (see right)

1 Rub the quail all over with basil oil and leave to marinate for a few hours, or overnight if possible.

2 Toast the pine nuts in a small frying pan over a moderate heat until lightly browned.

3 Season the birds well with salt and pepper, a sprinkling of ground coriander and freshly ground nutmeg. Place 2-3 basil leaves and 6 pine nuts in each quail cavity. Crush one of the garlic cloves and divide between the 4 birds.

4 To prepare the peppers, cut off the tops, making an opening large enough to accept the quails; reserve the tops. Remove the core and seeds.

5 Drizzle a little olive oil in each pepper and carefully place the quails inside. Cut the remaining garlic clove into 4 slices and add a sliver to each pepper. Replace the tops and stand the peppers in a shallow ovenproof dish.

6 Drizzle the remaining olive oil over the peppers and cook in a preheated oven at 200°C (400°F) mark 6 for about 30-40 minutes, basting the peppers occasionally.

7 To serve, carefully lift the peppers on to warm serving plates, spoon over some of the juices and garnish with herbs and the remaining toasted pine nuts. Serve with the corn muffins to soak up the juices.

Marion MacFarlane

Little Corn Muffins

60 g (2¼ oz) cornmeal (coarse-ground)
65 g (2¼ oz) plain flour
5 ml (1 tsp) sugar
7.5 ml (1½ tsp) baking powder
1.25 ml (¼ tsp) salt
1 small egg (size 5)
120 ml (4 fl oz) milk
15 ml (1 tbsp) corn oil
25 g (1 oz) sun-dried tomatoes in oil, drained

1 Stir all the dry ingredients together in a bowl and make a well in the centre. Beat the egg with the milk and oil, add to the well and mix into the flour to yield a smooth batter. Dry the excess oil from the tomatoes using kitchen paper, then chop finely and stir into the batter.

2 Spoon the batter into oiled small or medium muffin tins to half-fill the tins. Bake in a preheated oven at 220°C (425°F) mark 7 for 10-12 minutes until golden brown. Leave in the tins for a few minutes, then carefully remove and serve warm.

Marion MacFarlane

Stuffed Breast of Pheasant with Caramelised Calvados Apples

4 boneless, skinless pheasant breasts
600 ml (1 pint) game stock

Pâté:
1 Cox's apple
75 g (3 oz) unsalted butter
15 ml (1 tbsp) Calvados
1 slice smoked back bacon, cut into strips
25 g (1 oz) onion, finely chopped
leaves from 3 thyme sprigs
125 g (4 oz) chicken livers, trimmed and roughly chopped
salt and freshly ground black pepper

Caramelised Apples:
2 Cox's apples
50 g (2 oz) butter
30-45 ml (2-3 tbsp) Calvados
salt and freshly ground black pepper
30-45 ml (2-3 tbsp) double cream

To Serve:
few chopped toasted hazelnuts (optional)
flat-leaved parsley sprigs

1 First make the pâté. Peel, core and slice the apple. Melt 25 g (1 oz) of the butter in a pan, add the apple with the Calvados and cook until soft; set aside. Meanwhile melt the remaining butter in a frying pan, add the bacon and onion and cook gently until softened. Add the thyme and chicken livers. Cook for 1-2 minutes; do not overcook.

2 Place the apples and liver mixture in a food processor and process briefly to make a coarse paté. Season liberally with salt and pepper. Allow to cool slightly.

3 Carefully make a deep horizontal slit in each pheasant breast to form a pocket. Stuff with the paté, then wrap each one tightly in muslin and tie with string. Heat the stock in a wide shallow pan and season with salt and pepper. Add the parcels and poach for 7 minutes until just cooked; remove from the pan and leave to rest (still wrapped) in a warm place.

4 Meanwhile, prepare the caramelised apples. Peel, core and slice the apples. Heat the butter in a pan and add the apples and 15 ml (1 tbsp) Calvados. Cook until the apples are golden and brown at the edges. Season liberally with salt. Remove the apples with a slotted spoon and keep warm. Deglaze the pan with the rest of the Calvados, then whisk in the cream. Season with salt and pepper to taste.

5 To serve, open up the parcels and slice each pheasant breast very carefully into 5-6 slices. Arrange in a semi-circle to one side of each warmed serving plate. Place a spoonful of caramelised apples on the other side. Reheat the sauce if necessary and drizzle over the meat. Sprinkle a few chopped toasted hazelnuts onto the apple and garnish with flat-leaved parsley.

Clare Askaroff

Pan-fried Duck Breast on a Salad of Braised Red Cabbage

2.5 ml (½ tsp) salt
2 large duck breasts, each weighing 275 g (10 oz)
4 handfuls of mixed salad leaves, eg radicchio, curly endive, lamb's lettuce, sorrel

Braised Red Cabbage:
30 ml (2 tbsp) olive oil
1 large onion, chopped
1 small red cabbage, cored and finely sliced
1 large cooking apple
15 ml (1 tbsp) brown sugar
60 ml (4 tbsp) red wine vinegar (approximately)
2.5 ml (½ tsp) caraway seeds
1 bay leaf
4 allspice berries, crushed
salt and freshly ground black pepper

Orange Dressing:
1 orange
5 ml (1 tsp) white wine vinegar
5 ml (1 tsp) Dijon mustard
salt and freshly ground black pepper
15-25 ml (3-5 tsp) olive oil

To Serve:
15 ml (1 tbsp) raisins
15 ml (1 tbsp) toasted pine nuts

1 To prepare the braised red cabbage, heat the oil in a large pan and sauté the onion until soft, but not coloured. Add the red cabbage and cook, stirring, for 10 minutes.

2 Peel, core and chop the apple and add to the cabbage with the sugar. Cook for a further 5 minutes. Add the remaining ingredients and bring to a gentle simmer. Cover the pan and simmer very gently for 2 hours, adding a little more wine vinegar if the mixture becomes dry. Leave overnight at room temperature.

3 Sprinkle the salt into a heavy frying pan and heat. When hot, add the duck breasts, skin side down and sauté for 10 minutes; they will yield a lot of fat. Turn the breasts over and cook the meat side for 4 minutes until tender, but still pink inside. Remove from the pan. Leave in a warm place to rest for 10 minutes.

4 Meanwhile prepare the orange salad dressing. Finely pare the rind from half of the orange, cut into fine strips and reserve for the garnish. Squeeze the juice from the orange and mix with the vinegar, mustard and seasoning. Whisk in the olive oil to yield a thick emulsion.

5 Arrange the salad leaves on one half of each serving plate. Place 2 or 3 heaped spoonfuls of the cooled braised cabbage on top of the salad.

6 Slice the duck breasts into thin diagonal slices and arrange in a fan shape on the other side of each plate. Spoon the orange dressing over the duck and salad. Top with the raisins, pine nuts and the reserved orange rind to serve.

Mark James

Chicken Mousse with Mango and a Lemon Ginger Sabayon

Mousse:
2 chicken breasts, about 450 g (1 lb) total weight, filleted and skinned
salt and freshly ground white pepper
2 egg whites, beaten
120 ml (4 fl oz) double cream, chilled
120 ml (4 fl oz) milk
2.5 cm (1 inch) cube of fresh root ginger, peeled and finely grated
1-2 mangoes, peeled and thinly sliced

Lemon Ginger Sayabon:
2 egg yolks
125 g (4 oz) butter, clarified and melted
juice of ½ lemon
120 ml (4 fl oz) double cream
30 ml (2 tbsp) chicken stock
salt and freshly ground black pepper

To Garnish:
few chives

1 Put the chicken in a food processor, add salt and pepper, and process until smooth. Mix in the egg whites, cream, milk and ginger. Pass through a drum or tamis sieve, or a food mill; this is important and will result in a light-textured mousse when cooked.

2 Line 4 ramekins with a layer of mango slices and spoon in the chicken mousse. Stand the ramekins in a bain-marie or roasting tin containing enough boiling water to come two thirds of the way up the sides of the dishes. Cover the tin loosely with foil and cook in a preheated oven at 180°C (350°F) mark 4 for about 30 minutes until firm to the touch. Remove from the bain-marie to stop the cooking process.

3 Meanwhile make the lemon ginger sabayon. Whisk the egg yolks with 45 ml (3 tbsp) water in a saucepan over a gentle heat until thickened and doubled in volume. Remove from the heat and slowly add the melted butter, whisking constantly. Continue whisking over the heat and add the lemon juice, cream and chicken stock. Season with salt and pepper to taste. Whisk until the sauce resembles a custard in consistency.

4 To serve, gently unmould each mousse into the centre of a large warmed serving plate and surround with the sauce. Place a couple of chives on each mousse and position 2 or 3 slices of mango to one side on the sauce. Serve immediately.

Gill Tunkle

Chicken Livers with Salsa

125 g (4 oz) chicken livers
4 shallots
30 ml (2 tbsp) olive oil
50 g (2 oz) oyster mushrooms

Marinade:
125 ml (4 fl oz) sherry
2 cloves garlic, crushed
4 black peppercorns
salt and freshly ground pepper
handful of chopped basil
10 ml (2 tsp) sesame oil

Salsa:
1 red pepper
½ green pepper
2 small red chillis (or to taste)
2 shallots
15 ml (1 tbsp) capers
15-30 ml (1-2 tbsp) olive oil
15 ml (1 tbsp) white wine vinegar
juice of ½ lime
salt and freshly ground pepper

To Serve:
rocket leaves

1 Combine all the ingredients for the marinade in a shallow dish. Add the chicken livers and leave to marinate for 3-4 hours or overnight if possible. Drain the livers, then cut into strips.

2 To make the salsa, remove the core and seeds from the peppers and chillis. Chop the peppers, chillis, shallots and capers very finely. Place in a small bowl. Add the olive oil, vinegar, lime juice and seasoning, mix well and leave to stand.

3 Cut the shallots into bite-sized pieces. Heat 15 ml (1 tbsp) olive oil in a pan and cook the shallots gently for a few minutes. Add the sugar and cook until the shallots are soft and caramelised. Set aside.

4 Heat the remaining olive oil in the clean pan and sauté the chicken livers for 2-3 minutes. Add the mushrooms and cook for a further 30 seconds. Remove with a slotted spoon and mix with the caramelised shallots. Add the rocket leaves and toss very gently. Serve immediately, with the salsa.

Melanie Jappy

Fresh Pasta with Chicken Livers and Lemon Sauce

Pasta Dough:
225 g (8 oz) strong white flour (preferably Italian wheat flour type oo)
3.75 ml (½ tsp) salt
1 egg
1 egg yolk (egg white reserved)
small handful of flat-leaved parsley
small handful of chervil
5 ml (1 tsp) white wine
5 ml (1 tsp) olive oil

Sauce:
225 g (8 oz) chicken livers, trimmed
15 ml (1 tbsp) olive oil
250-300 ml (8-10 fl oz) homemade chicken stock
2-3 cloves garlic, crushed
25 g (1 oz) Parmesan cheese, freshly grated
45-60 ml (3-4 tbsp) double cream
strip of finely pared lemon zest, blanched
salt and freshly ground pepper

To Garnish:
flat-leaved parsley and chervil sprigs

1 To make the pasta dough, put the flour, salt, egg and egg yolk into a food processor and work until evenly mixed. Add the herbs, wine and oil, then process briefly until the dough begins to hold together, adding reserved egg white as necessary to bind. Wrap in cling film and leave to rest in the refrigerator for 30 minutes.

2 Put the pasta dough through a pasta machine until thin and silky, then cut into tagliatelle. If you do not have a pasta machine, roll out the dough as thinly as possible and cut into long thin strips.

3 To make the sauce, cut the chicken livers in half. Heat the oil in a large frying pan, add the livers and fry, turning, for 2 minutes. Drain on kitchen paper, then place in a dish and leave to rest in a low oven, set at 150°F (300°F) mark 2, while preparing the sauce.

4 Pour the stock into the pan and simmer until reduced by about half. Add the garlic, Parmesan, cream and lemon zest; reduce, then add seasoning to taste. Pass through a sieve.

5 Meanwhile, cook the pasta in boiling salted water until al dente; this will take only 30 seconds if cooked immediately; up to 2 minutes if the pasta has been left to dry for a short while. Drain thoroughly.

6 Arrange the pasta in a twirl on each serving plate. Surround with chicken livers and pour the sauce over them. Serve immediately, garnished with torn parsley and chervil leaves.

Sue Lawrence

Devilled Chicken Livers with Walnuts on a Mixed Leaf Salad

225 g (8 oz) chicken livers
45 ml (3 tbsp) Worcestershire sauce
5 ml (1 tsp) cayenne pepper
5 ml (1 tsp) powdered mustard
salt and freshly ground black pepper
50 g (2 oz) walnuts, coarsely chopped
a little walnut oil
15 ml (1 tbsp) light olive oil flavoured with garlic and chilli
5 ml (1 tsp) unsalted butter

Salad:
sufficient mixed salad leaves for 4 (eg lamb's lettuce, rocket)

Lime Vinaigrette:
30 ml (2 tbsp) olive oil (see note)
15 ml (1 tbsp) freshly squeezed lime juice
5 ml (1 tsp) thin honey
2.5 ml (½ tsp) powdered mustard
salt and freshly ground pepper

1 Trim the chicken livers of any fibrous parts, then cut each one into 3 even-sized pieces; set aside.

2 For the marinade, put the Worcestershire sauce in a small bowl and whisk in the cayenne, mustard and seasoning. Add the chicken livers, turn to coat with the marinade, then cover and leave to marinate in the refrigerator for about 2 hours.

3 Toss the walnuts in a little walnut oil until well coated, then spread on a baking tray and toast in a preheated oven at 200°C (400°F) mark 6 for 5-10 minutes. Drain on kitchen paper and allow to cool.

4 Combine the salad leaves in a bowl. Put all the ingredients for the lime vinaigrette in a small screw-topped jar and shake well until amalgamated. Pour the dressing over the salad leaves and toss to coat.

5 Drain the chicken livers. Heat the garlic and chilli flavoured oil with the butter in a heavy-based frying pan. Toss in the chicken livers and cook over a moderately high heat for a few minutes, moving them gently with a spatula, until firm and browned all over, but still pink in the centre. Add half of the walnuts and toss to mix.

6 Arrange the dressed salad leaves on individual serving plates. Spoon the hot chicken livers on top and sprinkle over the reserved walnuts. Serve at once.

Marian Freeman

Note: Keep a jar of light olive oil flavoured with chives, rosemary, marjoram and the zest of 1 lime, to use for the base of this salad dressing.

Black Pudding en Croûte with Mulberry-dressed Salad Leaves

40 g (1½ oz) butter
2 leeks, trimmed (white parts only), chopped
1 clove garlic, crushed
½ large potato, peeled and diced
2 apples, (preferably Granny Smith)
225 g (8 oz) black pudding (see note), diced
15 ml (1 tbsp) apache jelly (see note)
15 ml (1 tbsp) thyme jelly (see note)
salt and freshly ground black pepper
3 sheets filo pastry
a little melted butter, for brushing
15 ml (1 tbsp) Calvados

Salad:
sufficient mixed salad leaves for 4, (eg rocket, radicchio, oak leaf lettuce)

Dressing:
60 ml (4 tbsp) hazelnut oil
30 ml (2 tbsp) groundnut oil
30 ml (2 tbsp) mulberry or raspberry wine vinegar
5 ml (1 tsp) wholegrain mustard
5 ml (1 tsp) red wine vinegar

1 Heat 25 g (1 oz) of the butter in a frying pan, add the leeks, garlic and potato and sauté until softened. In the meantime, peel, core and dice 1 apple. Add to the pan with the black pudding and cook for 1-2 minutes. Stir in the apache and thyme jellies. Season with salt and pepper. Leave to cool.

2 When the mixture is cool, lay the 3 sheets of filo pastry one on top of the other on a lightly floured surface, then cut four 12 cm (5 inch) squares through the triple thickness.

3 Spoon the black pudding mixture in the centre of each and brush the pastry edges lightly with melted butter. Bring the edges up over the filling and twist together to form 4 purse shapes. Brush with melted butter. Transfer to a baking sheet and bake in a preheated oven at 200°C (400°F) mark 6 for 15-20 minutes until golden brown.

4 Meanwhile, peel, quarter and core the remaining apple. Cut into segments. Melt the remaining butter in a frying pan, add the apple and sauté until golden brown. Add the Calvados and flame. When the flame has died down, remove from the heat; keep warm.

5 Combine the salad leaves in a bowl. Put the ingredients for the dressing in a screw-topped jar and shake vigorously until amalgamated. Pour the dressing over the salad and toss lightly.

6 To serve, place a filo purse in the centre of each serving plate, surround with dressed salad leaves and place 3 or 4 sautéed apple wedges to one side.

Liz Franklin

Note: It is important to use a good quality black pudding, which is not too fatty.

Apache and thyme flavoured apple jellies are available from specialist shops. If unobtainable, use ordinary apple jelly and flavour with a little chilli sauce and finely chopped fresh thyme leaves.

Leek and Goat's Cheese Ravioli with Gremolata

Pasta Dough:
150 g (5 oz) durum wheat flour
50 g (2 oz) strong plain flour
pinch of salt
2 eggs (size 3)
2 egg yolks (size 3)

Filling:
2 large leeks (white and tender green parts only), cleaned
25 g (1 oz) unsalted butter
salt and freshly ground black pepper
freshly grated nutmeg
100 g (3½ oz) skinless chicken breast fillet
pinch of ground mace
1 small egg white (size 4 or 5)
150 ml (¼ pint) double cream
200 g (7 oz) firm goat's cheese

Gremolata:
handful of flat-leaf parsley, finely chopped
grated zest of 1 lemon
sea salt

To Finish:
beaten egg yolk, for brushing
flour, for dusting
75 g (3 oz) butter

1 To make the pasta dough, put the flours, salt, eggs and egg yolks in a food processor (or bowl of a mixer). Using the dough blade (or hook), work to a smooth, elastic ball of dough, adding a little water or more flour if necessary. Cover the bowl with a damp tea-towel and leave to rest.

2 To prepare the filling, finely slice the leeks. Heat the butter in a pan, add the leeks and sweat for about 5 minutes until softened. Season with salt, pepper and a little grated nutmeg. Let cool completely.

3 Roughly chop the chicken and place in a food processor. Add 5 ml (1 tsp) salt, some pepper and the mace. Process to a fine purée. Chill the mixture in the refrigerator for 15-20 minutes. Return to the processor and gradually work in the egg white, then the cream, using the pulse button if possible; do not overwork or the mousseline may separate. Pass through a fine sieve into a bowl. Add the cooled leeks, then crumble in the goat's cheese and mix well. Cover and refrigerate until needed.

4 Roll out the dough in manageable portions, using a pasta machine, keeping the rest of the dough wrapped. Pass the dough through the machine on its widest setting, then fold the dough and pass through the machine repeatedly, narrowing the setting by one notch each time until you reach the thinnest setting. Cut the sheets of pasta into 6.5 cm (2½ inch) squares; you will need about 32 in total.

5 Place a heaped teaspoonful of the filling in the centre of half of the pasta squares. Brush the edges of the pasta with a little egg yolk and cover with the remaining pasta squares. Pinch the edges together to seal and dust the ravioli with flour.

6 To make the gremolata, mix the chopped parsley with the grated lemon zest and season with a little sea salt.

7 Add the ravioli to a large pan of well-salted lightly boiling water and cook for about 7 minutes. Drain thoroughly.

8 Meanwhile, melt the butter in a frying pan large enough to hold all the ravioli, adding 15-30 ml (1-2 tbsp) water to form an emulsion. Stir in the gremolata and add the ravioli. Warm through, ensuring all the ravioli are coated with the melted butter and gremolata. Serve immediately.

Neil Haidar

Ravioli of Ricotta and Boursin Cheese with Fennel and Pine Nut Butter

Pasta Dough:
310 g (10½ oz) '00' flour
2.5 ml (½ tsp) salt
3 eggs (size 2)
25 ml (1 fl oz) olive oil (approximately)

Filling:
2 cloves garlic, crushed
15 ml (1 tbsp) olive oil
225 g (8 oz) ricotta cheese
175 g (6 oz) Boursin cheese
1 egg (size 2)
30 ml (2 tbsp) finely chopped basil

Topping:
75 g (3 oz) butter
60 ml (4 tbsp) olive oil
1 fennel bulb, cored and finely chopped
50 g (2 oz) pine nuts
3 ripe plum tomatoes, seeded and chopped
30 ml (2 tbsp) finely chopped basil
25 g (1 oz) Parmesan cheese, freshly grated

To Garnish:
basil leaves

1 To make the ravioli dough, put the flour, salt, eggs and olive oil in a food processor and process for about 30 seconds until a smooth dough is formed. If necessary, add a little more olive oil to help the dough come together. Wrap in cling film and flatten. Leave to rest in the refrigerator for 30 minutes.

2 To make the ravioli filling, sauté the garlic in the olive oil until softened, then transfer to a bowl. Add all of the remaining ingredients and whisk with an electric beater until smooth.

3 Cut off about one quarter of the ravioli dough and re-wrap the remainder. Flatten the piece of dough slightly and dust with flour. Pass through a pasta machine on its widest setting, then fold the dough and pass through the machine repeatedly, narrowing the setting by one notch each time until you reach the last but one setting. Dust lightly with flour, cover with a tea-towel and set aside. Repeat with the rest of the dough.

4 Using a 7.5 cm (3 inch) pastry cutter, cut 30 circles from the pasta dough. Place a rounded teaspoon of the filling in the centre of 15 circles. Moisten the edges of the other 15 circles and place over the filling. Press the edges together to seal. Leave the ravioli on a tea-towel and allow to dry slightly before cooking.

5 Meanwhile, prepare the topping. Heat the butter and 45 ml (3 tbsp) olive oil in a pan, add the fennel and sauté for 3 minutes or until soft; keep warm. Heat the remaining 15 ml (1 tbsp) olive oil in a frying pan and toast the pine nuts until browned. Warm the tomatoes through in a pan.

6 Cook the ravioli in a large pan of boiling water for 4-5 minutes until al dente (tender but firm to the bite). Drain and arrange on warmed serving plates. Top with the buttered fennel, pine nuts, chopped tomatoes and basil. Sprinkle the Parmesan on top and garnish with basil leaves. Serve immediately.

Holly Schade

Lemon Risotto with Fresh Herb Salad

15 ml (1 tbsp) oil
75 g (3 oz) butter
4 shallots, finely chopped
600 ml (1 pint) chicken stock (homemade)
salt and freshly ground black pepper
150 g (5 oz) carnaroli or Arborio rice
50 g (2 oz) Parmesan cheese, freshly grated
30 ml (2 tbsp) chopped herbs (eg basil, chives, thyme, parsley, rocket, sorrel)
finely grated zest of 1 lemon
dash of Noilly Prat

Fresh Herb Salad:
30 ml (2 tbsp) walnut oil
15 ml (1 tbsp) olive oil
15 ml (1 tbsp) blackberry vinegar
5 ml (1 tsp) red wine vinegar
5 ml (1 tsp) balsamic vinegar
50 g (2 oz) assorted herb leaves (eg rocket, baby spinach, sorrel, basil, parsley)

To Serve:
Parmesan Tuiles (see right)

1 Heat the oil with half of the butter in a medium heavy-based pan. Add the shallots and sauté until soft and translucent. In the meantime, bring the stock almost to the boil in another pan, season, lower the heat and keep at simmering point.

2 Add the rice to the shallots and stir over the heat for 1-2 minutes until the grains are shiny and coated with the butter and oil. Add a ladleful of stock and cook, stirring constantly, until all the liquid is absorbed. Continue adding the stock, a ladleful at a time, ensuring each addition is absorbed before adding the next, until the rice is *al dente* (cooked but firm to the bite). This should take approximately 18-20 minutes.

3 Add the remaining butter, cheese, herbs, lemon zest and Noilly Prat. Stir gently.

4 For the salad, combine the oils and vinegars in a screw-topped jar with seasoning to taste and shake vigorously to combine. Just before serving, toss the herb leaves in the dressing to coat.

5 Serve the risotto with the herb salad and Parmesan Tuiles.

Liz Franklin

Parmesan Tuiles

50 g (2 oz) Parmesan cheese, coarsely grated

1 Place a sheet of non-stick baking parchment on a baking tray and sprinkle the cheese into oval shapes on the paper. Cook in a preheated oven at 180°C (350°F) mark 4 for about 5 minutes until the cheese melts and turns golden brown.

2 Carefully remove with a spatula and lift over a rolling pin. Leave until cool and crisp, then transfer to an airtight tin to store until needed.

Liz Franklin

Tarte à l' Oignon

Sweet red onions are used for these rich, creamy individual flans. It is important to fry them very slowly until completely soft before filling the flan cases.

Pastry:
175 g (6 oz) plain flour
3 large pinches of salt
75 ml (5 tbsp) extra-virgin olive oil
2 cloves garlic, crushed
7.5 ml (1½ tsp) water

Filling:
65 ml (4½ tbsp) extra-virgin olive oil
2 medium red onions, halved and sliced
15 ml (1 tbsp) balsamic vinegar
15 ml (1 tbsp) caster sugar
250 m (8 fl oz) double cream
1 egg (size 2)
2 egg yolks (size 2)
salt and freshly ground black pepper

To Garnish:
basil leaves

1 To make the pastry, sift the flour and salt into a bowl. Heat the olive oil in a pan, add the garlic and water and heat until it begins to bubble, then gradually mix into the flour.

2 Divide the dough into 4 portions and use to line 4 greased 10 cm (4 inch) individual flan tins, pressing the dough against the sides and base with your fingers. Chill in the refrigerator for about 30 minutes.

3 Bake in a preheated oven at 220°C (425°F) mark 7 for 10 minutes. Remove from the oven and lower the oven setting to 190°C (375°F) mark 5.

4 For the filling, heat the olive oil in a heavy-based frying pan over a low heat. Add the onions, balsamic vinegar and sugar and cook slowly, stirring frequently, until the onions are soft.

5 In a mixing bowl, whisk together the cream, whole egg, egg yolks and seasoning. Stir in the cooked onions.

6 Spoon the onion filling into the pastry cases and cook in the centre of the oven for 15 minutes or until lightly golden brown. Serve garnished with basil leaves.

Charlotte Bircher

Double Tomato Tartlets

Pastry:
100 g (4 oz) plain flour, sifted
pinch of salt
50 g (2 oz) unsalted butter, diced
2 egg yolks
15 ml (1 tbsp) oil, from the sun-dried tomato jar

Filling:
4 cherry tomatoes
5 ml (1 tsp) salt
175 g (6 oz) mascarpone
75 g (3 oz) Jarlsberg cheese, grated
90 ml (6 tbsp) chopped basil leaves
salt and freshly ground black pepper
4 sun-dried tomatoes in oil, well drained and halved

To Serve:
a little oil from the sun-dried tomato jar

1 To make the pastry, place the flour, salt and butter in a food processor and work until the mixture resembles breadcrumbs. Mix the egg yolks and oil together; add to the rubbed-in mixture. Process briefly until the dough binds together, adding 1 or 2 drops of cold water, if necessary.

2 Wrap the dough in cling film and leave to rest in the refrigerator for 30 minutes.

3 Roll out the pastry thinly and use to line four 9 cm (3½ inch) lightly buttered tartlet tins (preferably loose-based ones). Prick the pastry bases with a fork and chill in the refrigerator for 20 minutes. (This pastry is 'short' so it may crack.)

4 Meanwhile, prepare the filling. Slice the cherry tomatoes into rounds, sprinkle with a little salt and place on a wire rack over kitchen paper. Cover with kitchen paper and leave to drain for 20 minutes; pat dry.

5 Place the mascarpone, Jarlsberg and half of the chopped basil in the food processor. Add seasoning and process until smooth and creamy.

6 Line the pastry cases with greaseproof paper and baking beans and bake in a preheated oven at 200°C (400°F) mark 6 for 10 minutes. Remove from the oven and let cool. Lower the oven setting to 180°C (350°F) mark 4.

7 Divide the cheese mixture between the pastry cases. Arrange a line of fresh tomato slices across the middle and put a sun-dried tomato half on either side. Season with pepper.

8 Place on a baking tray and bake in the oven for about 30 minutes, until the filling is set and golden brown. Leave to stand for 10 minutes.

9 Carefully remove the tartlets from the tins and place on warmed serving plates. Surround with the remaining chopped basil leaves, and drizzle with a little sun-dried tomato oil. Serve warm.

Louise Halfhide

Roquefort Tartlets with a Walnut Salad

Pastry:
120 g (4 oz) flour
pinch of salt
60 g (2½ oz) margarine, in pieces
25 ml (5 tsp) boiling water

Filling:
150 g (5 oz) Roquefort cheese
150 ml (¼ pint) double cream
1 large egg, lightly beaten
30 g (1 oz) walnuts, ground
freshly ground black pepper

Salad:
assorted salad leaves
15 ml (1 tbsp) wine vinegar
30 ml (2 tbsp) walnut oil
25 g (1 oz) walnuts

1 To make the pastry, put the flour, salt, margarine and boiling water into a bowl and mix together using a round-bladed knife. (Using boiling water will allow you to use the pastry immediately.) Roll out thinly and use to line 4 individual flan tins. Prick the bases with a fork.

2 Crumble the Roquefort into a bowl, add the cream and mix until smooth. Add the lightly beaten egg and the crushed walnuts. Season with pepper. Pour the filling into the pastry cases and cook in a preheated oven at 190°C (375°F) mark 5 for about 45 minutes.

3 Meanwhile prepare the salad leaves. For the dressing, mix the vinegar with salt and pepper, then add the walnut oil and whisk to combine. Toss the salad leaves in the dressing.

4 Serve the tartlets just warm, with the salad leaves. Garnish with the walnuts.

Anne May

Polenta with Home-dried Tomatoes, Mozzarella, Basil and Olive Tapenade

Polenta:
100 g (3½ oz) quick-cook (instant) polenta
500 ml (16 fl oz) water
salt and freshly ground black pepper
75 g (3 oz) pecorino cheese, grated
knob of butter

Filling:
1 buffalo mozzarella cheese, about 125 g (4 oz)
8 home-dried tomato halves (see below)
handful of basil leaves

Tapenade:
125 g (4 oz) black olives (pitted)
1 clove garlic, peeled
2 canned anchovy fillets
15 ml (1 tbsp) extra-virgin olive oil
5 ml (1 tsp) lemon juice

1 To cook the polenta, bring the water to the boil in a large saucepan. Add 2.5 ml (½ tsp) salt. Sprinkle in the polenta, whisking constantly. Lower the heat and cook, stirring continuously, for 5 minutes, until the polenta is smooth and very thick; it will leave the side of the pan. Add the grated cheese and knob of butter. Stir until evenly amalgamated.

2 Spread the polenta thinly on a baking tray, as evenly as possible, to a depth of about 5 mm (¼ inch). Leave to cool and set.

3 For the filling, chop the mozzarella, tomatoes and basil and combine in a bowl. Drizzle over a little olive oil (from the tomatoes) and set aside to infuse.

4 To make the tapenade, put the olives, garlic and anchovies in a blender or food processor and process until finely chopped. Add the olive oil and lemon juice and process until evenly mixed. Season with salt and pepper to taste.

5 When ready serve, cut the polenta into 5 cm (2 inch) squares, using a ravioli cutter or pastry cutter. Brown under a preheated grill on both sides. Sandwich the polenta squares together in pairs with the mozzarella and tomato filling.

Charlotte Bircher

Home-dried Tomatoes: Halve 16 ripe plum tomatoes lengthwise, then scoop out and discard the seeds and hard cores. Lay the tomato halves on 2 baking sheets and drizzle with 60 ml (4 tbsp) olive oil. Sprinkle with 15 ml (1 tbsp) sugar and 5 ml (1 tsp) salt. Bake in the oven on the lowest possible setting – 50°C (100°F) mark ⅛ for about 12-14 hours until crinkly. The tomatoes will be drier than sun-dried tomatoes and have a more intense flavour. They can be used straight away or stored in olive oil.

Cheese and Walnut Soufflé

50 g (2 oz) dry white breadcrumbs
100 ml (3½ fl oz) milk
30 g (1 oz) unsalted butter
15 g (½ oz) plain white flour
1 egg yolk
80 g (3¼ oz) mature soft cheese (eg chaumes, maroille, milleens)
3 egg whites
5 ml (1 tsp) lemon juice
75 g (3 oz) walnuts, chopped
salt and freshly ground pepper
60 g (2¼ oz) watercress, trimmed
45 ml (3 tbsp) walnut oil
15 ml (1 tbsp) white wine vinegar

1 Liberally butter 4 ramekins and coat with a generous layer of breadcrumbs.

2 Bring the milk to the boil in a small saucepan, then remove from the heat. In another saucepan, melt the butter, stir in the flour and cook for 1-2 minutes. Slowly add the milk, stirring constantly. Bring to the boil and simmer for 1 minute, stirring. Remove from the heat and stir in the egg yolk and soft cheese until smooth.

3 Whisk the egg whites in a large mixing bowl with a pinch of salt, until soft peaks form. Add the lemon juice and continue whisking until the mixture is smooth and stiff. Beat about a quarter of the egg white into the cheese mixture, then fold in the remainder. Season with salt and pepper.

4 Half fill the ramekins with the soufflé mixture. Sprinkle 50 g (2 oz) of the chopped walnuts evenly over the surface, then cover with the remaining soufflé.

5 Stand the ramekins in a bain-marie (roasting tin containing enough water to come halfway up the sides of the dishes). Bake in a preheated oven at 180°C (350°F) mark 4 for 8 minutes. Leave to cool for 10 minutes. Shake the soufflés to loosen them from the ramekins, then turn them out carefully onto a lightly oiled baking sheet. Allow to cool for a further 10 minutes (or longer if more convenient).

6 Just before serving, return the soufflés to the oven and bake at the same temperature for 5 minutes until the crusts are crisp.

7 Meanwhile toss the watercress leaves in the walnut oil and wine vinegar and arrange on individual serving plates. Sprinkle with the rest of the chopped walnuts. Serve the hot soufflés on the bed of watercress leaves.

Ashley Wilson

Layered Aubergines with Tomato, Feta and Basil, and Two Sauces

4 small aubergines
salt and freshly ground black pepper
90 ml (6 tbsp) olive oil
30 g (1 oz) butter
300 g (10 oz) good ripe tomatoes, blanched, peeled, seeded and coarsely chopped
pinch of sugar
30 g (1 oz) basil leaves, finely shredded
120 g (4 oz) Greek feta cheese

Tomato Sauce:
15 g (½ oz) butter
200 g (7 oz) can chopped tomatoes
pinch of sugar

Yogurt Sauce:
150 ml (¼ pint) natural yogurt
lemon juice, to taste

To Garnish:
few small basil leaves

1 Cut the aubergines into 1 cm (½ inch) slices. Season with pepper. Heat the olive oil in a frying pan until smoking, then quickly fry the aubergine slices on both sides; drain on kitchen paper.

2 Melt the butter in a frying pan, add the tomatoes and cook for 1 minute. Add the sugar and basil and season to taste with pepper. Crumble the cheese into the pan and remove from the heat.

3 Layer the tomato mixture with the aubergine slices in an ovenproof dish and bake in a preheated oven at 200°C (400°F) mark 6 for 7-10 minutes.

4 Meanwhile, to make the tomato sauce, melt the butter in a pan, add the chopped tomatoes, seasoning and sugar. Cook until reduced by half, then strain through a fine sieve.

5 For the yogurt sauce, mix the yogurt with a little lemon juice to taste.

6 Serve the terrine with the two sauces.

Vanessa Binns

Beetroot Mousse with Horseradish Sauce

Beetroot Mousse:
150 ml (¼ pint) vegetable stock
½ sachet powdered gelatine
225 g (8 oz) beetroot, cooked and peeled
juice and grated rind of ½ lemon
5 ml (1 tsp) balsamic vinegar
5 ml (1 tsp) sugar
salt and freshly ground black pepper
150 ml (¼ pint) whipping cream

Horseradish Sauce:
30 ml (2 tbsp) grated fresh horseradish root
10 ml (2 tsp) lemon juice
10 ml (2 tsp) sugar
pinch of powdered mustard
150 ml (¼ pint) double cream

To Garnish:
salad leaves

1 To make the beetroot mousse, warm the vegetable stock in a small pan over a low heat until hot but not boiling, then sprinkle the powdered gelatine over the surface. Allow the gelatine to dissolve completely, then remove from the heat and allow to cool slightly.

2 Put the beetroot, lemon rind and juice, balsamic vinegar and sugar in a food processor and work to a smooth purée. Add the cooled gelatine mixture, salt and pepper, and process briefly until evenly mixed. Cool until just beginning to set.

3 Lightly whip the cream and fold into the beetroot mixture. Check the seasoning. Pour into lightly greased ramekins and chill in the refrigerator until set.

4 To make the horseradish sauce, mix together the horseradish, lemon juice, sugar and mustard. Whip the cream until soft peaks form, then fold into the horseradish mixture.

5 To serve, turn the mousses out onto individual serving plates. Drizzle the horseradish sauce around the mousses and garnish with salad leaves.

Claire Ketteman

Parcels of Marinated Orkney Goat's Cheese with Salad

225 g (8 oz) goat's cheese (preferably Lairobell)
45 ml (3 tbsp) extra-virgin olive oil
15 ml (1 tbsp) chopped parsley
15 ml (1 tbsp) chopped thyme
30 ml (2 tbsp) chopped chives
½ clove garlic, crushed
freshly ground black pepper
1 yellow pepper
1 red pepper
4-8 large spinach leaves

Salad:
selection of salad leaves (eg frisée, rocket, oakleaf lettuce)
30 ml (2 tbsp) extra-virgin olive oil
10 ml (2 tsp) raspberry vinegar
salt and freshly ground black pepper

1 Cut the cheese into four slices. Pour the oil into a shallow dish, add the chopped herbs, garlic and black pepper, and mix well. Add the cheese, turning to coat well. Cover and leave to marinate for 2 hours at room temperature, or overnight in the refrigerator.

2 Halve the peppers and place-cut side down under a preheated high grill for about 10-15 minutes until the skin is blistered and blackened. Cover with a tea-towel and leave until cool enough to handle, then skin, de-seed and slice each pepper half into 6 strips.

3 Blanch the spinach leaves in boiling water for a few seconds only until pliable. Refresh in cold water, then drain well and dry on a tea-towel.

4 Wrap each piece of cheese in a spinach leaf, brush with a little olive oil and place in an ovenproof dish. Cover with foil, and bake in a preheated oven at 220°C (425°F) mark 7 for 8 minutes.

5 Meanwhile combine the olive oil, raspberry vinegar, salt and pepper for the salad dressing in a screw-topped jar and shake well to combine. Toss the peppers in a little of the dressing; use the rest to dress the salad leaves.

6 Arrange the salad leaves and peppers on individual plates. Top each with a goat's cheese parcel. Serve at once.

Katherine Rendall

Warm Salad of Puy Lentils and Spring Onions with a Mustard Dressing

10 ml (2 tsp) black mustard seeds
10 ml (2 tsp) yellow mustard seeds
salt and freshly ground black pepper
5 ml (1 tsp) Dijon mustard
15 ml (1 tbsp) balsamic vinegar
150 ml (¼ pint) olive oil, plus 30 ml (2 tbsp)
2 bunches of spring onions
200 g (7 oz) Puy lentils, rinsed
3 slices of white bread
a little olive oil, for brushing

To Serve:
selection of salad leaves (eg rocket, lamb's lettuce, oakleaf lettuce)

1 Roughly crush the black mustard seeds with 5 ml (1 tsp) of the yellow mustard seeds, using a pestle and mortar. Add a pinch of salt, some pepper, the Dijon mustard, balsamic vinegar and 150 ml (¼ pint) olive oil. Slice the spring onions into thin rounds, then toss in the dressing.

2 Add the lentils to a pan of boiling salted water and simmer over a moderate heat for about 15 minutes until just tender. Drain, rinse with boiling water, then drain thoroughly and toss with the dressing.

3 Brush the slices of bread with olive oil and grill on both sides until golden. Cut each into 4 triangles.

4 To finish, heat the 30 ml (2 tbsp) olive oil in a pan, then add the remaining yellow mustard seeds. Cook over a gentle heat until they just start to pop. Tip in the lentils and their dressing and just warm through. Arrange the salad leaves and lentils on individual plates. Garnish with the toast and serve.

Elaine Bates

Mixed Herb Salad with Quail's Eggs

12 quail's eggs
salt and freshly ground black pepper
50 g (2 oz) piece Parmesan cheese
30 ml (2 tbsp) virgin olive oil
50 g (2 oz) very thinly sliced pancetta, cut into strips
1 clove garlic, crushed
15 ml (1 tbsp) basil oil
15 ml (1 tbsp) balsamic vinegar
2.5 ml (½ tsp) caster sugar
sufficient mixed salad leaves to serve 4 (eg lamb's lettuce, frisée, radicchio)
few mixed herb leaves (eg basil, flat-leaved parsley, dill)

1 Cook the quail's eggs in a pan of boiling salted water for approximately 5 minutes. Drain and cool under running cold water until cold. Peel the eggs and halve lengthwise; set aside.

2 Thinly pare the Parmesan into shavings, using a potato peeler.

3 Heat 15 ml (1 tbsp) olive oil in a small non-stick frying pan. Add the pancetta and garlic and fry until crispy. Drain on kitchen paper.

4 For the dressing, whisk together the basil oil, remaining olive oil, balsamic vinegar, seasoning and sugar thoroughly.

5 Place the salad leaves and herbs in a large bowl, pour over the dressing and toss to coat the leaves thoroughly.

6 Divide the salad between 4 serving plates, arrange the halved quail's eggs around the edge and sprinkle the pancetta and fried garlic over the middle of the salad. Top with the wafer-thin shavings of Parmesan. Serve immediately.

Andrew Urbanek

Warm Goat's Cheese with Apple and Celeriac Salad

4 mature goat's cheeses (preferably Crottin de Chauvignole)
30 ml (2 tbsp) flour, for dusting
1 egg, lightly beaten
90 ml (6 tbsp) slivered almonds
olive oil, for frying

Salad:
¼ small celeriac, peeled
1 tart dessert apple (eg Granny Smith)
1 small Cos or sweet Romaine lettuce
handful of rocket leaves

Dressing:
7.5 ml (1½ tsp) hazelnut oil
45 ml (3 tbsp) sunflower oil
22 ml (1½ tbsp) cider vinegar
large pinch of salt
2-3 grinds of black pepper

Bread Croûtes:
4 slices French country-style bread
15 g (½ oz) butter

1 Lightly dust the goat's cheeses with flour. Dip into the beaten egg, then coat with the almonds. Place on a flat plate, cover and chill in the refrigerator until needed.

2 Cut the celeriac into fine julienne and immerse in a bowl of cold water acidulated with a squeeze of lemon juice. Peel, halve and core the apple; cut into julienne and add to the acidulated water.

3 For the bread croûtes, cut a round from each slice of bread just larger than the cheese. Heat the butter in a frying pan, add the bread slices and fry until golden on both sides. Drain on kitchen paper and keep warm.

4 Heat a thin film of olive oil in a frying pan, add the cheeses and fry gently for 1-2 minutes, turning carefully until coloured on all sides. Transfer to an oiled baking sheet and roast in a preheated oven at 200°C (400°F) mark 6 for about 3 minutes.

5 Meanwhile, whisk together the ingredients for the dressing. Roughly tear the salad leaves. Drain the celeriac and apple julienne and pat dry with kitchen paper. Toss the salad leaves and julienne separately with the dressing.

6 Arrange the salad leaves in the centre of each serving plate. Surround with the celeriac and apple julienne. Place each cheese on a bread croûte and position on the salad leaves. Serve at once.

Chumki Banerjee

Salad of Cooked Peppers with a Saffron Vinaigrette

3 green peppers
2 red peppers
80 ml (5 tbsp) olive oil
2.5 ml (½ tsp) ground cumin
2 cloves garlic, peeled
2 ripe, red plum tomatoes, skinned, seeded and roughly chopped
salt and freshly ground black pepper

Saffron Vinaigrette:
45 ml (3 tbsp) olive oil
small pinch of saffron threads
1 clove garlic, peeled
5 ml (1 tsp) wine vinegar
45 ml (3 tbsp) water
large pinch of salt
small pinch of cayenne pepper
pinch of sugar

Deep-fried Coriander:
24 coriander leaves
corn oil for deep-frying

To Garnish:
1 small tomato, skinned, seeded and finely chopped

1 Grill the peppers under a preheated hot grill, turning occasionally, until blistered and charred all over. Place in a bowl, cover and leave to cool; the steam created will help to lift the skins. Peel away the skins, then halve, core and cut the peppers into 1 cm (½ inch) wide strips.

2 Heat the olive oil in a saucepan. Add the pepper strips and cumin, and cook, stirring, for 1 minute. Add the garlic, tomatoes and seasoning. Simmer for 20 minutes, until the peppers are very tender. Leave to cool, then check the seasoning.

3 To make the saffron vinaigrette, heat the olive oil in a small pan, add the saffron and garlic, cover and sweat for about 1 minute. Add the vinegar, water, salt, cayenne and sugar. Remove from the heat and leave to cool and infuse for at least 30 minutes. Discard the garlic and check the seasoning.

4 Just before serving, prepare the deep-fried coriander. Wash the coriander leaves and pat dry thoroughly on kitchen paper. Heat the oil in a deep-fat fryer to 165°C (325°F), then add the coriander leaves. Deep-fry until the leaves stop bubbling. Remove with a slotted spoon and drain on kitchen paper.

5 Remove the garlic and as much cooking oil as possible from the cooked peppers. Pile a mound of peppers onto the centre of each serving plate. Drizzle the vinaigrette around them and scatter the diced tomato on the vinaigrette. Garnish with the deep-fried coriander.

Juliette Boisseau-Hardman

Spiced Cornucopia of Wild Mushrooms

450 g (1 lb) assorted mushrooms (see note)
120 ml (4 fl oz) olive oil
10 ml (2 tsp) cumin seeds
10 ml (2 tsp) coriander seeds
120 ml (4 fl oz) white wine
75 ml (2½ fl oz) water
rosemary sprig
juice of ½ lemon
freshly ground black pepper
30 ml (2 tbsp) chopped coriander leaves
1 clove garlic, crushed
4 thin slices white bread
few salad leaves, to garnish

1 Clean the mushrooms thoroughly. Heat half of the olive oil in a saucepan, add the cumin and coriander seeds and sauté for 1 minute, then add the mushrooms and sauté for 2 minutes. Add the wine, water, rosemary and lemon juice and simmer for about 10 minutes. Turn up the heat and boil rapidly until the liquid has reduced by half. Season with pepper to taste. Stir in the chopped coriander and keep warm.

2 To make the cornucopias, mix the remaining olive oil with the garlic. Brush each slice of bread liberally with the garlic oil, then wrap around a cream horn tin and press the edges together, cutting off any excess, to achieve a horn shape. Place on a baking tray and bake in a preheated oven at 180°C (350°F) mark 4 for 10-15 minutes until light golden. Carefully remove the bread horns from the tins.

3 To serve, spoon some of the mushrooms into each bread horn, then lay on a serving plate. Spoon the rest of the mushrooms onto the plates so that they look as if they are spilling out of the cornucopias. Pour some of the mushroom juices around the plate and garnish with a few salad leaves. Serve at once.

Elaine Bates

Note: Use a mixture of different mushrooms, such as chanterelles, pied de moutons, oyster and button mushrooms – depending on whatever is available.

Warm Salad of Wild Mushrooms with Deep-fried Polenta and Balsamic Dressing

Polenta:
900 ml (1½ pints) salted water
150 g (5 oz) polenta
25 g (1 oz) butter
25 g (1 oz) freshly grated Parmesan cheese
oil for deep-frying

Salad:
175 g (6 oz) young spinach leaves
1 bunch rocket leaves
22 ml (1½ tbsp) olive oil
25 g (1 oz) butter
275 g (10 oz) wild mushrooms (see note), cleaned
1 large clove garlic, chopped
15 ml (1 tbsp) chopped flat-leaved parsley
salt and freshly ground black pepper

To Serve:
12 ml (½ tbsp) balsamic vinegar
30 ml (2 tbsp) extra-virgin olive oil
freshly shredded Parmesan cheese

1 First make the polenta. Bring the salted water to the boil in a pan and slowly trickle in the polenta, whisking continuously until evenly combined and smooth. Lower the heat and cook, stirring continuously with a wooden spoon, for 30-40 minutes, making sure the polenta does not stick to the base of the pan. The polenta is cooked when it leaves the sides of the pan clean.

2 Stir in the butter and grated Parmesan and pour into a shallow square dish. Allow to cool for about 30 minutes until set, then cut into 1 cm (½ inch) cubes.

3 Heat the oil in a deep-fat fryer. When it is hot, deep-fry the polenta cubes in batches until crisp and golden. Drain on kitchen paper.

4 Combine the spinach and rocket in a large salad bowl.

5 Heat the olive oil and butter in a frying pan and sauté the mushrooms and garlic over a moderate to high heat for 2-3 minutes. Remove from the heat, stir in the parsley and seasoning to taste, then spoon over the salad in the bowl.

6 Add the balsamic vinegar to the pan and heat, stirring to scrape up the sediment, then pour over the salad. Add the polenta cubes, drizzle with the olive oil and adjust the seasoning. Toss the salad gently and serve immediately, topped with slivers of Parmesan cheese.

Alastair Hendy

Note: Use whichever wild mushrooms are in season for this salad, such as chanterelles, hedgehog mushrooms, horn of plenty and oyster mushrooms.

Fish & Shellfish

Scallops and Prawns in a Ginger and Citrus Butter Sauce

16 large scallops, shelled
20 large raw prawns, shelled and deveined
lemon juice, to taste

Sauce:
5 cm (2 inch) piece fresh root ginger, peeled and sliced
170 ml (6 fl oz) Sauternes or other dessert wine
60 ml (4 tbsp) double cream
175 g (6 oz) unsalted butter, cubed
juice of ½ lemon
juice of ½ lime
salt and freshly ground black pepper

To Serve:
steamed baby vegetables, eg carrots, sweetcorn, courgettes, fine beans, cherry tomatoes

To Garnish:
dill sprigs
wild celery leaves
lemon and lime zest

1 First make the sauce. Put the sliced ginger and wine in a saucepan over gentle heat and allow to reduce very slowly, for about 30 minutes to about 15 ml (1 tbsp) syrup. Add the double cream and bring to the boil. Take off the heat and whisk in the butter cubes, two at a time. Strain, then add the citrus juices and seasoning to taste.

2 Cut each scallop in half and season with salt, pepper and lemon juice. Season the prawns with salt and pepper. Put the prawns into a steamer and gently steam for 2 minutes. Add the scallops and steam for 1 minute.

3 Remove the scallops and prawns from the steamer and arrange on heated serving plates. Pour over the sauce. Arrange the steamed baby vegetables on the plates, alternating colours for maximum effect.

4 Garnish with dill sprigs and dot with a few wild celery leaves. Sprinkle over a little lemon and lime zest.

Alan Spedding

Gingered Crab and Sole Layer with a Rhubarb Sauce

100 g (3½ oz) filo pastry
30 g (1 oz) butter
450 g (1 lb) filleted white fish (eg sole, plaice, cod)
100 g (3½ oz) young spinach leaves
15 ml (1 tbsp) crème fraîche
2 pieces preserved stem ginger in syrup, finely chopped
15 ml (1 tbsp) stem ginger syrup
225 g (8 oz) dressed crab meat
salt and freshly ground white pepper
cayenne pepper, to taste

Rhubarb Sauce:
450 g (1 lb) rhubarb
75 g (3 oz) sugar
30 ml (2 tbsp) stem ginger syrup

1 First make the sauce. Put the rhubarb and sugar in a saucepan with 200 ml (7 fl oz) water. Place over a low heat until the sugar is dissolved, then bring to the boil. Lower the heat and simmer for 10-15 minutes. Strain the sauce through a sieve, pressing through as much juice from the rhubarb as possible. Add the stem ginger syrup and set aside.

2 Place 3 sheets of filo pastry one on top of another, brushing each sheet with melted butter, then cut out 8 rectangular or diamond shapes, each about 8 x 5 cm (3 x 2 inches). Place on a greased baking sheet and bake in a preheated oven at 200°C (400°F) mark 6 for 5-10 minutes until golden and crisp.

3 Meanwhile, cut the fish into eight similar-sized pieces.

4 Blanch the spinach in boiling water for 1 minute; drain thoroughly.

5 In a bowl, mix the crème fraîche, ginger and ginger syrup with the crab and season with salt, pepper and cayenne to taste.

6 Place 4 pieces of fish on a foil-lined baking sheet and cover with half of the spinach. Spoon the crab meat on top, then cover with the remaining spinach. Lay the other fish pieces on top to form 4 neat stacks. Bake in a preheated oven at 200°C (400°F) mark 6 for 10 minutes until the fish is just cooked. Meanwhile reheat the sauce.

7 Sandwich each 'fish stack' between the cooked filo pastry pieces and serve on warmed plates on a pool of rhubarb sauce, with accompaniments of your choice.

Ashley Wilson

Pan-fried Fillet of Tuna with a Basil Salsa

4 tuna fillets, each about 175 g (6 oz), cut from the middle to the tapering end of the fillet if possible

Marinade:
60 ml (4 tbsp) extra-virgin olive oil
juice of 1 lemon
handful of fresh mixed herbs (bay, thyme, oregano, parsley, chervil)
2 cloves garlic, very roughly chopped
salt and freshly ground black pepper

Basil Salsa:
90 ml (3 fl oz) agrumato (see note)
25 ml (1 fl oz) lemon juice
5 ml (1 tsp) coriander seeds, crushed
8 basil leaves, shredded
2 tomatoes, skinned, seeded and diced

To Finish:
a little oil for cooking

1 Wipe the tuna fillets with kitchen paper, then place in a shallow dish. Mix together the ingredients for the marinade, then pour over the tuna to cover evenly. Cover the dish with cling film and leave to marinate for at least 2 hours.

2 To prepare the basil salsa, heat the oil gently in a small pan. Add the lemon juice. Remove from the heat, add the crushed coriander seeds and leave to infuse. Set aside the shredded basil and diced tomato.

3 To cook the tuna, heat a little oil in a heavy-based frying pan or griddle until searing hot. Lift the tuna out of the marinade, discarding any bits of herb that may be sticking to the fillets. Add the tuna to the pan, pressing down firmly to sear the fillets. Cook for 1 minute each side only; the tuna should still be pink in the centre.

4 Place on a tuna fillet each warmed serving plate. Add the basil and tomato to the basil salsa and spoon over the tuna and sparingly around the plate. Serve at once, with baby fennel and potato galettes.

Gill Tunkle

Note: Agrumato is extra-virgin olive oil flavoured with lemon. If unobtainable, use a good quality extra-virgin olive oil instead.

Seared Tuna Fillets with a Slow-cooked Tomato Sauce

4 pieces fresh tuna fillet, each about 125 g (4 oz) and 1 cm (½ inch) thick
4 large basil leaves, torn
15 ml (1 tbsp) olive oil

Tomato Sauce:
450 g (1 lb) plum tomatoes
15 ml (1 tbsp) olive oil
5 ml (1 tsp) sugar
2 cloves roasted garlic (from the ½ head, see note)

To Garnish:
basil leaves
½ head garlic, roasted (see note)

1 Place the tuna fillets in a shallow dish, sprinkle with the torn basil leaves and olive oil and turn to coat. Cover and leave to marinate in the refrigerator for about 2 hours.

2 Meanwhile, make the tomato sauce. Immerse the tomatoes in a bowl of boiling water for 30 seconds, then remove and peel away the skins. Deseed and chop the tomato flesh. Heat the olive oil in a large pan. Add the chopped tomatoes and sugar and cook for 2-3 minutes. Reduce the heat and cook very gently for 40 minutes, stirring occasionally. Add the garlic and purée in a blender or food processor until smooth. Season with salt and pepper to taste.

3 To cook the tuna, preheat a griddle or heavy-based frying pan over a high heat for 3-4 minutes (without any oil) until very hot. Place the tuna fillets on the griddle (or in the pan) and cook for 1-2 minutes each side.

4 To serve, place the tuna fillets on warmed serving plates and top with the tomato sauce. Garnish with basil and roasted garlic. Serve with accompaniments of your choice.

Abigail Barlow

Note: To roast the garlic for the sauce and garnish, wrap the ½ head garlic in foil and bake in a moderate oven for 30 minutes.

Crispy Skin Salmon with Morels and Trompette de Mort on Curly Kale with Spiced Puy Lentils

575 g (1¼ lb) middle-cut salmon fillet, with skin
7.5 ml (1½ tsp) hazelnut oil
sea salt

Lentils:
125 g (4 oz) Puy lentils
25 g (1 oz) butter
50 g (2 oz) leek (white part only), shredded
1 clove garlic
2.5 ml (½ tsp) fennel seeds, freshly ground
2.5 ml (½ tsp) coriander seeds, freshly ground
2.5 ml (½ tsp) cardamom seeds, freshly ground
2.5 ml (½ tsp) cumin seeds, freshly ground
150 ml (¼ pint) chicken stock

Sauce:
12 small dried morels
12 dried trompette de mort
120 ml (4 fl oz) Noilly Pratt
150 ml (¼ pint) chicken stock
120 ml (4 fl oz) double cream
15 g (½ oz) butter

Kale:
5 ml (1 tsp) oil
25 g (1 oz) derinded bacon, finely chopped
125 g (4 oz) curly kale, finely chopped
4 juniper berries, crushed

1 Soak the lentils in cold water to cover for 2 hours. Cut the salmon fillet into four rectangular pieces and keep covered in a cool place until required.

2 To make the sauce, soak the dried mushrooms in warm water to cover for 30 minutes; drain. Simmer the Noilly Pratt in a pan until reduced by about two thirds. Add the stock and reduce again by about half. Add the cream and butter and bring to a simmer. Stir in the reconstituted mushrooms and cook gently until softened. Set aside to allow the flavours to infuse, until required.

3 To cook the lentils, melt the butter in a pan, add the leek and sauté until softened. Add the garlic and spices and cook for a further 1 minute. Drain the lentils and put into a saucepan with the stock and the leek and spice mixture. Cook for about 10 minutes until al dente, tender but firm to the bite.

4 To cook the curly kale, heat the oil in a wok, add the bacon and toss over a medium-high heat for 1 minute. Add the kale and juniper berries and toss over a moderate heat for 2-3 minutes until just wilted.

5 Meanwhile heat the hazelnut oil in a heavy-based frying pan until very hot. Place the salmon fillets, skin-side down, in the pan and cook for 1 minute then, using tongs, seal each of the other surfaces. Now place skin-side down for 2 minutes, turn and cook the opposite side for 1 minute, then turn again and cook skin-side down for a further 1-2 minutes; the skin should be dark brown and crisp.

6 To serve, place a mound of kale on each serving plate and scatter over the lentils. Position a portion of salmon on top and spoon the sauce and mushrooms around. Sprinkle the salmon with sea salt and serve at once.

Marion MacFarlane

Pan-fried Fillet of Salmon with a Tomato and Basil Vinaigrette

15 ml (1 tbsp) butter
5 ml (1 tsp) chopped herbs
5 ml (1 tsp) crushed or finely chopped garlic
4 Scottish salmon fillets, skinned

Vinaigrette:
175 ml (6 fl oz) olive oil
60 ml (4 tbsp) cider vinegar
5 ml (1 tsp) honey
1 clove garlic, crushed
15 ml (1 tbsp) finely chopped tomato flesh
15 ml (1 tbsp) chopped basil
salt and freshly ground black pepper

To Garnish:
lemon wedges
basil sprigs

1 First make the vinaigrette. Place all the ingredients in a screw-topped jar and shake well. Season with salt and pepper.

2 Melt the butter in a heavy-based frying pan, add the herbs and garlic, then add the salmon fillets and cook over a high heat for about 10-15 seconds each side to seal. Turn the heat down to medium and cook for 6-8 minutes, until the salmon is just cooked and flakes easily when tested with a fork.

3 Place one salmon fillet in the middle of each warmed serving plate. Give the vinaigrette a good shake and spoon over the salmon. Garnish with lemon and basil to serve.

Betsy Anderson

Wild Salmon filled with Spinach Mousse in a Puff Pastry Parcel

4 fillets of wild salmon
1 egg, beaten
450 g (1 lb) ready-prepared puff pastry

Spinach Moulds:
1 kg (2¼ lb) trimmed baby spinach leaves
25 g (1 oz) butter, melted
200 ml (7 fl oz) crème fraîche
salt and freshly ground black pepper
2 egg whites (size 2)

Tomato Butter Sauce:
300 g (10 oz) ripe, full-flavoured tomatoes
40 g (1½ oz) unsalted butter, chilled and diced
5 ml (1 tsp) caster sugar
2.5 ml (½ tsp) cayenne pepper

To Garnish:
diced skinned tomato
8 baby spinach leaves

1 First cook the spinach in a steamer or a covered pan with just the water clinging to the leaves after washing for 3 minutes. Refresh in cold water and squeeze dry. Thoroughly pat dry on kitchen paper.

2 Butter 4 individual moulds. Put the remaining butter in a pan on a high heat, add the spinach and cook for 2-3 minutes; do not allow to brown. Drain, then chop finely or purée in a food processor.

3 Put the crème fraîche in a small pan and reduce by one third over a medium heat. Add to the chopped spinach and season. In a bowl, whisk the egg whites until soft peaks form, then fold into the spinach. Set aside a small quantity for stuffing the salmon.

4 Spoon the remaining mixture into the prepared moulds and place in a bain-marie, or roasting tin containing enough hot water to come halfway up the sides. Bake in a preheated oven at 180°C (350°F) mark 4 for 15-20 minutes.

5 Meanwhile make the salmon parcels. Roll out the pastry to a 3-5 mm (⅛-¼ inch) thickness. Cut out 4 rectangles large enough to wrap the salmon fillets in. Cut a slit in the centre of each salmon fillet and insert the reserved spinach mousse; do not overfill.

6 Place a stuffed salmon fillet on one side of each pastry rectangle. Brush the pastry edges with beaten egg and fold the pastry over the salmon to enclose and form a neat parcel. Press the edges together firmly. Brush the top of the parcel with more beaten egg. Decorate with shapes cut from the pastry trimmings. Brush with beaten egg to glaze. Make two small slits in the top of each parcel. Bake in a preheated oven at 200°C (400°F) mark 6 for 15 minutes or until the pastry is crisp and golden brown.

7 Meanwhile, make the tomato butter sauce. Halve, skin and deseed a third of the tomatoes. Place in a blender or food processor with the rest of the tomatoes and blend well. Pass the blended tomatoes through a sieve into a small pan, pressing them through with the back of a spoon. Warm gently over a low heat; do not to allow to boil or it will separate. Whisk in the butter, a piece at a time, on and off the heat. Taste and add sugar, salt and cayenne pepper.

8 To serve, place a salmon parcel on each warmed serving plate. Unmould a spinach mousse onto each plate and add a portion of tomato butter sauce. Garnish with diced tomato and spinach leaves. Serve at once.

Connie Stevens

Mosaic of Salmon and Cod with Sorrel Sauce

2 thick cod fillets, skinned, each about 300 g (10 oz)
2 thick salmon fillets, skinned, each about 225 g (8 oz)
juice of 1 lemon
salt and freshly ground white pepper
16-20 large spinach leaves
Japanese dried seaweed, for steaming (optional)

Sorrel Sauce:
225 g (8 oz) sorrel
50 g (2 oz) butter
250 ml (8 fl oz) single cream
250 ml (8 fl oz) double cream
30-45 ml (2-3 tbsp) reduced fish stock
few drops of lemon juice

1 Trim the top of each fish fillet as necessary, to give an even 2 cm (¾ inch) thickness. Cut each cod fillet lengthways into 8 strips, each about 10 x 2 x 2 cm (4 x ¾ x ¾ inch). If it isn't possible to cut 10 cm (4 inch) lengths, wrap shorter pieces together to achieve the required length. Cut each salmon fillet widthways into 8 strips, about 2 cm (¾ inch) wide. Sprinkle with lemon juice and season with salt and pepper.

2 Wash the spinach leaves thoroughly and remove the thick stalks. Blanch the spinach in boiling water for 1 minute or so until pliable. Drain thoroughly. Wrap each cod strip in a spinach leaf. Weave four strips of each fish together to form a chequerboard, trimming the salmon as necessary. Season well with salt and pepper.

3 If using seaweed, cover with cold water and leave to soak for 10 minutes; drain. Half-fill a large frying pan with water and bring to the boil. Take a large steamer and line with the seaweed if using. Lay the fish in the steamer. Set over the frying pan. Cover and steam for about 8-10 minutes until the salmon flakes easily when tested.

4 Meanwhile prepare the sauce. Wash the sorrel leaves thoroughly and remove the thick stalks. Melt the butter in a saucepan, add the sorrel leaves and cook gently until wilted. In a separate pan, gently heat the creams together, taking care not to allow the mixture to boil. Add the fish stock and sorrel; stir well. Add the lemon juice and season with salt and pepper to taste.

5 To serve, place a mosaic on each warmed serving plate and pour on some of the sorrel sauce. Hand the extra sorrel sauce separately, in a small jug. Serve immediately, with wild rice and vegetable julienne.

Sara Douglas

Prince of Wales Salmon

700 g (1½ lb) middle-cut salmon
30 ml (2 tbsp) wholegrain mustard
450 g (1 lb) leeks
50 g (2 oz) butter
15 ml (1 tbsp) tarragon leaves
salt and freshly ground pepper
15 ml (1 tbsp) dry white wine

Stock:
450 g (1 lb) white fish or salmon bones and heads
1 onion
1 leek, white part only
4 button mushrooms
25 g (1 oz) butter
100 ml (4 fl oz) dry white wine
1 bouquet garni

1 First prepare the stock. Discard the gills, then chop up the fish heads and break up the fish bones; rinse well. Chop the vegetables. Heat the butter in a saucepan and sweat the vegetables until soft. Add the fish heads and bones and sweat for 3 minutes. Add the wine, bring to the boil and reduce by half. Cover the contents of the pan with cold water, add the bouquet garni and simmer, uncovered, for 30 minutes. Strain the stock into a bowl.

2 Meanwhile, remove the skin from the salmon and cut out the bone, leaving the fillets attached at one side. Open out like a book, tweeze out any small bones then spread with the mustard and chill in the refigerator while preparing the stuffing.

3 Thinly slice the leeks, place in a saucepan with the fish stock and cook until soft. Drain, reserving the stock. Purée the leeks in a blender or food processor with the butter and tarragon until smooth. Season to taste.

4 Spread half of the leek purée over the mustard-coated inside of the salmon and sandwich together. Lay the salmon on a sheet of foil, sprinkle with the wine and seal the foil. Bake in a preheated oven at 200°C (400°F) mark 6 for 25 minutes, then leave to rest in the foil for 5 minutes.

5 Mix the remaining leek purée with the fish stock to make a sauce and reheat gently. Add the cooking juices from the salmon. Cut the salmon vertically into 4 portions. Place one on each plate and pour on a little of the sauce. Serve the rest of the sauce separately.

Kate Whiteman

Salmon Fillet on a bed of Courgette and Ginger with an Orange Butter Sauce

4 skinless salmon fillets, each about 140 g (4½ oz)
4 courgettes, about 525 g (1¼ lb) total weight
salt and freshly ground black pepper
olive oil and butter, for frying
10 ml (2 tsp) grated fresh root ginger
30 ml (2 tbsp) chopped chives
30 ml (2 tbsp) chopped tarragon

Dressing:
juice of 1 lime, ie 22 ml (1½ tbsp)
60 ml (4 tbsp) sunflower oil
10 ml (2 tsp) caster sugar
5 ml (1 tsp) coarse-grain mustard
freshly ground black pepper, to taste

Sauce:
120 ml (4 fl oz) fish stock
juice of 1 very large orange, ie 120 ml (4 fl oz)
15 ml (1 tbsp) wine vinegar
3 egg yolks
225 g (8 oz) unsalted butter
rind of 1 orange, removed in thin strips with a zester

To Garnish:
4-8 cherry tomatoes, halved and grilled
few steamed asparagus tips
deep-fried strips of courgette skin

1 Coarsely grate the courgettes, place in a colander and sprinkle with salt. Leave to stand (over a plate to collect the degorged juices) for 2 hours.

2 Meanwhile, prepare the dressing. Put all of the ingredients into a screw-topped jar and shake well to combine; set aside. Prepare the garnish at this stage too.

3 For the sauce, put the fish stock and orange juice in a pan and boil to reduce by half. In a separate pan, bring the wine vinegar to the boil. Immediately pour onto the egg yolks, whisking constantly, preferably using a hand-held blender. Melt the butter in a pan, then very slowly add to the yolk mixture, whisking all the time; it will become very thick. Whisk in enough of the reduced stock and orange juice to give a smooth pouring consistency. Stir in the orange zest.

4 Season the salmon fillets liberally with salt and pepper. Brush with oil and cook under a preheated hot grill for 2-3 minutes each side. (Alternatively, fry in a little oil and butter for 1-2 minutes, then finish off under the grill for 1 minute).

5 Meanwhile, squeeze excess water from the courgettes, then toss with the ginger and steam for 1 minute to just heat through. Mix with the herbs and 30 ml (2 tbsp) of the dressing.

6 To serve, pile the courgette mixture onto warmed serving plates and surround with the sauce. Arrange the salmon on the courgette and top with the fried courgette skin. Garnish the plates with the cherry tomatoes and asparagus tips. Serve accompanied by Parsnip and Potato Cakes (page 229).

Clare Askaroff

Salmon Parcels with Lime and Coriander Beurre Blanc

For this recipe, the salmon must be taken from the centre of the fish; it should be approximately 10 cm (4 inches) across.

900 g (2 lb) middle portion filleted salmon

Stuffing:
2 leeks
1 courgette
2 carrots
salt and freshly ground black pepper

Beurre Blanc:
50 g (2 oz) shallots, peeled and very finely diced
30 ml (2 tbsp) wine vinegar
90 ml (3 fl oz) dry white wine
finely pared zest and juice of 1 lime
15 ml (1 tbsp) whipping cream
225 g (8 oz) unsalted butter, diced
5 ml (1 tsp) ground coriander
salt and freshly ground black pepper

1 Remove the skin from the salmon and pull out any small residual bones with tweezers. (You will have 2 fillets.) Slice the salmon into 4 pieces, cutting two from each fillet. Set aside in a cool place.

2 For the stuffing, thinly slice the leeks, courgette and carrots on the diagonal. Steam the vegetables until just tender, allowing approximately 6 minutes for the carrots, 4 minutes for leeks and 2 minutes for the courgette. Leave to cool slightly.

3 Divide the steamed vegetables between the salmon fillets, placing them at the end of one short side. Season with salt and pepper, then roll the fillet to enclose the vegetables. Place the rolled fish parcels on a large sheet of lightly greased foil. Bring the sides of the foil together and seal tightly. Set aside.

4 To make the beurre blanc, place the shallots in a heavy-based pan and add the vinegar, white wine and half the lime juice. Cover and simmer over a low heat until almost all of the liquid has evaporated, about 15-20 minutes.

5 Meanwhile blanch the lime zest in boiling water for about 4 minutes. Allow to cool, then chop finely.

6 Remove the shallots from the heat and allow to cool slightly, then whisk in the cream. Gradually whisk in the butter, one piece at a time, ensuring each piece is incorporated before adding the next. Once all of the butter is incorporated, add the chopped lime zest and ground coriander. Season with salt and pepper to taste, adding a little more lime juice if necessary. Cover and keep warm.

7 Place the foil-wrapped salmon parcels in a preheated oven at 200°C (400°F) mark 6 and cook for 10-12 minutes until the salmon is just opaque. Carefully place each salmon parcel on a warmed serving plate and add a generous swirl of sauce. Serve at once, with Potato and Courgette Soufflés (see page 229).

Claire Ketteman

Grilled Salmon Steaks with a Dill, Cucumber and Green Peppercorn Sauce

4 salmon steaks
30 ml (2 tbsp) olive oil
juice of ½ lemon
salt and freshly ground black pepper

Sauce:
10 ml (2 tsp) olive oil
2.5 ml (½ tsp) finely chopped garlic
125 ml (4 fl oz) dry white wine
125 ml (4 fl oz) fish stock
2.5 ml (½ tsp) plain flour
150 ml (¼ pint) double cream
5 ml (1 tsp) green peppercorns in brine, drained
¼ cucumber, peeled, seeded and chopped
75 ml (5 tbsp) chopped dill

To Serve:
rocket leaves

1 First make the sauce. Heat the oil in a saucepan and lightly fry the chopped garlic, then add the wine and fish stock and reduce by half. Mix the flour with the cream, then add to the sauce and reduce for a further 2 minutes. Add the peppercorns, cucumber, salt, pepper and dill. Set aside.

2 Brush the salmon steaks liberally with the olive oil and lemon juice. Season with salt and pepper. Grill under a moderately high heat for 8-10 minutes, turning once.

3 Arrange a bed of rocket on each plate. Position a salmon steak on top and pour on the sauce. Serve with new potatoes tossed in butter, and broccoli with sesame seeds.

Nicholas Hocking

Red Mullet and Grilled Vegetables with a Peppered Fish Sauce and Rouille

3-4 red mullet, each about 225 g (8 oz), filleted (bones and trimmings reserved for the stock)
salt and freshly ground black pepper
22 ml (1½ tbsp) olive oil

Stock:
fish bones and trimmings from the red mullet
1 onion, quartered
few parsley and thyme sprigs
300 ml (½ pint) dry white wine

Sauce:
30 ml (2 tbsp) olive oil
1 shallot, or ½ small onion, chopped
1 carrot, diced
2 cloves garlic, peeled
30 ml (2 tbsp) chopped flat-leaved parsley
1 bay leaf
30 ml (2 tbsp) tomato purée
large pinch of cayenne pepper, or to taste
600 ml (1 pint) dry white wine

Rouille:
1 red pepper
2 cloves garlic, blanched
5 ml (1 tsp) tomato purée
15 ml (1 tbsp) olive oil
15 ml (1 tbsp) fresh white breadcrumbs
15 ml (1 tbsp) crème fraîche
large pinch of cayenne pepper, or to taste

Vegetables:
2 red peppers
1 aubergine
salt
2 red onions
1 fennel bulb
2 large courgettes
60 ml (4 tbsp) olive oil, flavoured with garlic and herbs to taste

To Serve:
225 g (8 oz) spinach or samphire
black olives, to garnish

1 Put all the ingredients for the stock in a large pan, bring to the boil, lower the heat and simmer for 15 minutes, skimming frequently. Strain through a fine sieve, then return the stock to the pan and boil to reduce to 150 ml (¼ pint).

2 To make the sauce, heat the oil in a pan, add the shallot, carrot and garlic cloves and sauté for 2 minutes. Add all of the remaining sauce ingredients. Bring to the boil, lower the heat and simmer for 15 minutes, then increase the heat and boil to reduce to 150 ml (¼ pint). Strain through a fine sieve and add the fish stock; set aside.

3 Season the red mullet fillets with salt and pepper and rub with a little olive oil. If they are large, cut the fillets in half.

4 Place all 3 red peppers, including the one for the rouille, on a baking sheet, drizzle with a little oil and bake in a preheated oven at 200°C (400°F) mark 6 for 25 minutes. Remove from the oven, place in a dish, cover and leave until cool enough to handle, then peel off the skins. Halve, core and deseed the peppers.

5 To make the rouille, put 1 red pepper in a food processor or blender with the blanched garlic and tomato purée and work to a purée. With the motor running, add the oil in a thin steady stream through the feeder tube to form a thick, glossy mixture. Turn into a bowl and fold in the breadcrumbs to thicken the rouille. Add the crème fraîche and season with cayenne pepper and salt to taste.

6 To prepare the vegetables, slice the aubergine into thick rounds, sprinkle liberally with salt and leave to degorge for at least 20 minutes. Thickly slice the red onions, to give 4 solid rounds from each one. Trim the fennel and cut lengthways into 8 slices. Cut the courgettes into thick slices on the diagonal. Slice the 2 red peppers into strips.

7 To cook the vegetables, place the onion and fennel slices on a baking sheet, drizzle with 30 ml (2 tbsp) of the flavoured oil and roast in the oven at 180°C (350°F) mark 4 for 20 minutes, turning once. Add the pepper strips for the last 5 minutes.

8 Rinse the aubergine slices thoroughly in cold water to remove the salt and bitter juices and pat dry with kitchen paper.

9 Heat a ribbed chargrill pan until smoking hot. Brush the courgette and aubergine slices with a little of the flavoured oil and chargrill in batches until just cooked; keep warm while cooking the remainder. (Alternatively, these can be roasted in the oven with the onions and fennel).

10 Blanch the spinach in boiling water until just wilted and drain thoroughly, pressing the spinach to squeeze out excess moisture; keep warm. Reheat the fish sauce and keep warm.

11 To cook the fish, heat 15 ml (1 tbsp) olive oil in a large non-stick frying pan and gently fry the fish fillets, flesh-side down, for 5 minutes, then turn and fry the skin side for 2 minutes.

12 To serve, place a small mound of spinach in the centre of each warmed serving plate. Arrange a selection of vegetables with the red mullet in a circle on top. Pour the sauce around the fish and vegetables. Add a spoonful of rouille to each portion and garnish with black olives.

Alastair Hendy

Steamed Fillets of Red Snapper with Courgettes and Shallots, on a Watercress Sauce

2 courgettes
4 red snapper fillets, each about 175 g (6 oz)
few chives
few parsley sprigs
few thyme sprigs
salt and freshly ground black pepper
30 ml (2 tbsp) unsalted butter
4 shallots, sliced

Watercress Sauce:
small bunch of watercress, stalks removed
20 ml (4 tsp) butter
3 shallots, sliced
30-45 ml (2-3 tbsp) fish stock
15 g (1 tbsp) wine vinegar

1 Trim the courgettes and pare into long strips, using a swivel vegetable peeler. Immerse in a bowl of iced water and place in the refrigerator.

2 To make the watercress sauce, blanch the watercress leaves in a pan of boiling water for 1 minute, then drain and refresh in a bowl of iced water; drain thoroughly. Heat a quarter of the butter in a small pan, add the shallots and sauté until just transparent, then place in a blender with the watercress. Process in short bursts until smooth, adding a little fish stock if necessary. Strain the sauce into a small pan and heat gently, adding just enough stock to give a pouring consistency. Add the wine vinegar and seasoning to taste; set aside.

3 Lay the herbs in a steamer and place the fish fillets on top. Season well and dot with half of the butter. Bring the water in the steamer pan to a gentle boil and position the steamer. Cook for about 8 minutes, depending on the thickness of the fish fillets.

4 Meanwhile, heat the remaining butter in a pan and sauté the shallots until softened. Drain the courgette, pat dry and add to the shallots; cook for 1 minute.

5 Just before serving, gently reheat the sauce and beat in the remaining unsalted butter, a little at a time, until the sauce is glossy and smooth.

6 Spread a pool of watercress sauce on each warmed serving plate and pile the courgette and shallot mixture in the middle. Position the fish fillets on top. Serve at once, accompanied by Cheese and Sesame Tuiles filled with Baby Vegetables (see page 212) and fried potato shavings.

Marian Freeman

Fillet of Baby Halibut with Fennel, Shallots and Roasted Red Pepper

1 red pepper
75 g (3 oz) butter
1 fennel bulb, sliced
4 shallots, sliced
salt and freshly ground black pepper
4 skinned baby halibut fillets, each about 125-150 g (4-5 oz)
½ lime
2 spinach leaves

1 Roast the pepper under a preheated hot grill, turning frequently until it is black all over. Place it in a covered bowl until cool enough to handle, then peel, remove the core and seeds, and dice the flesh.

2 Heat 50 g (2 oz) butter in a pan, add the fennel and shallots, cover and soften, without browning, for 10 minutes. Add the pepper, then season with salt and pepper.

3 Butter 4 pieces of foil, each about 30 x 40 cm (12 x 16 inches). Divide the fennel mixture between them, then top each with a halibut fillet, a squeeze of lime juice, a sprinkling of salt and a knob of butter. Fold the foil to make loose parcels, sealing the edges well.

4 Place the parcels on a heated baking tray and cook in a preheated oven at 200°C (400°F) mark 6 for 6-8 minutes, depending on the thickness of the fish.

5 While the fish is cooking, shred the spinach, immerse briefly in boiling water and drain thoroughly.

6 Place a fillet of fish on each warmed serving plate, surround with the fennel mixture and top with a few strands of spinach. Serve immediately, accompanied by new potatoes.

Jan Gilberthorpe

Brill with Mushroom Hollandaise and Herb Sauce

For the herb sauce, you need to prepare a fish stock in advance (see below).

4 fillets of brill, each about 225 g (8 oz), skinned
225 g (8 oz) fresh wild mushrooms, or mixed wild and cultivated
10 ml (2 tsp) truffled sauce or porcini mushroom spread with truffles, or 15 ml (1 tbsp) crème fraîche
salt and freshly ground black pepper
small knob of butter
olive oil, for frying

Herb Sauce:
150 ml (¼ pint) fish stock (see below)
20 ml (4 tsp) chopped thyme
60 ml (4 tbsp) chopped parsley
juice of ½ lemon
20 g (¾ oz) unsalted butter

Hollandaise:
2 egg yolks
15 ml (1 tbsp) water
squeeze of lemon juice, to taste
225 g (8 oz) unsalted butter

1 Finely chop the mushrooms and cook in a dry frying pan, without any fat, over a high heat, until all the liquid from the mushrooms has evaporated. Taste and stir in the truffle sauce or spread if using or, alternatively, the crème fraîche. Season with salt and pepper to taste and set aside.

2 Season the fish fillets with salt and pepper. Heat a small knob of butter together with a film of olive oil in a frying pan. Add the fish fillets and fry briefly for about 1 minute on each side to colour. Transfer to a baking sheet and roast in a preheated oven at 230°C (450°F) mark 8 for 10-15 minutes, depending on the thickness of the fillets. Meanwhile, make the herb and hollandaise sauces.

3 For the herb sauce, pour the fish stock into a saucepan and reduce over a high heat by one third. Stir in the herbs, lemon juice and butter. Season with salt and pepper to taste; set aside in a warm place.

4 For the hollandaise, put the egg yolks, water and a squeeze of lemon juice in a blender. Melt the butter in a pan. With the motor running, pour the hot butter through the blender feeder tube in a steady stream. Spoon the hollandaise into a bowl. Gently reheat the mushrooms and fold into the hollandaise. Season with salt and pepper to taste, adding a little extra lemon juice if required.

5 To serve, place a brill fillet in the centre of each warmed serving plate. Pour some of the herb sauce onto the fish and spoon a pool of mushroom hollandaise to one side. Serve immediately, with Stoved New Potatoes (see page 233) and Glazed Green Beans (see page 205).

Chumki Banerjee

Fish Stock: Rinse 1.4 kg (3 lb) fish bones under cold running water to remove all traces of blood, then chop roughly. Finely chop 2 leeks, 1 onion, 4 celery sticks (including leaves), ½ head fennel and 2 cloves garlic. Place in a large saucepan and add a small wine glass of Noilly Prat. Boil rapidly until nearly all of the liquid has evaporated. Add the fish bones and 1.8 litres (3 pints) water. Bring to the boil and skim off any scum. Add 10 black peppercorns, a handful of parsley stalks and 2 thyme sprigs. Simmer gently for 20 minutes. Strain through a fine sieve.

Turbot with Leeks and Wild Mushrooms

4 turbot fillets, each about 150 g (5 oz)
75 g (3 oz) butter
6 leeks, white and tender pale green parts only, cleaned and chopped
salt and freshly ground black pepper
4 shallots, finely chopped
125 g (4 oz) button mushrooms, finely chopped
90 ml (3 fl oz) white wine
25 ml (1 fl oz) Madeira (preferably Malmsey)
125 g (4 oz) wild mushrooms (eg trompettes, pied de mouton, chanterelles)
60 ml (2 fl oz) chicken stock
10 ml (2 tbsp) tarragon mustard

To Garnish:
dill sprigs

1 Melt 25 g (1 oz) butter in the pan, add the leeks and sauté until soft. Place in a blender and purée until smooth. Season with salt and pepper to taste; keep warm.

2 Melt 15 g (½ oz) butter in the pan, add the shallots and sauté until softened, then add the button mushrooms and cook for a further 1-2 minutes. Add the wine and Madeira and bring to the boil. Transfer to an ovenproof dish.

3 Lay the turbot fillets on top of the shallot and mushroom mixture. Cover the dish and cook in a preheated oven at 180°C (350°F) mark 4 for 8-10 minutes, taking care to avoid overcooking this delicate fish. Leave to rest in a warm place whilst cooking the wild mushrooms.

4 Sauté the wild mushrooms in 15 g (½ oz) butter until tender. Season with salt and pepper to taste.

5 Combine the cooking juices from the fish and the wild mushroom cooking liquor in a pan. Add the chicken stock and bring to the boil. Reduce by one third, then add the tarragon mustard. Whisk in the remaining diced 25 g (1 oz) butter, a piece at a time, then pass through a sieve to remove the shallots and chopped button mushrooms.

6 Season the turbot fillets and warm through if necessary. Place a mound of puréed leeks on each warmed serving plate and lay a turbot fillet on top. Surround with the sauce and scatter the wild mushrooms on top. Garnish with sprigs of dill and serve immediately.

Neil Haidar

Turbot with a Herb Topping on a Beurre Blanc

4 turbot steaks, each 150-175 g (5-6 oz)
30 ml (2 tbsp) chopped parsley
15 ml (1 tbsp) chopped dill
15 ml (1 tbsp) chopped thyme
5 ml (1 tsp) finely chopped rosemary leaves
600 ml (1 pint) fish stock

Sauce:
60 ml (4 tbsp) reduced fish stock
15 ml (1 tbsp) white wine vinegar
1 shallot, chopped
225 g (8 oz) unsalted butter, chilled and cut into small pieces
salt and freshly ground black pepper
juice of ½ lemon, or to taste

1 Mix the chopped herbs together and press 15 ml (1 tbsp) onto the top of each turbot steak. Bring the fish stock to the boil in a steamer.

2 To make the sauce, put the stock, vinegar and shallot in a wide pan and bring to the boil, then boil to reduce to about 30 ml (2 tbsp). Strain and return to the pan. Place over a low heat and whisk in the butter, a piece at a time, until the sauce is thick and creamy. Season with salt and pepper to taste and add enough lemon juice to sharpen the sauce. Transfer to a bowl set over a pan of hot, but not boiling, water to keep warm for no longer than 15 minutes, whisking gently from time to time.

3 Meanwhile, steam the turbot over the fish stock for 8-10 minutes, depending on thickness. The fish should be just opaque in the middle. Remove the skin from the fish and take out the central bone, taking care to avoid disturbing the topping too much.

4 To serve, spread some of the sauce on each warmed serving plate and place the turbot on top. Serve at once, with accompaniments of your choice.

Judi Geisler

Pan-fried John Dory with Wild Mushrooms and Chinese 'Seaweed'

900 g (2 lb) spring greens, washed and stalks removed
4 shallots
30 ml (2 tbsp) olive oil
350 ml (12 fl oz) good quality fish stock
350 ml (12 fl oz) fruity red wine (eg Grenache or Gamay)
4 thyme sprigs, leaves only
5-10 ml (1-2 tsp) balsamic vinegar
40 g (1½ oz) unsalted butter
400 g (14 oz) wild mushrooms (eg hedgehog fungus, chanterelles), cleaned and sliced
salt and freshly ground black pepper
groundnut oil for deep-frying
a little caster sugar
4 John Dory fillets, each about 200 g (7 oz)
seasoned flour, for dusting
knob of clarified butter
squeeze of lemon juice

1 Roll up each spring green leaf tightly into a cylinder and slice across the roll, as finely as possible, to yield long, fine strands. Dry thoroughly.

2 Finely dice 2 shallots; chop the others.

3 Heat 15 ml (1 tbsp) olive oil in a pan, add the finely diced shallots and cook until softened. Add the fish stock, wine, thyme and balsamic vinegar. Bring to the boil and simmer to reduce to about one third of the original volume. Strain through a fine sieve into a clean pan; keep warm.

4 Heat half of the butter with the remaining oil in a frying pan. Add the chopped shallots and sauté until softened. Add the sliced mushrooms and seasoning. Sauté over a high heat for 6-7 minutes until tender. Set aside; keep warm.

5 Heat the groundnut oil in a deep-fat fryer to 190°C (375°F) and deep-fry the greens in batches until they change colour. Remove and drain thoroughly on kitchen paper. Season liberally with salt and pepper and sprinkle with sugar. Keep warm.

6 Dust the John Dory fillets lightly with seasoned flour. Heat a large frying pan until fairly hot, then add a knob of clarified butter. Add the fish, flesh-side down, and cook for 1-1½ minutes, then turn and cook on the other side for 1-1½ minutes.

7 Meanwhile, return the sauce to the heat and whisk in the remaining butter, a piece at a time, until the sauce is glossy.

8 Squeeze a little lemon juice over the mushrooms and pile into the centre of the warmed serving plates. Place the fish on top and arrange a mound of 'Chinese seaweed' alongside. Flood the plates with the red wine sauce and serve immediately.

Neil Haidar

Cod wrapped in Parma Ham, with Roasted Peppers, Tomatoes and Aubergines

2 large potatoes
50 g (2 oz) butter (approximately)
salt and freshly ground black pepper
1 large onion, finely sliced
200 g (7 oz) pork caul
4 thick pieces cod fillet, each about 175 g (6 oz), skinned
8 slices Parma ham
5 orange peppers
5 yellow peppers
about 200 ml (7 fl oz) olive oil flavoured with garlic and thyme
12 large plum tomatoes, skinned, seeded and quartered
1 aubergine
30 ml (2 tbsp) balsamic vinegar
30 ml (2 tbsp) chopped fresh basil
salt and freshly ground black pepper

1 Peel and finely slice the potatoes. Heat 25 g (1 oz) butter in a pan, add the potato slices and sauté gently until soft but not coloured; drain on kitchen paper and season with salt and pepper. Add the onion to the pan, with a little more butter if needed and sauté in the same way. Drain and season.

2 Wash the pig's caul well and squeeze out all the water. Spread it out flat on a clean surface and cut into 4 squares.

3 Season the cod fillets. Lay each one on two overlapping slices of Parma ham and place a layer of onion and a layer of potato on each piece of fish. Wrap the Parma ham around the fish and topping to enclose, then wrap each parcel in a square of caul. Cover and set aside in the refrigerator.

4 Put the peppers in a shallow roasting tins and drizzle over 90 ml (3 fl oz) of the flavoured olive oil. Roast in a preheated oven at 200°C (400°F) mark 6 for 30-40 minutes until tender, but still slightly retaining their shape. Transfer to a bowl and cover tightly. Pour the oil remaining in the roasting tin into a bowl; set aside.

5 When cool enough to handle, skin, halve and deseed the peppers, adding any juices to the reserved oil. Cut the flesh into large strips. Season with salt and pepper and set aside in a warm place.

6 Put the tomatoes in a shallow roasting tin and drizzle over 45 ml (1½ fl oz) of the flavoured oil. Roast in the oven for 10-15 minutes, making sure they retain some firmness. Season with salt and pepper; set aside in a warm place. Add any oil remaining in the roasting tin to the reserved pepper juices and oil.

7 Heat 30 ml (2 tbsp) flavoured oil in a non-stick frying pan with the remaining 25 g (1 oz) butter. Add the cod parcels and fry gently for 3-4 minutes, until golden brown on all sides. Transfer to an oiled baking sheet and bake in the oven for about 8 minutes until the fish is tender.

8 Meanwhile, dice the aubergine. Heat 30 ml (1 fl oz) flavoured oil in a non-stick frying pan. Add the aubergine and fry until golden. Drain on kitchen paper. Season with salt and pepper and keep warm.

9 Just before serving, gently heat the peppers and tomatoes with the reserved juices and oil, an extra 20 ml (4 tsp) of the flavoured oil and the balsamic vinegar. Stir in the basil. Spoon onto warmed serving plates, place the fish on top and scatter the aubergine around. Serve at once.

Chumki Banerjee

Cod and Coriander on a bed of Leeks with Parmesan

4 thick pieces of cod fillet, each about 150 g (5 oz)
salt and freshly ground black pepper
flour, for coating
15 ml (1 tbsp) butter
25 ml (1 fl oz) olive oil
25 g (1 oz) chopped coriander leaves

Leeks with Parmesan:
olive oil, for cooking
225 g (8 oz) leeks, trimmed and roughly chopped
50 g (2 oz) Parmesan cheese, freshly grated

To Serve:
Saffron Mash (see page 234)

To Garnish:
roasted red pepper diamonds (see note)
coriander leaves

1 Season the cod fillets with salt and pepper, and coat evenly with flour.

2 Melt the butter in a non-stick frying pan, then add the olive oil. Add the cod fillets with the coriander and pan-fry over a high heat for about 10 minutes until golden brown on both sides, turning the fish halfway through cooking.

3 Meanwhile, cover the base of another frying pan with a thin layer of olive oil. Add the leeks, and season with salt and pepper. Fry gently for about 5 minutes; the leeks should still be slightly crunchy. Add the grated Parmesan and toss to mix.

4 To serve, arrange a ring of roasted red pepper diamonds around the edge of each warned serving plate. Place a mound of Saffron Mash in the centre and top with the leeks. Place the pan-fried fish on the top and garnish with coriander leaves. Serve at once.

Amanda Farnese

Note: To prepare the garnish, quarter, core and deseed 1 large red pepper and place on a baking tray. Sprinkle with sea salt and drizzle with olive oil. Bake in a preheated oven at 180°C (350°F) mark 4 for 1 hour. Remove from the oven and cover with a tea-towel. When cool enough to handle, peel away the skin and cut the flesh into diamonds.

Rolled Fillets of Sole and Mixed Peppers on a Cream and Chive Sauce

12 sole fillets, each about 50 g (2 oz), skinned
1 large lemon
½ red pepper
½ green pepper
½ yellow pepper

Sauce:
90 ml (3 fl oz) dry white wine
15 ml (1 tbsp) Noilly Prat
1 small shallot, finely chopped
250 ml (8 fl oz) fish stock
200 ml (7 fl oz) double cream
salt and freshly ground pepper
22 ml (1½ tbsp) finely chopped chives

To Garnish:
snipped chives

1 Place the sole fillets in a shallow dish. Grate 5 ml (1 tsp) zest from the lemon, then squeeze the juice and sprinkle the lemon juice and zest over the sole. Leave to marinate in a cool place for 2 hours.

2 Halve, core and deseed the peppers, then cut into thin strips. Blanch in boiling water for 3 minutes, then refresh under cold water.

3 To make the sauce, put the wine, Noilly Prat and shallot in a saucepan and simmer to reduce by half. Add the fish stock and reduce to one quarter. Stir in the cream and let the sauce simmer for 5 minutes until slightly thickened. Strain the sauce through a fine sieve or muslin and season with salt and pepper. Stir in the chopped chives.

4 Lay the sole fillets on a board and place 3 pepper strips, one of each different colour, on top. Roll up and place, seam-side down, in a steamer. Steam for 6-8 minutes.

5 To serve, ladle the chive sauce onto warmed serving plates and arrange the rolled sole fillets on top. Serve immediately, garnished with chives.

James Doering

Sole Fillets stuffed with Smoked Salmon Mousse

125 g (4 oz) smoked salmon
125 g (4 oz) salmon fillet
1 egg white
200 ml (8 fl oz) single cream
salt and freshly ground pepper
5 ml (1 tsp) chopped dill
8 sole fillets
45 ml (3 tsp) dry white wine
few dill sprigs
5 ml (1 tsp) tomato purée
lemon juice to taste
dill sprigs, to garnish

1 Cut half of the smoked salmon into strips; reserve for garnish. Chop the remaining smoked salmon and the fresh salmon, then work in a blender or food processor with the egg white, 30 ml (2 tbsp) cream and a pinch of salt. Stir in the chopped dill.

2 Lay the sole fillets on a board, season, then divide the salmon mixture between them. Roll up and place in a buttered shallow ovenproof dish. Pour over the wine and add the dill sprigs. Cover with foil and cook in a preheated oven at 180°C (350°F) mark 4 for about 20 minutes.

3 Carefully lift out the fish rolls and keep warm. Pour the cooking juices into a saucepan and boil rapidly until reduced by about half. Add the remaining cream and the tomato purée, stir well and boil for a few minutes. Season carefully, possibly adding a little lemon juice.

4 To serve, halve each rolled fillet and arrange on serving plates. Pour over the sauce and garnish with the reserved smoked salmon and dill.

Daphne Nelson

Turbans of Salmon and Sole with a Watercress Sauce

Turbans:
8 small salmon fillets
8 small sole fillets
salt and freshly ground white pepper
25 g (1 oz) butter, melted

Mousseline:
225 g (8 oz) mixed white fish fillets (bream, whiting, haddock, etc)
1 egg white, size 2
250 ml (8 fl oz) double cream
25 g (1 oz) pistachio nuts, chopped

Fish Fumet:
450 g (1 lb) fish bones, heads and trimmings
1 onion, chopped
1 carrot, chopped
1 leek, chopped
1 bouquet garni
250 ml (8 fl oz) dry white wine

Watercress Sauce:
25 g (1 oz) butter
25 g (1 oz) plain flour
600 ml (1 pint) fish fumet
½ bunch watercress

1 To prepare the mousseline, purée the white fish in a food processor until smooth. Add the egg white and process briefly until evenly blended. Transfer to a pyrex bowl and cover the surface closely with cling film. Place in a large bowl containing ice and refrigerate for 1 hour. Uncover and gradually work in the cream. Fold in the pistachio nuts and season with salt. Cover and refrigerate until required.

2 To prepare the fish fumet, put the fish bones, heads and trimmings in a large saucepan with the vegetables. Add 600 ml (1 pint) water, the bouquet garni and white wine. Bring to the boil, cover and simmer gently for 20 minutes. Strain through a fine sieve and check the seasoning. Measure 600 ml (1 pint) for the watercress sauce.

3 To prepare the turbans, brush 4 dariole or baba moulds with melted butter. Season the salmon and sole fillets and use to line the moulds: alternate the fillets and allow to overhang the edges of the moulds by about 2.5 cm (1 inch). Pack the mousseline into the moulds and fold the overhanging fillets over the mousseline to enclose.

4 Cover each mould with a circle of greaseproof paper. Place on a wire rack in an ovenproof dish and pour enough hot water into the dish to come halfway up the sides of the moulds. Cook in a preheated oven at 170°C (325°F) mark 3 for 35-40 minutes until the turbans are set and springy to the touch. Remove from the oven and leave to rest for 10 minutes.

5 Meanwhile, make the watercress sauce. Melt the butter in a pan, stir in the flour and cook for 1-2 minutes. Remove from the heat and gradually stir in the fish fumet. Bring to a simmer, stirring, and cook, stirring, for 2-3 minutes until thickened and smooth. Set aside a few watercress sprigs for garnish; finely chop the rest and stir into the sauce; keep warm.

6 Remove the greaseproof paper from the moulds. Invert, one at a time, onto a plate, drain off any liquid, then invert onto a warmed serving plate. Soak up any remaining liquid with kitchen paper. Brush the turbans with melted butter and garnish with sprigs of watercress. Serve with the watercress sauce and creamed potatoes.

Tony Davis

Medallions of Skye Monkfish with a Trompette and Tarragon Sauce

700 g (1½ lb) monkfish
16 cherry tomatoes
25 g (1 oz) dried trompettes (or other dried mushrooms)
300 ml (½ pint) wine fish stock
200 ml (⅓ pint) double cream
maldon salt
freshly ground white pepper
175 g (6 oz) spinach, thoroughly cleaned
tiny knob of butter
lemon juice, to taste
40 g (1½ oz) tarragon, chopped

Potato and Courgette Topping:
175 g (6 oz) potatoes, peeled
2 courgettes
oil for deep-frying

To Garnish:
tarragon sprigs

1 Cut the monkfish into medallions, ½-1 cm (¼-½ inch) thick, and pat dry with kitchen paper; cover and set aside in a cool place.

2 Place the cherry tomatoes on an oiled baking tray and roast in a preheated oven at 150°C (300°F) mark 2 for 2-3 hours.

3 Meanwhile soak the mushrooms in warm water to cover for 20 minutes. Transfer to a small pan and cook until the mushrooms are tender and the liquid has evaporated.

4 In another pan, heat the fish stock until bubbling. Stir in the cream and adjust the seasoning. Add the mushrooms to the sauce, then set aside.

5 To prepare the potato and courgette topping, using a vegetable peeler, finely pare thin strips from the potatoes. Repeat with the courgettes. Pat dry with kitchen paper. Heat the oil in a deep-fryer to 190°C (375°F). Add the potato strips and fry until they just stop bubbling and begin to change colour. Remove and drain on kitchen paper; keep warm. Repeat with the courgette strips; keep warm.

6 Remove any tough stalks from the spinach. Place a frying pan over moderate heat. Add the butter, then the spinach and cook, turning constantly, until tender. Season with salt and pepper, and add lemon juice to taste. Set aside; keep warm.

7 To cook the monkfish, place a heavy-based frying pan over a high heat. Add a few drops of oil, then place the fish medallions in the pan, moving them a little initially to prevent sticking (then don't move again). Cook for about 1 minute, then turn and cook for 45 seconds. (The cooking time will depend on the thickness of the fish.) Season with salt and pepper, and sprinkle with a little lemon juice; keep warm.

8 Bring the sauce to the boil and stir in the chopped tarragon. Place a bed of spinach on each warmed serving plate and arrange the monkfish on top. Place 2 cherry tomatoes at each end of the fish and pour the sauce around. Sprinkle the crispy courgette and potatoes on top of the fish. Serve immediately, garnished with tarragon sprigs.

Gerry Goldwyre

Monkfish in a White Wine Sauce

450 g (1 lb) monkfish fillet
5 ml (1 tsp) salt
15 ml (1 tbsp) cornflour
2 egg whites
300 ml (½ pint) corn oil

White Wine Sauce:
2 slices of fresh root ginger, crushed, juice reserved
60 ml (4 tbsp) dry white wine
60 ml (4 tbsp) chicken stock
2 cloves garlic, crushed
5 ml (1 tsp) sugar
15 ml (1 tbsp) cornflour

To Garnish:
shredded spring onion

1 Cut the monkfish into small cubes. Sprinkle with the salt, then dust with the cornflour to coat lightly. Lightly beat the egg whites in a bowl with 7.5 ml (1½ tsp) of the oil.

2 Heat the rest of the oil in a wok or deep frying pan over a moderate heat. When it is hot, fry the fish in batches. Dip the cubes of fish in the egg white mixture, one at a time, then fry in the oil for 2 minutes or until crisp and golden on the outside and cooked in the middle.

3 Drain the fish on kitchen paper and keep warm while cooking the remainder. Clean the wok.

4 To make the sauce, combine the ginger juice, wine, stock, garlic and sugar in the wok. Blend the cornflour with 45 ml (3 tbsp) water, add to the wok and bring to the boil, stirring. Cook, stirring, for 1½ minutes until thickened.

5 Add the fish to the wok and heat through for 45 seconds. Serve at once, garnished with spring onion.

Betsy Anderson

Poultry & Game

Roasted Chicken with Wild Mushrooms, and Potato and Celeriac Mash

2 free-range chickens, each about 1.4 kg (3 lb) in weight

Stuffing:
80 g (3 oz) flat-leaf parsley, stalks removed, finely chopped
40 g (1½ oz) fresh breadcrumbs
40 g (1½ oz) unsalted butter, at room temperature
salt and freshly ground black pepper

Jus:
600 ml (1 pint) good chicken stock
few thyme sprigs

Mushrooms:
30 ml (2 tbsp) olive oil
400 g (14 oz) wild mushrooms (eg hedgehog fungus or chanterelles), cleaned and sliced

Potato and Celeriac Mash:
600 g (1 lb 2 oz) waxy potatoes, (such as Charlotte)
300 g (10 oz) celeriac
50 g (2 oz) unsalted butter
50 g (2 oz) Parmesan cheese, freshly grated

1 Carefully remove the legs and wings from the chickens (see note), making sure that the skin over the breasts is not broken. (You may also prefer to remove the wishbone at this point to make carving easier.)

2 To prepare the stuffing, in a bowl mix together the parsley, breadcrumbs, butter and seasoning.

3 Put the stuffing into a piping bag fitted with a plain nozzle and pipe inbetween the skin and breast meat. Smooth the stuffing evenly under the skin. Season the chicken breasts with salt and pepper. Place in a roasting tin and roast in a preheated oven at 200°C (400°F) mark 6 for 25 minutes.

4 Meanwhile, peel the potatoes and celeriac and cut into even-sized chunks. Cook in salted water to cover until tender. Drain well, then mash smoothly. Beat in the unsalted butter and Parmesan. Season with salt and pepper to taste; keep warm.

5 In the meantime pour the chicken stock into a small saucepan, bring to the boil and reduce by half to concentrate the flavour. Take off the heat, add a few thyme sprigs and set aside to infuse for 15 minutes. Check the seasoning and keep warm.

6 Remove the chicken from the oven and leave to rest in a warm place for 15 minutes. Heat the olive oil in a frying pan, add the wild mushrooms and sauté over a high heat for 6-7 minutes until tender.

7 To serve, remove the chicken breasts from the bone. Spoon some mash onto each warmed serving plate, place a chicken breast on top and scatter the mushrooms around. Pour over the jus and serve at once.

Neil Haidar

Note: Use the chicken legs and wings as the basis for the stock.

Chicken with Roast Garlic in Sauternes Sauce

1 boned chicken, cut into 4 pieces (use carcass for sauce)
120 ml (4 fl oz) crème fraîche
salt and freshly ground black pepper
4 baby carrots, scrubbed

Sauternes Sauce Base:
30 ml (2 tbsp) olive oil
450 g (1 lb) onions, sliced
450 g (1 lb) carrots, sliced
1 leek, sliced
1 chicken carcass, in pieces
1 kg (2 lb) veal bones
1 bottle Sauternes
450 ml (¾ pint) light chicken stock
bouquet garni, ie parsley sprigs, 2 thyme sprigs, celery and bay leaves
75 ml (5 tbsp) double cream
salt and freshly ground black pepper
10 ml (2 tbsp) lemon juice, or to taste

Roast Garlic:
2 heads garlic, unpeeled
15 g (½ oz) butter
10 ml (2 tsp) sugar

To Finish:
15 ml (1 tbsp) chopped parsley

1 Place the chicken in a dish, pour over the crème fraîche and season with salt and pepper to taste. Leave to marinate in a cool place while preparing the sauce.

2 To make the Sauternes sauce base, heat the oil in a large pan and add the onions, carrots and leek. Cover and cook for 5 minutes, then uncover and cook for about 15 minutes until browned. Add the chicken carcass and veal bones. Cook for about 10 minutes until browned.

3 Add a cupful of Sauternes and cook for about 20 minutes until reduced to a glaze. Repeat until all the Sauternes is used. Lower the heat and add the stock and bouquet garni. Cover and cook for 1 hour. Strain through a fine sieve into a clean pan, pressing to extract as much juice as possible. Cook until reduced to a cupful, about 10 minutes. Allow to cool, then remove any fat from the surface.

4 To prepare the garlic, add to a small pan of boiling water and boil for 3 minutes, then drain and remove the skins. Heat the butter in an ovenproof dish, add the garlic and sprinkle with the sugar. Cook in a preheated oven at 120°C (250°F) mark ½ (or at the bottom of a hotter oven while other dishes cook) for about 2 hours. The garlic should be tender and golden; if necessary cover with foil during cooking to prevent browning.

5 Cook the chicken under a preheated grill for 5-10 minutes, then turn over and grill for 5-10 minutes until tender and cooked through. Remove the chicken as it is cooked; the legs will take longer.

6 Meanwhile cook the carrots in salted water for 1 minute; drain.

7 Bring the sauce to the boil, then add the cream and reduce slightly. Correct the seasoning and add lemon juice if necessary. Slice the chicken attractively and arrange on individual serving plates.

8 Spoon over the sauce and garnish with the carrots, roast garlic and parsley. Serve with tagliatelle flavoured with tarragon.

Orlando Murrin

Chicken Sauté in Ginger Sauce with Japanese Mushroom Fritters

4 chicken breast fillets
10 g (⅓ oz) fresh root ginger, peeled and grated
150 ml (¼ pint) soy sauce
75 ml (5 tbsp) saké (Japanese rice wine)
15 ml (1 tbsp) vegetable oil
10 g (⅓ oz) butter
15 ml (1 tbsp) cornflour, blended with 30 ml (2 tbsp) water

Japanese Mushroom Fritters:
100 g (3½ oz) flour
pinch of salt
150 ml (¼ pint) lukewarm water (approximately)
2 egg whites
200 g (7 oz) Japanese mushrooms (eg shiitake, maitake)
corn oil for deep-frying

1 Put the chicken fillets in a shallow non-reactive dish with the grated ginger, soy sauce and saké. Turn to coat with the mixture and leave to marinate for about 15 minutes.

2 Meanwhile, make the mushroom fritter batter. Sift the flour and salt into a bowl, then gradually mix in the water to form a smooth, thick batter. In a separate bowl, whisk the egg whites until stiff, then fold into the batter.

3 Remove the chicken from the marinade, reserving the marinade. Heat the oil in a frying pan and add the butter. When melted together, add the chicken and fry over a high heat for about 1 minute. Reduce the heat to moderate and fry for 5 minutes on each side until tender.

4 Meanwhile cook the mushroom fritters. Heat the oil for deep-frying in a deep saucepan or deep-fat fryer to 190°C (375°F). When it is hot, cook the mushrooms in batches. Dip them into the batter, one at a time, then immerse in the hot oil. When the mushroom fritters rise to the surface, remove with a slotted spoon and drain well on kitchen paper; keep hot.

5 Transfer the chicken to a warmed dish; keep warm. Strain the reserved marinade into the pan and boil to reduce for about 3 minutes. Add the blended cornflour and cook, stirring, for 1 minute.

6 Pour the sauce over the chicken and arrange the mushroom fritters alongside. Serve accompanied by Parsley Rice (see page 238) and Three-colour Vegetable Stir-fry (see page 208).

Noriko Anzai-Jackson

Poached Chicken 'Hindle Wakes' with Lemon Sauce and Forcemeat Balls

2 large, free-range chicken breasts, each about 225 g (8 oz)
600 ml (1 pint) well-flavoured reduced chicken stock

Stuffing:
1 black pudding, about 175 g (6 oz), skinned and coarsely chopped
125 g (4 oz) 'no soak' prunes, roughly chopped
50 g (2 oz) blanched almonds
salt and freshly ground black pepper

Forcemeat Balls:
125 g (4 oz) thick-cut, smoked streaky bacon, derinded and diced
1 celery stick, diced
175 g (6 oz) fatty pork, coarsely minced
50 g (2 oz) fresh breadcrumbs
2.5 ml (½ tsp) ground mace
15-30 ml (1-2 tbsp) finely chopped parsley
freshly ground black pepper
flour, for coating
1 egg, beaten
125 g (4 oz) dried breadcrumbs
oil for deep-frying

Lemon Sauce:
300 ml (½ pint) well-flavoured reduced chicken stock
grated rind and juice of 1 lemon
110 g (4 oz) unsalted butter, diced
10 ml (2 tsp) plain flour

1 To prepare the stuffing, heat a non-stick frying pan, then add the black pudding and prunes. Fry until the pudding changes colour and the mixture is slightly amalgamated. Add the almonds and season liberally with salt and pepper. Let cool.

2 To make the forcemeat balls, combine the bacon, celery, minced pork, fresh breadcrumbs, mace and parsley together in a bowl. Season well with pepper (the bacon should provide sufficient salt). Mix the ingredients together thoroughly. Form the mixture into 12 walnut-sized balls.

3 Using a sharp knife, cut a deep pocket in the side of each chicken breast. Mould the black pudding stuffing into two plump cylinders, using your hands, then use to fill the chicken breasts. Secure with bamboo skewers.

4 Heat the stock in a shallow pan, add the stuffed chicken breasts and poach very gently for 20-30 minutes until tender.

5 In the meantime, cook the forcemeat balls. Roll each one in seasoned flour, dip in beaten egg, then coat in dry breadcrumbs. Heat the oil for deep-frying in a deep-fat fryer until a piece of bread dropped in will turn golden in 1 minute. Add the forcemeat balls and deep-fry for 4-5 minutes until golden brown. Remove and drain on kitchen paper; keep hot.

6 Meanwhile, make the sauce. Put the stock in a saucepan with the lemon rind and juice. Bring to the boil and boil to reduce by half. Blend the flour with 10 ml (2 tsp) of the butter to make a beurre manié. Whisk the remaining butter into the sauce, a piece at a time. Finally whisk in the beurre manié and cook until the sauce thickens without boiling.

7 Remove the skewers from the chicken and carve each breast into 6 thick slices. Arrange 3 slices on each warmed serving plate. Spoon over the sauce and serve with the forcemeat balls and Spinach and Cucumber Ribbons (see page 204).

Mandy Ford

Macadamia and Sesame Chicken

500 g (1 lb) chicken fillets
30 ml (2 tbsp) light soy sauce
125 g (4 oz) macadamia nuts, finely chopped
75 ml (5 tbsp) sesame seeds
1 egg white
salt
30 ml (2 tbsp) cornflour
peanut oil, for shallow-frying

To Serve:
Thai-style salad (see page 202)
red chillies, to garnish
soy sauce flavoured with chilli slices, for dipping

1 Cut the chicken into thin slices and place in a shallow dish. Add the soy sauce, turn to coat and leave to marinate for 1 hour.

2 Combine the chopped nuts and sesame seeds in a flat dish. Beat the egg white with a pinch of salt until light and frothy. Dip the chicken pieces into the cornflour, then in the egg white. Finally coat with the nut mixture, pressing it on firmly.

3 Heat the oil for shallow-frying in a frying pan until a heat haze rises. Shallow-fry the chicken in batches until golden brown. Drain well on kitchen paper and keep warm while cooking the remainder.

4 To serve, divide the salad between serving plates and top with the warm chicken. Garnish with chillies and serve at once, accompanied by the dipping sauce.

Alison Fiander

Note: If macadamia nuts are unobtainable use cashew nuts instead.

Chicken Moroccan-style

6-8 chicken thighs (depending on size)

Stuffing:
30 ml (2 tbsp) chopped coriander
30 ml (2 tbsp) chopped parsley
1 preserved lemon (see note)
10 ml (2 tsp) ground cumin
freshly ground black pepper
8 green olives, stoned
3 cloves garlic
30 ml (2 tbsp) olive oil

Marinade:
large pinch of saffron strands

Sauce:
125 ml (4 fl oz) white wine
15 ml (1 tbsp) chopped coriander
15 ml (1 tbsp) chopped parsley
15 g (½ oz) stoned green olives, cut into slivers
few slivers of preserved lemon rind (see note)
150 ml (¼ pint) double cream
salt and freshly ground pepper
squeeze of lemon juice (optional)

1 Using sharp kitchen scissors, bone the chicken thighs. Put the bones in a roasting tin and brown in a preheated oven at 180°C (350°F) mark 4 for 30-45 minutes.

2 Meanwhile, put all the stuffing ingredients in a blender or food processor and work until the mixture is well blended. Spread a little of this mixture over the inside of each chicken thigh, roll up and tie loosely if necessary with fine string. Place in a shallow dish.

3 Steep the saffron strands in 300 ml (½ pint) boiling water for about 10 minutes, then strain the liquid over the chicken and leave to marinate for several hours, turning occasionally.

4 Remove the chicken from the marinade, wipe dry and place in the roasting tin with the bones; reserve 150 ml (¼ pint) marinade. Roast the chicken in the oven for 25-30 minutes until cooked through and crispy on the outside; increase the heat towards the end of the cooking time if necessary. Discard the bones. Transfer the chicken to a warmed plate; keep warm.

5 Deglaze the pan with the wine. Add the reserved marinade and allow to bubble over a medium heat until syrupy. Strain if necessary, then add the herbs, olives, preserved lemon rind and a little cream. Simmer until rich and creamy. Check the seasoning and add a little lemon juice if preferred.

6 To serve, slice the chicken. Pour a pool of sauce on to each serving plate and arrange the chicken slices on top. Serve immediately.

Sue Longden

Note: To prepare preserved lemons, wash and dry 450 g (1 lb) unwaxed lemons, then cut lengthwise into quarters, leaving them attached at the base. Sprinkle the inside flesh with 30-40 ml (2-3 tbsp) salt. Reshape and pack into a small sterilised jar. Fill to the brim with cooled boiled water. Seal and store in a cool place for about 3 weeks.

Breast of Chicken with Comté Cheese Sauce

4 boneless chicken breasts, skinned
salt and freshly ground black pepper
flour, for coating
60 g (2½ oz) butter
350 ml (12 fl oz) dry white wine
300 ml (½ pint) chicken stock
pinch of freshly grated nutmeg
pinch of cayenne pepper

Comté Cheese Sauce:
35 g (1¼ oz) butter
25 g (1 oz) plain flour
2 egg yolks
150 ml (¼ pint) crème fraîche
30 g (1 oz) Comté cheese, finely grated

To Finish:
60 g (2-2½ oz) Comté cheese, grated
blanched red pepper diamonds

1 Cut the chicken breasts into bite-sized pieces. Season with salt and pepper and coat evenly with flour, shaking off any excess. Heat the butter in a wide, shallow pan and brown the chicken pieces on all sides over a medium heat. Stir in the white wine; bring to the boil, then add the chicken stock with the nutmeg and cayenne. Bring to a simmer and gently poach the chicken pieces for a few minutes until tender.

2 Remove the chicken with a slotted spoon and transfer to a greased 1.5 litre (2½ pint) baking dish. Skim off the fat from the cooking liquid. Strain the liquid and reserve.

3 To make the sauce, melt the butter in a saucepan and stir in the flour. Let it bubble for 1 minute, then gradually whisk in the strained cooking liquid. Simmer, stirring occasionally, for 5-10 minutes until thickened to a coating consistency. Check the seasoning.

4 In a bowl, beat the egg yolks with the crème fraîche. Whisk a little of the sauce into the yolk mixture, then whisk this mixture into the remaining sauce. Heat gently, without boiling, until slightly thickened. Remove from the heat and add the Comté cheese, stirring until melted. Check the seasoning.

5 Pour the sauce over the chicken. Sprinkle with grated cheese and bake in a preheated oven at 220°C (425°F) mark 7 for 5 minutes until golden brown.

6 Arrange on warmed plates, and garnish with red pepper diamonds. Serve immediately, with spinach flavoured tagliatelle.

Tony Davis

Stuffed Breast of Chicken in Filo Pastry with a Wild Mushroom Sauce

4 chicken breasts (preferably free-range or corn-fed)
4 sheets of filo pastry
125 g (4 oz) butter, melted
1 egg, beaten, to glaze

Mousse:
125 g (4 oz) boneless chicken breast or thigh meat
75 g (3 oz) spinach leaves
150 ml (¼ pint) double cream
freshly grated nutmeg, to taste
salt and freshly ground pepper
15 g (½ oz) butter
350-450 g (¾-1 lb) wild mushrooms, eg oyster, shiitake

Sauce:
1.2 litres (2 pints) good homemade chicken stock
Madeira, to taste
wild mushrooms(reserved from mousse)
25-50 g (1-2 oz) butter

1 First prepare the mousse. Put the chicken and spinach in a food processor and work until smooth. Pass through a sieve into a bowl, cover and chill thoroughly, then add the cream, nutmeg and seasoning. Heat the butter in a pan and sauté the mushrooms for no longer than 1 minute. Set aside three quarters of them for the sauce.

2 Open out the chicken breasts as flat as possible. Season, then add a spoonful of mousse together with some sautéed mushrooms. Carefully close the chicken breasts and wrap securely in foil.

3 Bring the stock to the boil in a large pan. Add the chicken and poach for 10 minutes. Remove from the stock and leave to cool, then unwrap. Reduce the stock and reserve.

4 Brush a sheet of filo pastry with melted butter and fold in half. Brush the top again with butter. Place a chicken breast in the centre and wrap the filo around, folding in the ends, to make a parcel. Repeat with the remaining filo and chicken.

5 Brush the filo parcels with beaten egg and place on a well buttered baking tray. Cook in a preheated oven at 190°C (375°F) mark 5 for 25 minutes. Just before you serve, add the Madeira to the chicken stock, and check the seasoning. Add the remaining mushrooms and poach briefly, then strain.

6 Arrange the filo parcels on individual plates with the mushrooms. Whisk the butter into the stock in pieces; serve separately as a sauce.

Louise Solden

Piquant Chicken with Coriander and Lime Sauces

finely grated rind and juice of 2 limes
2 cloves garlic, crushed
50 g (2 oz) unsalted butter
10 ml (2 tsp) ground coriander
4 chicken breast fillets
salt and freshly ground black pepper

Coriander Sauce:
125 ml (4 fl oz) full-cream milk
225 g (8 oz) block creamed coconut
225 g (8 oz) fresh coriander leaves, finely chopped
125 ml (4 fl oz) double cream

Lime Sauce:
finely grated rind and juice of 6 limes
5 ml (1 tsp) light soft brown sugar

1 Mix the lime rind and juice with the garlic, butter and coriander; set aside.

2 Remove any sinews from the chicken. Lay out each chicken breast flat, cover with greaseproof paper and beat lightly to flatten, ensuring that the flesh is not broken.

3 Spread both sides of each chicken breast with the flavoured butter, then roll up and wrap tightly in foil, so that none of the juices may escape. Chill in the refrigerator for 30 minutes, then cook in a preheated oven at 190°C (375°F) mark 5 for 40 minutes.

4 Meanwhile prepare the sauces. For the coriander sauce, place the milk and creamed coconut in a saucepan and heat gently, stirring, until all of the coconut is dissolved. Add the coriander and cook very gently, stirring frequently, for 10 minutes. Purée the sauce in a blender or food processor, then stir in the cream and heat through gently.

5 For the lime sauce, heat the lime juice and grated rind with the sugar. Unwrap the chicken and add the pan juices to the lime sauce. Reduce to a glaze.

6 Place the chicken on individual plates, spoon over the lime sauce to glaze and serve with the coriander sauce, spiced rice and French beans.

Tim Robinson

Pan-fried Duck on a Port and Wine Sauce

4 duck breast fillets
salt and freshly ground black pepper

Sauce:
60 ml (4 tbsp) vegetable oil
2 shallots, roughly chopped
1 celery stick, roughly chopped
1 carrot, roughly chopped
30 g (1¼ oz) brown sugar
100 ml (3½ fl oz) port
200 ml (⅓ pint) red wine
300 ml (½ pint) chicken stock
50 g (2 oz) unsalted butter, diced

1 To make the sauce, heat the oil in a pan, add the shallots, celery and carrot and fry until well browned. Add the sugar and cook until lightly caramelised. Add the port and wine and reduce to about 100 ml (3½ fl oz). Add the stock and reduce until the sauce is thick enough to lightly coat the back of a wooden spoon. Pass through a sieve into a clean pan and gradually whisk in the butter a piece at a time, over a low heat.

2 Place a heavy-based frying pan over a high heat. Season the duck breasts, add to the pan, skin-side down, and sear for 2 minutes. Turn the duck breasts over and sear the other side for 2 minutes.

3 Transfer to a roasting tin and cook in a preheated oven at 190°C (375°F) mark 5 for 8-12 minutes, or longer if preferred, according to taste and the size of the duck breasts; they should still be pink in the centre. Leave to rest in a warm place before carving.

4 To serve, slice the duck and arrange on warmed serving plates. Pour on the sauce and serve with Potatoes Lyonnaise (see page 232), Braised Cabbage Rolls (see page 214) and Root Vegetable Purée (see page 223).

James Hurd

Duck Breast with Dried Cherry and Orange Sauce

3-4 duck breasts
salt and freshly ground black pepper
45 ml (3 tbsp) cherry preserve

Sauce:
350 ml (12 fl oz) duck or brown stock
350 ml (12 fl oz) red wine
125 ml (4 fl oz) port
2.5 ml (½ tsp) thyme leaves
30 ml (2 tbsp) grated orange rind
juice of ½ orange
75 g (3 oz) dried cherries
10 ml (2 tsp) arrowroot

1 To make the sauce, boil the stock to reduce by half, then add the rest of the ingredients except the dried cherries and arrowroot. Simmer until reduced by half, then add the cherries and cook for a further 10 minutes. Mix the arrowroot with 5 ml (1 tsp) water, then add to the sauce and stir over a medium heat until thickened. Keep warm until ready to serve.

2 Rub the fat side of the duck breasts with salt and pepper, then spread with the cherry preserve. Preheat a heavy-based frying pan, then add the duck breasts, skin-side down, and sear over a high heat for 2 minutes. Turn the duck breasts over and sear the other side for 2 minutes. Transfer to a roasting tin and cover lightly with foil.

3 Cook the duck in a preheated oven at 200°C (400°F) mark 6 for 10-15 minutes until cooked through but still pink in the centre. Slice the duck breasts and fan out on warmed individual serving plates. Pour on the sauce and serve at once, with Potato Rösti (see page 233), and courgettes flavoured with thyme.

Holly Schade

Duck Breast in a Pastry Lattice with Grapes and Green Lentils

2 Barbary ducks
45 ml (3 tbsp) olive oil
½ carrot, diced
½ small onion, diced
5 cm (2 inch) white part of leek, diced
½ celery stick, diced
1 thyme sprig
1 glass dry white wine
450 ml (¾ pint) good chicken stock
15 g (½ oz) butter
125 g (4 oz) seedless grapes, peeled

Pastry:
125 g (4 oz) plain flour
pinch of salt
75 g (3 oz) butter, chilled
beaten egg yolk, to glaze

Lentils:
50 g (2 oz) green lentils, soaked in cold water for 4 hours
1 thyme sprig
½ carrot, very finely diced
½ celery stick, very finely diced
5 cm (2 inch) piece white leek, finely diced
15 g (½ oz) butter

1 Remove the breast fillets from the ducks; discard the skin and any excess fat. Set aside.

2 Chop the duck legs and carcasses and place in a roasting tin containing 30 ml (2 tbsp) of the oil. Roast in a preheated oven at 220°C (425°F) mark 7 for 20 minutes, then add the diced vegetables and thyme and roast for a further 10 minutes. Pour off the fat, then add the wine to the roasting tin and reduce over a moderate heat. Add the chicken stock and simmer, uncovered, for 20 minutes, skimming occasionally. Remove the bones and strain the sauce through a fine sieve. Whisk in the butter and season to taste.

3 Season the duck fillets with salt and pepper. Heat remaining 15 ml (1 tbsp) oil in a heavy-based frying pan and quickly seal the duck breasts on both sides. Remove from the pan and let cool.

4 To make the pastry, sift the flour and salt into a bowl, grate in the butter and mix with a round-bladed knife, adding a little cold water if necessary to bind the dough. Wrap in cling film and chill for 20 minutes.

5 Cut the pastry into 4 portions. Roll each out to a rectangle, 3 mm (⅛ inch) thick and large enough to wrap around the duck fillets. Roll with a lattice roller (see note on page 139) to make 4 pastry lattices. Wrap around the duck fillets and brush with egg yolk. Cover with cling film and chill for 20 minutes.

6 Drain the lentils and cook in boiling salted water, with a sprig of thyme added, for 15 minutes. Sweat the finely diced vegetables in the butter until tender. Drain the lentils, add to the vegetables and stir to mix. Season with salt and pepper to taste.

7 Meanwhile cook the duck parcels in a preheated oven at 220°C (425°F) mark 7 for 8 minutes or until golden. Leave to rest on a rack in a warm place for 4 minutes.

8 Just before serving, add the grapes to the sauce and heat through. Spoon a portion of lentils onto each warmed serving plate. Place a duck breast alongside and pour around some of the sauce. Hand the remaining sauce separately. Serve accompanied by mangetouts, carrots and turnips.

Katherine Rendall

Pan-fried Breast of Gressingham Duck with a Jasmine-scented Sauce

2 Gressingham ducks
15 g (½ oz) unsalted butter
15 g (½ oz) caster sugar
150 ml (¼ pint) orange juice
5 ml (1 tsp) soy sauce
120 ml (4 fl oz) cherry brandy
juice of ¼ lime
salt and freshly ground black pepper
1 jasmine tea bag
15 ml (1 tbsp) clarified butter

1 Remove the breasts from the ducks, discard the skin, then set aside.

2 Chop the duck carcasses and place in a roasting tin. Roast in a preheated oven at 230°C (450°F) mark 8 for about 20 minutes until well browned. Transfer to a large pan and add water to cover. Bring to the boil, then lower the heat and simmer for about 30 minutes. Pass through a sieve into a clean pan, then reduce over a moderate heat to 200 ml (7 fl oz). Skim off any fat from the surface.

3 Melt the butter in a separate pan, add the sugar and dissolve over a low heat. Increase the heat and cook until caramelised. Add the orange juice and soy sauce and reduce by about half.

4 Pour the cherry brandy into another pan and reduce over a moderate heat by two thirds. Add to the orange sauce with the duck stock and reduce to the desired consistency. Add the lime juice and check the seasoning.

5 Heat the clarified butter in a heavy-based frying pan and fry the duck breasts, skinned-side down, for 5 minutes. Turn and cook the other side for about 3 minutes until browned. Cover and leave to rest in a warm place for a few minutes. Immerse the tea bag in the sauce for a few seconds just before serving.

6 Carve the duck breasts into thin slices and arrange on warmed serving plates. Serve with roast parsnips flavoured with Parmesan, and seasonal vegetables, such as new potatoes, leeks and fine green beans.

Graham Underwood

Duck Breast with a Mediterranean Salsa and Potato Rösti

3 duck breasts, skinned
45 ml (3 tbsp) olive oil
juice of 1 lemon
15 ml (1 tbsp) chopped basil
salt and freshly ground black pepper
a little olive oil, for frying

Salsa:
4 baby sweet peppers, cored and seeded
3 sun-dried tomatoes
few green olives, stoned
1 large clove garlic, peeled
finely grated rind of 1 lemon
45 ml (3 tbsp) set yogurt

Rosti:
2 baking potatoes
30 ml (2 tbsp) melted butter

To Garnish:
basil sprigs

1 Put the duck breasts in a shallow dish with the olive oil, lemon juice and basil. Turn to coat, then leave to marinate for 1½-2 hours.

2 To prepare the salsa, chop the peppers, sun-dried tomatoes, olives and garlic. Place in a bowl with the lemon rind and yogurt. Mix well and season with salt and pepper to taste. Set aside.

3 Peel and grate the potatoes for the rösti. Dry in a tea-towel to remove excess moisture, then place in a bowl. Stir in the melted butter and season liberally with salt and pepper. Divide into 4 portions.

4 Heat a large heavy-based frying pan until it is very hot. Add the rosti, pressing each one into a flat round cake, using the back of a fish slice. Cook over a moderate heat for about 5 minutes until golden brown underneath, then turn the rösti and cook the other side until crisp and golden brown. Transfer to a warmed plate and keep hot in a warm oven.

5 Meanwhile, remove the duck breasts from the marinade. Heat a little olive oil in a heavy-based frying pan, add the duck breasts, skin-side down, and fry over a moderate heat for 6-8 minutes. Turn the duck breasts over, lower the heat and cook for 6-8 minutes until tender but still pink inside. Remove from the pan, wrap in foil and leave to rest for 5 minutes.

6 To serve, carve the duck breasts crosswise into thick slices. Place a rösti on each warmed serving plate and arrange the slices of duck alongside. Spoon the salsa on top of the rosti and garnish with basil sprigs. Serve at once, accompanied by braised leeks and carrots.

Sarah Dyson

Breast of Gressingham Duck Wildfowler-style

2 oven-ready Gressingham ducks
salt and freshly ground black pepper

Sauce:
reserved duck bones
1 carrot, chopped
1 onion, chopped
1 celery stick, chopped
dash of Madeira
10 ml (2 tsp) chopped tarragon
1.5 litres (2½ pints) duck or chicken stock

Stuffing:
25 g (1 oz) rindless streaky bacon, minced
25 g (1 oz) butter
50 g (2 oz) button mushrooms, minced
50 g (2 oz) morels, minced
2.5 ml (½ tsp) crushed garlic
½ bay leaf
4 sage leaves
1 thyme sprig
25 ml (1 fl oz) Madeira
1 egg white
120 ml (4 fl oz) double cream

1 Take the legs from the ducks and remove the meat from the bones, trimming away any tendons and fat and reserving the bones for the sauce. Dice the leg meat and set aside in the refrigerator. Remove the outer wing joints, leaving the inner part attached to the breast; leave the breast on the bone.

2 To make the sauce, put the duck bones in a deep heavy-based pan with the chopped vegetables and brown over a moderate heat. Deglaze the pan with the Madeira, then add the chopped tarragon. Cover with stock. Bring to the boil, skim the surface, then simmer for 1-2 hours. Strain through a fine sieve and return to the pan. Reduce by about half until the sauce is shiny and a deep mahogany colour.

3 Meanwhile, prepare the stuffing. Put the minced bacon in a heavy-based pan over a medium heat until the fat starts to run. Add the butter and melt, then add the mushrooms and morels and sauté for 3-4 minutes. Add the garlic and sauté for a further 3 minutes. Add the herbs and Madeira, then simmer over a medium heat until the liquid is evaporated and the mixture is almost dry. Discard the herbs and allow to cool.

4 Put the chilled duck leg meat in a food processor and process until smooth. With the motor running, add the egg white through the feeder tube and process for 20-30 seconds. Scrape down the side of the bowl, then add the cream and process briefly until evenly incorporated. Transfer to a bowl and fold in the cooled mushroom mixture.

5 Transfer the mixture to a piping bag fitted with the plain nozzle. Loosen the skin on the duck breasts and pipe a quarter of the mixture under the skin of each duck breast. Leave in refrigerator until needed.

6 Season the duck breasts with salt and pepper and bake in a preheated oven at 180°C (350°F) mark 4 for 25 minutes until just cooked. Leave to rest in a warm place for 5-10 minutes. Reheat the sauce.

7 To serve remove the whole breasts from the duck carcasses and slice each one into 4 or 5 pieces. Fan out on warmed serving plates and surround with the sauce. Serve with Potato Galettes (see page 235), a creamed purée of leeks, and steamed and sautéed carrots, parsnips and celeriac.

Michael Boning

Barbary Duck Breast with Honey and Thyme

30 ml (2 tbsp) oil or butter
4 Barbary duck breasts
4 shallots, diced
juice of 1 lemon
10 ml (2 tsp) chopped thyme
30 ml (2 tbsp) clear honey
10 ml (2 tsp) soy sauce
finely pared rind of ½ lemon, thinly sliced

1 Heat the oil or butter in a large heavy-based frying pan, add the duck breasts skin-side down and fry over a moderate heat for 6-8 minutes. Turn the duck breasts over, lower the heat and cook until almost tender.

2 Add the shallots, lemon juice and thyme. Bring to the boil, add the honey and soy sauce and cook for 2 minutes.

3 Remove the duck breasts and strain off the fat from the pan. Add the lemon rind shreds to the juices remaining in the pan and bring back to the boil.

4 Meanwhile slice the duck breasts and arrange them on individual plates. Pour the pan juices and lemon rind over the duck and serve immediately, with seasonal vegetables.

Robin Machin

Grilled Breast of Duck in Red Wine Sauce

4 duck breasts, each about 175 g (6 oz), boned (carcasses reserved)
15 ml (1 tbsp) each finely chopped basil, rosemary, sage and thyme

Sauce:
15 ml (1 tbsp) butter
15 ml (1 tbsp) oil
150 ml (¼ pint) red wine
2 shallots, chopped
15 ml (1 tbsp) tomato purée
30 ml (2 tbsp) brandy
600 ml (1 pint) rich brown poultry stock
beurre manié, ie 15 ml (1 tbsp) butter blended with 15 ml (1 tbsp) flour

To Garnish:
thyme sprigs

1 To prepare the sauce, chop the duck carcasses into small pieces. Heat the butter and oil in a large pan and add the duck bones. Cook, turning occasionally, until browned. Remove the excess fat from the pan, then deglaze with the red wine, stirring to scrape up the sediment.

2 Add the chopped shallots, tomato purée and brandy, then flambé. When the flames subside, add the brown poultry stock. Boil to reduce by half. Strain through a sieve lined with a double thickness of muslin, correct the seasoning and return to the cleaned pan. Thicken the sauce with beurre manié, adding it a little at a time, until the sauce reaches a coating consistency. Set aside.

3 To prepare the duck breasts, remove the tendon from each one. Press the chopped herbs on to the breasts and cook under a preheated grill for about 4 minutes each side until browned on the outside, but still rare in the middle. Leave to rest for 5-10 minutes before carving.

4 Pour a pool of sauce on to each warmed plate and arrange the duck on top. Garnish with thyme sprigs. Serve with Individual Potato and Mushroom Cakes (see page 230), and seasonal vegetables.

Martha Spencer

Breast of Duck with Prune and Pistachio Stuffing

For the stuffing, you will need to soak the prunes and pistachio nuts in the Madeira overnight.

150 g (5 oz) dried prunes
20 g (¾ oz) pistachio nuts
100 ml (3½ fl oz) Madeira
4 duck breast fillets
30 ml (2 tbsp) thin honey
2 cloves garlic, chopped
15 ml (1 tbsp) olive oil
200 ml (⅓ pint) lamb stock
25 ml (5 tsp) double cream
salt and freshly ground pepper

1 Put the dried prunes and pistachio nuts in a small bowl, pour on the Madeira and leave to soak overnight.

2 The next day, drain the prunes and nuts, reserving the marinade.

3 Prick the skin of each duck breast in several places, then turn the duck breasts over and make horizontal cuts, three-quarters of the way through the meat, so that the duck breasts open out flat.

4 Arrange a line of prunes down the centre of two of the fillets. Sprinkle with pistachio nuts, then cover with the other fillets; reserve the remaining prunes and nuts (approximately one third) for the sauce. Tie the fillets together securing with string at 1 cm (½ inch) intervals.

5 Smear the honey and garlic over the joints and place in a shallow dish. Pour on the reserved marinade and leave for 1 hour.

6 Remove the duck breast joints from the marinade with a slotted spoon; reserve the marinade for the sauce.

7 Heat the oil in a frying pan. Season the duck breast joints with salt and pepper, add to the hot oil and sear over a high heat, turning the joints until the skin is golden brown all over.

8 Transfer the joints to a roasting tin and cover with foil. Cook near the bottom of a preheated oven at 190°C (375°F) mark 5 for 40 minutes.

9 Meanwhile to make the sauce, bring the lamb stock to the boil in a pan. Add the remaining prunes and pistachio nuts, with the reserved marinade. Boil to reduce for 10 minutes. Transfer to a blender or food processor and work until smooth. Pass through a fine sieve into a clean pan. Heat through over a medium heat, add the cream and season with salt and pepper to taste. If necessary, sieve the sauce again before using.

10 To serve, slice the duck breasts, remove the string and arrange on warmed serving plates. Pour the sauce around one side of the meat and serve at once, with Potato and Wild Mushroom Bake (see page 230), and Tiered Shredded Vegetable Crowns (see page 219).

Glen Tabor

Guinea Fowl in Red Wine with Chestnuts

4 guinea fowl breasts

Stock:
30 ml (2 tbsp) olive oil
2 guinea fowl carcasses
2 onions, roughly chopped
2 carrots, roughly chopped
½ bottle full-bodied red wine
5 ml (1 tsp) juniper berries
1 bay leaf
bouquet garni

To Finish:
15 ml (1 tbsp) olive oil
¼ bottle full-bodied red wine
300 ml (½ pint) guinea fowl stock
30 ml (2 tbsp) black treacle
1 bay leaf
225 g (8 oz) frozen chestnuts, defrosted
salt and freshly ground black pepper
10 ml (2 tsp) arrowroot

1 First make the stock. Heat the oil in a large pan, add the guinea fowl carcasses and brown well. Add the onions and carrots and sauté until lightly browned. Add 600 ml (1 pint) water and all the other stock ingredients. Bring to the boil, lower the heat and simmer gently for about 3 hours.

2 Strain the stock into a bowl and allow to cool. Refrigerate when cold so that the fat sets on the surface. Discard this fat layer before use.

3 To cook the guinea fowl, heat the oil in a heavy-based frying pan over a medium-high heat. Add the guinea fowl breasts and brown on both sides. Add the wine, stock, treacle, bay leaf, chestnuts and salt and pepper. Bring to the boil, lower the heat and simmer for 15-20 minutes.

4 Mix the arrowroot to a paste with a little cold water. Remove the guinea fowl breasts from the pan and keep warm. Stir the arrowroot paste into the sauce. Cook, stirring, for 2-3 minutes.

5 To serve, slice the guinea fowl breasts and arrange on warmed individual serving plates with the chestnuts. Spoon over the sauce and serve at once, with accompaniments of your choice.

Keely Smith

Note: Ask your poulterer or butcher to bone the guinea fowl for you, remembering to ask for the carcasses which you will need for the stock.

Guinea Fowl Breasts with Calvados, Apple and Onion Sauce

60 ml (4 tbsp) olive oil
1 onion, halved and thinly sliced
1 cox's apple
45 ml (3 tbsp) Calvados
300 ml (½ pint) homemade chicken stock
4 guinea fowl breasts, with skin
30-45 ml (2-3 tbsp) double cream (optional)
salt and freshly ground black pepper

To Garnish:
1 cox's apple
15 g (½ oz) unsalted butter
7.5 ml (1½ tsp) brown sugar

1 Heat 30 ml (2 tbsp) of the oil in a heavy-based frying pan. Add the onion and fry gently until softened and starting to brown.

2 Meanwhile, peel, core and slice the apple. Add to the onions and fry over a low heat until softened and beginning to brown. Increase the heat, add the Calvados and bubble to reduce. Add the chicken stock, a little at a time, continuing to reduce the sauce to a fairly thick consistency. Transfer to a blender or food processor and work to a purée, then pass through a sieve into a clean pan.

3 In the meantime, heat the remaining oil in the frying pan. Add the guinea fowl breasts, skin-side down, and fry quickly over a high heat until the skin is golden brown. Turn the breasts over in the pan and immediately remove from the heat. Transfer the guinea fowl to a roasting tin, skin-side up, and cook in a preheated oven at 180°C (350°F) mark 4 for about 10 minutes until tender.

4 Meanwhile, prepare the garnish. Peel the apple and slice horizontally into rings. Remove the core from each slice with a small pastry cutter. Melt the unsalted butter in a pan. Add the apple rings, sprinkle with the brown sugar and cook over a high heat until caramelised.

5 Reheat the sauce, stir in the cream (if using) and season with salt and pepper to taste.

6 To serve, spoon the sauce onto warmed serving plates and place the guinea fowl on top. Garnish with the caramelised apple slices and serve at once, with Broccoli Timbales (see page 206) and Butternut Squash Balls (see page 223).

Charlotte Bircher

Stuffed Guinea Fowl Breast

2 guinea fowl
2 carrots, finely chopped
4 shallots, finely chopped
2 garlic cloves, finely chopped
salt and freshly ground black pepper
120 ml (4 fl oz) Vin Santo (strong sweet Tuscan wine), or a sweet Sauternes
5-10 ml (1-2 tsp) chopped mixed herbs (thyme, rosemary and marjoram), to taste
pinch of dried oregano
1 egg

Garlic Butter:
25 g (1 oz) butter, melted
½ garlic clove, crushed

Beurre Rouge Sauce:
15 g (½ oz) butter
2 shallots, finely chopped
175 ml (6 fl oz) red wine
75-100 g (3-4 oz) butter, chilled and diced

1 Skin the guinea fowl, then carefully remove the breasts by slicing down each carcass from the breastbone; set aside. Strip the flesh from the wings, legs and carcasses, discarding any fatty tissue. Chop this meat for the stuffing.

2 To prepare the stuffing, sprinkle the chopped carrots, shallots and garlic over the base of a baking dish. Add the reserved chopped guinea fowl. Season with salt and pepper and sprinkle with 60 ml (2 fl oz) wine. Cover and cook in a preheated oven at 180°C (350°F) mark 4 for 15 minutes.

3 Allow the mixture to cool slightly, then transfer to a food processor. Add the herbs and egg and work to a coarse cream.

4 To prepare each guinea fowl breast, hold down on the work surface with one hand and, using a sharp knife, slice into the breast horizontally to make a pocket, but do not cut right through. Open up carefully, then cover with a sheet of greaseproof paper. Beat with a meat mallet or rolling pin until it is almost 12 cm (5 inches) in diameter, without splitting in half.

5 Mound 2 tablespoonfuls of the stuffing into each pocket, then roll up and tie neatly with string; reserve the remaining stuffing. Put the guinea fowl breasts in the baking dish (used for the stuffing).

6 For the garlic butter, mix the melted butter with the garlic. Brush the guinea fowl breasts with garlic butter and season with salt and pepper. Sprinkle with the remaining wine. Cook in the oven at 180°C (350°F) mark 4 for 20 minutes.

7 To make the beurre rouge sauce, melt the butter in a pan, add the shallots and sauté gently for 2 minutes. Meanwhile press the reserved stuffing through a fine sieve to extract the juices. Add this liquid to the pan with the red wine and bring to the boil. Boil the sauce until it is well reduced and the shallots are just visible.

8 Remove the pan from the heat and whisk in the butter a piece at a time, making sure each piece is thoroughly incorporated before adding the next. Continue whisking until the sauce is the consistency of mayonnaise.

9 Remove the string from the guinea fowl breasts and replace with blanched chive strips. Place on warmed serving plates and spoon on the sauce. Serve immediately, with Celeriac Rösti (see page 225), mangetouts and carrots.

Derek Johns

Stuffed Pigeon Breast with a Lattice Puff Pastry Crust served with an Elderberry Sauce

150 g (5 oz) ready-made puff pastry
4 pigeon breasts
4 slices Prosciutto (or Parma ham)
1 egg yolk, beaten

Stuffing:
15 g (½ oz) unsalted butter
1 shallot, finely diced
70 g (2½ oz) open cap mushrooms, finely chopped
salt and freshly ground black pepper
pinch of freshly grated nutmeg

Elderberry Sauce:
400 ml (14 fl oz) pigeon stock
20 g (¾ oz) unsalted butter
20 g (¾ oz) plain flour
100 ml (3½ fl oz) elderberry juice
a little sugar, to taste

1 To prepare the stuffing, melt the butter in a frying pan, add the shallot and cook until soft. Add the mushrooms and increase the heat. Continue to cook until all the liquid from the mushrooms has evaporated and you are left with a paste. Season with salt, pepper and nutmeg to taste. Leave to cool.

2 To make the elderberry sauce, put the pigeon stock in a saucepan and boil to reduce by approximately two thirds. In a separate pan, heat the butter until melted, then stir in the flour. Cook for 1 minute, then gradually stir in the reduced pigeon stock and elderberry juice. Season with salt and pepper and add a little sugar to taste; keep warm.

3 Roll out the puff pastry to a 3 mm (⅛ inch) thickness and cut four rectangles, about 15 x 10 cm (6 x 4 inches). Roll with a pastry lattice roller (see note).

4 Cut a deep, horizontal slit in each pigeon breast to make a pocket. Fill each pocket with the mushroom stuffing. Wrap each pigeon breast in a slice of prosciutto, then carefully envelope in a pastry lattice. Brush with egg yolk to glaze and place on a baking tray. Cook in a preheated oven at 220°C (425°F) mark 7 for about 7-8 minutes until the pastry is golden brown.

5 To serve, carefully transfer each pigeon breast to a warmed serving plate and surround with the sauce. Serve with Puréed Parsnip Timbales (see page 227) and Lemon-glazed Carrot Ribbons (see page 219).

Andrew Whiteley

Note: A pastry lattice roller is a plastic or perspex cylinder with inset 'blades'. As the lattice roller moves over the pastry it cuts slits and, when the pastry is lifted from the surface, these slits open up to form the lattice. You can obtain lattice rollers from good kitchen shops and mail order cookware suppliers.

Pan-fried Breast of Wood Pigeon with a Wild Rowanberry Sauce

4 wood pigeons, plucked and drawn

Marinade:
¼ bottle full-bodied red wine
30 ml (2 tbsp) olive oil
1 clove garlic, crushed
2 bay leaves
1 thyme sprig or 5 ml (1 tsp) dried thyme
6 black peppercorns
salt and freshly ground black pepper

Sauce:
150 ml (¼ pint) well-flavoured pigeon stock (see right)
30 ml (2 tbsp) rowan jelly
½ square dark bitter chocolate
40 g (1½ oz) unsalted butter, in pieces

Croûtons:
4 slices wholemeal bread
25 g (1 oz) butter
15 ml (1 tbsp) hazelnut oil

To Garnish:
lamb's lettuce
12 steamed sugar snap peas

1 Remove the breasts from the pigeons, using a sharp knife. Use the carcasses to make the stock (see right).

2 For the marinade, combine the red wine, olive oil, garlic, bay leaves, thyme, black peppercorns and a pinch of salt in a large bowl. Add the pigeon breasts, turn to coat and leave to marinate for at least 5 hours, preferably overnight.

3 Shortly before serving, prepare the croûtons. Using a mug or similar-sized guide, cut a disc from each slice of bread. Melt the butter in a frying pan with the hazelnut oil. When hot, add the bread rounds and fry, turning once, until crisp and golden brown on both sides. Drain on kitchen paper and keep warm.

4 Lift the pigeon breasts out of the marinade and pat dry with kitchen paper. Strain the marinade and reserve. Place a non-stick frying pan over a moderate heat (without any fat). When it is very hot, add the pigeon breasts and sear for 2-3 minutes each side. Remove, cover with foil and leave to rest in a warm place.

5 Add the strained marinade to the pan, stirring with a wooden spoon to scrape up any sediment. Transfer to a saucepan and add the pigeon stock. Slowly bring to the boil, skim, then add the rowan jelly and stir until melted. Add the chocolate and again stir until incorporated. Simmer to reduce by one third or until the sauce has a syrupy consistency. Whisk in the butter, a piece at a time, and season with salt and pepper to taste.

6 To serve, slice each pigeon breast horizontally in two. Pool the sauce on the warmed serving plates and float a croûton in the centre. Arrange the pigeon slices on the croûton and top with a little lamb's lettuce. Garnish with sugar snap peas and serve with accompaniments.

Roger Hemming

Pigeon Stock: Chop the pigeon carcasses, place in a roasting tin and roast in a preheated oven at 450°C (230°F) mark 8 for 30 minutes until well browned. Transfer to a large saucepan and add 1.2 litres (2 pints) water, 1 chopped onion, 1 chopped carrot, 1 chopped celery stick and a bouquet garni. Bring to the boil and simmer for 3-4 hours. Strain.

Wood Pigeons with Wild Rice Stuffing and a Juniper and Port Sauce

4 wood pigeons

Stuffing:
25 g (1 oz) wild rice
175 g (6 oz) brown rice
25 g (1 oz) butter
2 rashers streaky bacon, finely chopped
1 shallot, finely chopped
grated rind of 1 orange
25 g (1 oz) walnuts, skinned and finely chopped
salt and freshly ground pepper
15-30 ml (1-2 tbsp) chopped coriander leaves

Sauce:
30 ml (2 tbsp) oil
50 g (2 oz) butter
1 onion, chopped
4 juniper berries, crushed
few thyme sprigs
300 ml (½ pint) homemade stock
125 ml (4 fl oz) port
15 ml (1 tbsp) redcurrant jelly
salt and freshly ground pepper

1 Wash and dry the pigeons. For the stuffing, wash the wild rice and brown rice separately. Cook the wild rice in boiling salted water in a covered pan for 30 minutes or until tender; drain.

2 Heat the butter in a pan, add the bacon and shallot and sauté until the shallot is softened. Add the brown rice and cook, stirring continuously, until the rice becomes translucent. Add 275 ml (9 fl oz) water and bring to the boil, then simmer covered for 20-25 minutes or until the rice is tender. Add the orange rind, wild rice, walnuts, seasoning and coriander.

3 To make the sauce, heat the oil and half of the butter in a pan and quickly seal the pigeons, then remove. Add the onion to the pan and fry until softened. Stir in the juniper berries, thyme, stock and port and bring to the boil. Simmer until the sauce has reduced by half. Strain the sauce into a clean pan. Add the redcurrant jelly and stir over moderate heat until the jelly has melted. Beat in the remaining butter, a little at a time, and adjust the seasoning. Keep warm.

4 Stuff the pigeons with the rice mixture and truss with fine string. Place in a roasting dish. Cook in a preheated oven at 220°C, (425°F) mark 7 for 20-25 minutes or until tender. Remove string. Place the pigeons on warmed plates and spoon over the sauce to serve.

Amita Baldock

Pheasant Breast with Chanterelles and Grapes on a Potato Pancake

4 pheasant breasts
90 g (3½ oz) chanterelles or other wild mushrooms
150 g (5 oz) red grapes
salt and freshly ground black pepper
15 ml (1 tbsp) oil
40 g (1½ oz) butter, chilled and diced
85 ml (6 tbsp) white wine
300 ml (½ pint) pheasant stock

Potato Cakes:
350 g (12 oz) large potatoes
50 g (2 oz) clarified butter

To Serve:
chervil sprigs, to garnish
few drops of truffle oil (optional)

1 Trim the pheasant breasts. Clean the mushrooms thoroughly. Halve and deseed the grapes.

2 To make the potato cakes, peel and thinly slice the potatoes, then mix with the clarified butter. Season with salt and pepper. Form into 4 potato cakes, each approximately 10 cm (4 inches) across and 5 mm (¼ inch) deep. Fry the potato cakes in a preheated heavy-based frying pan, pressing down firmly, until crisp and golden brown on both sides; keep warm.

3 Heat 15 ml (1 tbsp) oil and 25 g (1 oz) butter in another pan, add the pheasant breasts and fry briefly over a high heat until well browned. Turn and repeat on the other side. The cooked pheasant breasts must remain pink inside otherwise they become dry. Using a slotted spoon, transfer to an ovenproof dish.

4 Add the mushrooms to the pan and sauté gently, adding the grapes when the mushrooms are almost cooked. Add to the pheasant and keep warm. Drain off the oil from the pan.

5 Deglaze the pan with the white wine. Reduce until almost completely evaporated, then add the stock. Boil rapidly to reduce until the sauce starts to thicken. Strain through a muslin-lined sieve into a clean pan and reheat.

6 Reheat the pheasant, mushrooms and grapes in a preheated oven at 220°C (425°F) mark 7 for 1 minute. Meanwhile whisk the remaining 15 g (½ oz) butter into the sauce, a piece at a time.

7 Place a potato cake on the centre of each warmed serving plate. Slice the pheasant and arrange on top of the potato cakes. Arrange the mushrooms, grapes and sprigs of chervil around the pheasant and moisten with the sauce. Sprinkle the pheasant with a drop of truffle oil to add richness to the dish, if desired. Serve immediately, accompanied by vegetable purées, such as carrot and potato, and parsnip purées.

Ross Burden

Pan-fried Breast of Pheasant with a Date and Red Wine Sauce

4 pheasant breasts
25 g (1 oz) butter
30 ml (2 tbsp) olive oil
salt and freshly ground black pepper

Date and Red Wine Sauce:
knob of butter
4 shallots, finely chopped
3 cloves garlic, finely chopped
75 ml (5 tbsp) red wine
30 ml (2 tbsp) brandy
6 fresh dates, stoned and roughly chopped
24 peppercorns, crushed
15 ml (1 tbsp) plain flour
600 ml (1 pint) chicken stock (see right)

To Garnish:
4 fresh dates

1 First make the sauce. Melt the knob of butter in a saucepan, add the shallots and garlic, cover and sweat gently until softened. Add the red wine and reduce until the wine has almost completely evaporated. Add the brandy and reduce again.

2 Add the chopped dates and crushed peppercorns; cook for 2-3 minutes. Add the flour and mix well, then stir in the chicken stock. Allow to simmer for 10 minutes, then pass through a conical sieve into a clean saucepan, pressing the ingredients through to extract as much flavour as possible. Check the seasoning. Keep warm while cooking the pheasant.

3 To cook the pheasant breasts, heat the butter and oil in a large frying pan. When sizzling, add the pheasant breasts and fry, turning constantly, for 8-10 minutes or until cooked through. Transfer to a warmed plate, season with salt and pepper and leave to rest in a low oven for a few minutes.

4 To serve, place the pheasant breasts on warmed serving plates and pour over the sauce. Garnish with dates and serve immediately, with accompaniments of your choice.

Chris Rand

Chicken Stock: Put 1.4 kg (3 lb) chicken wings in a large saucepan and pour on about 1.7 litres (3 pints) water. Bring to the boil and skim. Add 2 carrots, peeled and quartered; 1 stick celery, chopped; 2 leeks, sliced; 2 small onions quartered; salt, pepper and a bouquet garni. Lower the heat, cover and simmer for 2 hours. Strain and use as required.

Salmis of Pheasant with Chestnuts and Redcurrants

2 pheasants
16 fresh chestnuts (or vacuum-packed chestnuts)
175 g (6 oz) unsalted butter
10 ml (2 tsp) sugar
600 ml (1 pint) pheasant stock (see right)
salt and freshly ground black pepper
15 ml (1 tbsp) red wine vinegar
30 ml (2 tbsp) brandy
150 ml (¼ pint) red wine (eg Burgundy)
10 ml (2 tsp) redcurrant jelly
50 g (2 oz) redcurrants

1 Remove the breasts and wing tips from the pheasants by scraping a knife between the bone and the breast along to the wing, cutting through the bone at the wing end if necessary. Use the carcasses to make the stock (see right).

2 If using fresh chestnuts, make a slit in their shells, then add to a pan of boiling water and cook for about 30 minutes. Drain and cool slightly, then peel off the shells and skins.

3 Melt 50 g (2 oz) butter in a non-stick pan, then add the sugar, chestnuts and 60 ml (2 fl oz) pheasant stock. Cook over a very low heat, turning occasionally, until the liquid has almost evaporated and the chestnuts are glazed.

4 Season the pheasant breasts with salt and pepper. Heat 50 g (2 oz) of the butter in a large pan. Add the pheasant breasts, skin-side down, and cook until golden brown, then turn and brown the underside. Add the wine vinegar, then the brandy and half of the stock. Bring to the boil, reduce the heat and simmer gently for 10-15 minutes, depending on the thickness of the breasts, until just slightly pink in the middle. Remove from the pan and keep warm.

5 Add the rest of the stock to the pan with the wine and redcurrant jelly and boil rapidly until reduced by half. Whisk in the remaining 50 g (2 oz) butter, a piece at a time, until the sauce is glossy. Stir in the redcurrants.

6 To serve, cut the pheasant breasts into fine slices, leaving a portion attached to the wing. Fan the slices out on warmed serving plates. Garnish with the chestnuts and spoon the sauce around. Serve at once, accompanied by Wild Rice with Lemon Grass (see page 238) and Braised Celery Hearts (see page 216).

Elaine Bates

Pheasant Stock: Heat 30 ml (2 tbsp) oil in a large pan and brown the pheasant carcasses. Roughly chop 2 onions and 2 carrots; add these to the pan and brown. Add a sprig of thyme and 600 ml (1 pint) water. Bring to the boil, then lower the heat and simmer for 10 minutes. Add a bottle of full-bodied red wine (eg Burgundy), 5 ml (1 tsp) juniper berries, a bay leaf and a bouquet garni. Bring back to the boil, lower the heat and simmer gently for about 3 hours. At this stage, there should be about 600 ml (1 pint). Strain the stock into a bowl and allow to cool. Refrigerate when cold so that the fat sets on the surface. Remove this before use.

Pheasant Pie with Potato Pastry

1 cock pheasant
25 g (1 oz) butter
100 g (4 oz) British smoked bacon rashers, derinded and chopped
1 onion, sliced
1 Bramley apple, peeled, cored and sliced
450 ml (¾ pint) cider
bouquet garni, ie sprig each of marjoram, parsley and thyme
4 cloves
salt and freshly ground black pepper
squeeze of lemon juice

Potato Pastry:
175 g (6 oz) self-raising flour
125 g (4 oz) butter
175 g (6 oz) cold mashed potato
beaten egg for brushing

1 Carefully remove the breasts and legs from the pheasant. (Use the rest of the meat and carcass to make stock for another dish.) Slice the meat, discarding the bones.

2 Heat the butter in a heavy-based pan and fry the bacon and onion until golden. Add the pheasant slices together with the apple slices and fry turning for a few minutes. Add the cider, bouquet garni, cloves, seasoning and lemon juice. Cover and cook for 45 minutes to 1 hour until the pheasant is tender. Discard the bouquet garni.

3 Meanwhile make the potato pastry. Sift the flour into a bowl, rub in the butter until the mixture resembles breadcrumbs, then add the mashed potato to bind the pastry. Wrap and leave to rest in the refrigerator for about 15 minutes.

4 Transfer the pheasant mixture to a pie dish. Roll out the pastry on a lightly floured surface to make a pie lid. Moisten the rim of the pie dish and position the pastry over the meat. Decorate the top of the pie with shapes cut from the trimmings. Brush with beaten egg and cook in a preheated oven at 200°C (400°F) mark 6 for 25 minutes. Serve immediately, with vegetables of your choice.

Linda Yewdall

Pheasant Stock: Make this from the leftover pheasant carcass. Put the pheasant carcass in a saucepan or pressure cooker with water to cover and flavouring ingredients – 1 onion, 1 leek, 1 carrot, chopped; 1 clove garlic, crushed; and seasoning. Bring to the boil and cook for 1½ hours, or 30 minutes in a pressure cooker. Strain before using as required.

Pan-fried Supremes of Quail with Grapes and a Sauternes Sauce

8 quails
60 ml (4 tbsp) butter
175 g (6 oz) seedless grapes, peeled
150 ml (¼ pint) Sauternes wine

Croûtons:
4 slices homemade white bread, each 5 mm (¼ inch) thick
clarified butter, for frying

To Garnish:
4 slices canned 'block' foie gras, each 5 mm (¼ inch) thick
30 ml (2 tbsp) Sauternes wine

1 To prepare the quails, slip your fingers between the skin and flesh, then pull away the skin. Cut against the ridge of the breastbone to loosen the flesh from the bone. Disjoint the wing where it joins the carcass and continue down along the rib cage, pulling flesh from bone as you cut until the meat from one side of the breast separates from the bone in one piece. Repeat on the other side.

2 To make the croûtons, cut the bread into rounds using a fluted cutter. Heat a 3 mm (⅛ inch) depth of clarified butter in a frying pan and sauté the bread rounds on each side until very lightly browned. Drain on absorbent kitchen paper.

3 Place the foie gras slices in a covered dish and baste with the Sauternes. Ten minutes before serving, set the dish over a pan of barely simmering water, to heat through.

4 Heat the butter in a sauté pan until it is foaming. Quickly roll the quail supremes in the butter and cook briefly until the flesh springs back with gentle resilience. Transfer the supremes to a warm platter, using a slotted spoon, and cover while making the sauce.

5 Warm the grapes in the butter remaining in the pan, then remove with a slotted spoon. Keep warm with the supremes.

6 Pour the wine into the sauté pan and reduce quickly over a high heat until the liquid is syrupy. Remove from the heat and check the seasoning, then strain through a muslin-lined sieve.

7 To serve, arrange the quail supremes and grapes on warmed serving plates. Pour over the Sauternes sauce and garnish with the foie gras and croûtons. Serve with vegetables of your choice.

Martha Spencer

Pan-fried Fillet of Wild Rabbit in a Juniper and Hermitage Sauce

8 fillets of wild rabbit
15-30 ml (1-2 tbsp) light olive oil, for frying

Marinade:
60 ml (4 tbsp) Hermitage red wine
30 ml (2 tbsp) port
30 ml (2 tbsp) cognac
2 thyme sprigs
2 bay leaves
salt and freshly ground black pepper

Sauce:
600 ml (1 pint) well-flavoured stock
reserved marinade ingredients
12 juniper berries
125 g (4 oz) button mushrooms, chopped
10 ml (2 tsp) rowan jelly
15 g (½ oz) unsalted butter, chilled and diced
25 g (1 oz) chanterelles

1 Mix together the ingredients for the marinade in a shallow dish. Add the rabbit fillets and turn to coat with the marinade. Cover and leave in the refrigerator for at least 1½ hours. Remove the rabbit fillets, reserving the marinade.

2 Pour the stock into a saucepan and add the marinade ingredients, juniper berries, mushrooms and rowan jelly. Bring to the boil, lower the heat and simmer, uncovered, for 20-30 minutes. Strain the sauce into a clean saucepan. Reduce by half, tossing in the chanterelles towards the end of the reduction. Just before serving, whisk in the butter, a piece at a time, and check the seasoning.

3 To cook the rabbit, heat the oil in a heavy-based frying pan. Add the rabbit fillets and fry, turning constantly, over a high heat for 3-4 minutes. Remove from the pan, wrap in foil and leave to rest in a warm place for 5-10 minutes.

4 To serve, slice the rabbit fillets at an angle to give long thin slices and arrange in rosettes on warmed serving plates. Spoon the sauce and chanterelles around the rabbit. Serve at once, accompanied by the vegetables of your choice.

Elaine Ford

Note: If possible use rabbit and veal bones to make the well-flavoured stock for the sauce.

Wild Rabbit in Cider and Rosemary

4 rabbit joints
15 ml (1 tbsp) flour
15 ml (1 tbsp) English mustard powder
30 ml (2 tbsp) sunflower oil
30 ml (2 tbsp) olive oil
knob of butter
1 onion, chopped
150 ml (¼ pint) cider
300 ml (½ pint) rabbit stock
1 rosemary sprig
1 bay leaf
5 ml (1 tsp) brown sugar
salt and freshly ground black pepper
chopped parsley, to garnish

1 If the joints are from an older rabbit, remove the sinews in the hind legs. Toss the rabbit joints in the flour and mustard powder (it is easiest to do this in a plastic bag). Reserve the excess flour mixture.

2 Heat the sunflower and olive oils in a flameproof casserole, add the rabbit joints and seal on all sides. Remove the rabbit and set aside.

3 Add the butter to the casserole dish, add the onion and sweat until softened. Stir in the remaining flour and cook, stirring, for 1-2 minutes. Gradually stir in the cider, followed by the stock. Bring to the boil, adding the rosemary, bay leaf, seasoning and brown sugar.

4 Return the rabbit joints to the casserole, cover and cook in a preheated oven at 160°C (325°F) mark 3 for 1¼-1½ hours.

5 Serve garnished with parsley and accompanied by prune-stuffed baked apples, puréed parsnips and mangetouts.

Sarah Marsh

Fillet of Highland Hare with Wild Mushrooms in a Creamy Marsala Sauce

2 saddles of hare
10 ml (2 tsp) hazelnut oil
8 dried morels
175 g (6 oz) mixed wild and cultivated mushrooms (eg chanterelles, boletus, pied de mouton, chestnut mushrooms)
salt and freshly ground black pepper
10 ml (2 tsp) olive oil
40 g (1½ oz) unsalted butter
300 ml (½ pint) hare stock
120 ml (4 fl oz) Marsala
150 ml (¼ pint) double cream

Forcemeat Balls:
50 g (2 oz) reserved hare meat
50 g (2 oz) chestnut mushrooms
7.5 ml (1½ tsp) double cream
salt and freshly ground black pepper

To Garnish:
chervil sprigs

1 Carefully remove the fillets and the tiny fillets mignon from the saddles of hare, reserving the carcasses to make the stock. Place the meat in a shallow dish, drizzle with the hazelnut oil and rub in. Leave to marinate for about 24 hours. Trim the ends off the fillets; reserve the trimmings and the fillets mignon for the forcemeat balls.

2 The next day soak the dried morels in warm water to cover for 30 minutes; drain, straining and reserving a little of the liquid. Slice all of the fresh mushrooms and set aside.

3 To make the forcemeat balls, put the reserved hare meat and mushrooms in a food processor and process until finely chopped. Mix with the cream and season with salt and pepper. Divide into 4 equal portions and roll into balls. Cover and keep in a cool place until needed, then bake in a preheated oven at 190°C (375°F) mark 5 for 5-6 minutes until set.

4 Season the hare fillets with salt and pepper. Heat the oil and a knob of butter in a frying pan. When hot, add the hare fillets and sear on both sides over a high heat for 3-5 minutes, depending on size; the fillets should still be quite pink. Remove and keep warm.

5 Pour off the fat, then add the remaining butter to the pan and sauté the fresh mushrooms for a few minutes. Season with salt and pepper, remove from the pan and keep warm. Add the stock and reserved morel soaking liquid. Reduce almost by half, then add the Marsala and reduce again. When the alcohol has evaporated, add the cream and reduce until the sauce thickens. Add the morels and heat through.

6 To serve, carve the hare fillets into 6-7 collops and arrange on warmed serving plates in a circle around a mound of stir-fried leeks. Garnish with the mixed mushrooms and spoon over the sauce. Position a forcemeat ball on the leeks and garnish the plates with chervil.

Marion MacFarlane

Note: It is essential to use young hare, and to marinate the fillets for 24 hours before cooking.

Medallions of Venison in a Rich Red Wine Sauce

575 g ($1\frac{1}{4}$ lb) venison fillet (plus the bones from the saddle)
salt and freshly ground black pepper
a little oil, for cooking

Marinade:
30 ml (2 tbsp) olive oil
50 g (2 oz) shallots, finely chopped
50 g (2 oz) carrots, diced
125 g (4 oz) celery, diced
50 g (2 oz) mushrooms, diced
45 ml (3 tbsp) red wine vinegar
500 ml (16 fl oz) full-bodied red wine
5 ml (1 tsp) juniper berries
small bunch of thyme sprigs
1 bay leaf
2 cloves garlic, finely chopped

Sauce:
30 ml (2 tbsp) dark treacle or molasses
60 ml (4 tbsp) light soy sauce

To Garnish:
thyme sprigs

1 To prepare the marinade, heat the oil in a heavy-based pan until hot, then brown the venison bones. Transfer to a large bowl. Add the shallots, carrots, celery and mushrooms to the pan and cook until golden. Deglaze the pan with the vinegar, transfer to the bowl and allow to cool. Cut the venison into 4 equal portions and add to the bowl, with the wine, juniper berries, thyme, bay leaf and garlic. Cover and leave to marinate in the refrigerator for up to 3 days.

2 Remove the venison from the marinade, pat dry and set aside in a cool place. Transfer the marinade (including the bones and vegetables) to a pan, bring to the boil and reduce by half. Stir in the treacle or molasses, 200 ml (7 fl oz) water and the soy sauce. Simmer for 1 hour or until reduce to a shiny sauce-like consistency.

3 About 20 minutes before the sauce has finished reducing, cut the venison into medallions, about 2.5 cm (1 inch) thick. Flatten slightly with the palm of your hand and season with salt and pepper. Heat a thin film of oil in a heavy-based frying pan until very hot, add the medallions and seal on each side. Transfer to a lightly oiled baking tray then roast in a preheated oven at 190°C (375°F) mark 5 for about 5 minutes; keep warm.

4 Strain the sauce through a fine sieve and season with pepper to taste.

5 Arrange the venison medallions on warmed serving plates and pour the sauce over and around them. Garnish with thyme and serve with accompaniments of your choice.

Michael Deacon

Venison with a Sloe Gin and Bramble Sauce

450 g (1 lb) fillet of venison
olive oil, for brushing

Marinade:
300 ml (½ pint) red wine
30 ml (2 tbsp) olive oil
salt and freshly ground pepper

Sauce:
450 ml (¾ pint) demi glace (see below)
75-90 ml (5-6 tbsp) blackberry juice
45 ml (3 tbsp) red wine
5 juniper berries, crushed
4 pink peppercorns, crushed
45 ml (3 tbsp) sloe gin
125 g (4 oz) blackberries
knob of butter

To Garnish:
thyme sprigs

1 Place the venison in a shallow dish. Mix together the ingredients for the marinade and pour over the venison. Leave to marinate for 1½ hours.

2 Remove the venison from the marinade, pat dry and brush with olive oil. Roast in a preheated oven at 200°C (400°F) mark 6 for 15-20 minutes.

3 Meanwhile, prepare the sauce. Put the demi glace, blackberry juice, wine, juniper berries and pink peppercorns in a saucepan and bring to the boil. Simmer until reduced by a third; the sauce should be thick enough to coat the back of a spoon. Add the sloe gin and transfer to a bain marie, or a heatproof bowl over a pan of hot but not boiling water. Add the blackberries and leave to cook gently for 10 minutes, then remove with a slotted spoon.

4 Place a small mound of blackberries in the centre of each plate. Whisk the knob of butter into the sauce and season with salt and pepper to taste. Cut the venison into 3mm (⅛ inch) slices and arrange overlapping around the blackberries. Spoon the sauce over the venison slices and serve immediately, garnished with thyme and accompanied by vegetables.

Jo Eitel

Demi glace: Measure 1 litre (1¾ pints) well-flavoured brown veal stock into a clean pan. Whisk in 3 egg whites and simmer for 10 min-utes, then strain through a muslin-lined stainless steel sieve into another pan. Tie 15 ml (1 tbsp) dried Provençal herbs in a muslin bouquet, add to the beautifully clear stock and simmer until reduced to 450 ml (¾ pint).

Sliced Fillet of Venison with Damson Sauce

450 g (1 lb) boned loin of venison
150 ml (¼ pint) good red wine
5-10 ml (1-2 tsp) juniper berries, lightly crushed
2.5 ml (½ tsp) sea salt
freshly ground black pepper
15 ml (1 tbsp) sunflower oil

Damson Sauce:
25 g (1 oz) damson cheese (or damson jam), cut into small pieces
10 ml (2 tsp) crème fraîche

To Garnish:
flat-leaved parsley

1 Cut the venison into 4 equal slices. Place in a shallow dish and pour over the red wine. Add the juniper berries, salt and a generous grinding of pepper. Stir, then cover and leave to marinate for 2 hours.

2 Remove the meat from the marinade and pat dry with kitchen paper; strain the marinade through a fine sieve and set aside. Heat the oil in a sauté pan over a high heat until smoking. Add the meat and cook quickly, turning constantly, for 4 minutes. Remove the meat from the pan and keep warm.

3 Add the marinade to the pan with the damson cheese. Simmer gently until the cheese has melted. Adjust the seasoning, remove from the heat and stir in the crème fraîche.

4 To serve, place the venison slices on warmed serving plates and pour on the damson sauce. Garnish with parsley and serve with accompaniments of your choice.

Derek Morris

Venison with Elderberry Jelly and Thyme

2 venison fillets, each about 350 g (12 oz), trimmed
30 ml (2 tbsp) hazelnut oil (approximately)
small handful of thyme sprigs
15 ml (1 tbsp) olive oil
50 g (2 oz) butter
2 glasses (good) red wine
450 ml (¾ pint) venison stock
30 ml (2 tbsp) elderberry jelly
salt and freshly ground pepper

To Garnish:
few elderberries (fresh or frozen)
thyme sprigs

To Serve:
Braised Red Cabbage *(see page 215)*

1 Brush the venison fillets with hazelnut oil and press thyme sprigs all over them. Cover and leave to marinate for 1-2 hours.

2 Heat the olive oil and half of the butter in a frying pan, then add the venison. Cook, turning, for about 6 minutes until sealed and browned on all sides.

3 Transfer to an ovenproof dish and leave to rest in a preheated oven at 150°C (300°F) mark 2 for no longer than 8 minutes.

4 Meanwhile, add the wine to the frying pan, stirring to deglaze, then reduce to about half of the volume. Add the stock and reduce by about half. Add a few thyme sprigs with the elderberry jelly. Stir well and reduce slightly. Add the remaining butter, in pieces, to give a glossy finish. Check the seasoning. Strain the sauce into a jug.

5 To serve, cut the venison into 1 cm (½ inch) medallions. Arrange in an overlapping circle on each plate, with the braised red cabbage in the centre. Spoon the sauce around the meat. Garnish with elderberries and thyme sprigs.

Sue Lawrence

Fillet of Spiced Venison with Mulled Fruits

For this recipe you will need to marinate the venison and fruits 24 hours ahead.

4 venison fillets, trimmed
16 dried figs or prunes
16 dried apricots
600 ml (1 pint) red wine
2 sachets of mulling spices
(or 3 cinnamon sticks, 8 crushed juniper berries and 12 cloves)
15 ml (1 tbsp) olive oil
salt and freshly ground black pepper

To Serve:
Grilled Polenta (see page 236)

1 Lay the venison fillets in a shallow dish with the dried fruits. Pour in the wine and add the spices. Cover and leave to marinate for 24 hours.

2 Lift the venison fillets out of the marinade. Remove and discard the spices from the marinade. Heat the olive oil in a frying pan, add the venison fillets and cook for about 3 minutes each side, depending on the thickness of the meat. Ideally it should still be quite pink inside. Remove the meat from the pan; cover and keep warm.

3 Add the marinade and fruit to the pan, stirring to scrape up the sediment. Allow the sauce to simmer, uncovered, for about 15 minutes, until reduced by half and slightly thickened. Season with salt and pepper to taste.

4 Cut each venison fillet into 6 slices and return to the pan. Heat through for 1-2 minutes, then arrange the venison slices in a fan-shape on each warmed serving plate. Surround with the mulled fruits and sauce. Serve at once, accompanied by the Grilled Polenta and steamed asparagus or mangetouts.

Andrea Ferrari

Tuscan-style Venison

15 g (½ oz) dried porcini mushrooms
700-900 g (1½-2 lb) venison
salt and freshly ground black pepper
flour, for coating
olive oil and butter, for cooking
125 g (4 oz) pancetta, derinded and chopped
1-2 cloves garlic, chopped
2 onions, finely chopped
2 carrots, finely chopped
2 sticks celery, finely chopped
500 ml (16 fl oz) dry red wine
500 ml (16 fl oz) passata
a little stock (optional)

Dolce Forte:
125 ml (4 fl oz) red wine vinegar
40 g (1½ oz) raisins
25 g (1 oz) pine nuts
40 g (1½ oz) plain chocolate chips
15 ml (1 tbsp) sugar

1 Soak the dried porcini in 150 ml (¼ pint) hot water for 20 minutes; drain.

2 Cut the venison into chunks and toss in seasoned flour to coat. Heat some olive oil and butter together in a heavy-based pan or braising pot, then brown the venison in batches on all sides, adding more oil and butter as necessary. Remove and set aside.

3 Add the pancetta and the garlic to the pan and sauté briefly, then add the onions and sauté for a few minutes. Add the porcini, carrots and celery and cook, stirring, for a few minutes. Add the red wine and cook for about 5 minutes. Stir in the passata and cook, uncovered, for about 15 minutes.

4 Return the venison to the pan and cook for 15 minutes. Add the *dolce forte* ingredients and cook for a further 5 minutes. Leave the lid off the pot throughout the cooking time. If the sauce is too thick, thin with a little stock.

5 Serve accompanied by creamed potatoes flavoured with chives, and green beans.

Alison Fiander

Venison with Black Pudding and a Mushroom Sauce

4 venison fillets, each about 150 g (5 oz)
30 ml (2 tbsp) olive oil

Marinade:
150 ml (¼ pint) olive oil
150 ml (¼ pint) red wine
30 ml (2 tbsp) balsamic vinegar
1 celery stalk, chopped
20 juniper berries, crushed
salt and freshly ground black pepper

Mushroom Sauce:
15 ml (1 tbsp) demerara sugar
15 ml (1 tbsp) balsamic vinegar
475 ml (15 fl oz) chicken stock
120 ml (4 fl oz) well-flavoured mushroom stock
10 ml (2 tsp) redcurrant jelly

Black Pudding Purée:
225 g (8 oz) black pudding
30 ml (2 tbsp) olive oil
50 ml (2 fl oz) chicken stock (approximately)

1 Mix all the marinade ingredients together in a shallow dish. Add the venison fillets, cover and leave to marinate in the refrigerator for 2-4 hours.

2 Meanwhile, make the sauce. Melt the sugar in a small heavy-based saucepan over a low heat, then continue to cook over a medium heat without stirring until caramelised. Carefully add the balsamic vinegar and about 30 ml (2 tbsp) of the stock (protect your hand with a cloth as the mixture will boil and spurt furiously). Continue heating and stirring until the caramel has dissolved; if necessary, stubborn pieces of caramel can be removed with a slotted spoon and discarded. Add the rest of the stock, and the redcurrant jelly. Bring to the boil and reduce to approximately 300 ml (½ pint). Strain through a fine sieve and season with salt and pepper to taste.

3 Steam the black pudding for 10 minutes, then transfer to a food processor or blender with the olive oil. Process, adding sufficient stock to make a fairly smooth purée (the purée will not be perfectly smooth but should be processed long enough to be reasonably so).

4 Heat the olive oil in a heavy-based frying pan, add the venison fillets and fry over a medium-high heat for 2 minutes on each of the four sides. Wrap in foil and leave to rest in a warm place for 5-10 minutes. Reheat the sauce and the black pudding purée.

5 Slice each venison fillet into 6 or 8 pieces. Arrange the venison slices on a bed of swede purée, sandwiched with a little of the black pudding and fanned out. Serve surrounded by a pool of sauce.

Ashley Wilson

Meat Dishes

Fillet of Beef with a Herb Crust

750 g (1 lb 10 oz) middle-cut fillet of beef, in one piece
freshly ground black pepper
45 ml (3 tbsp) olive oil
1 egg yolk, beaten

Herb Crust:
4 slices smoked back bacon
25 g (1 oz) pistachio nuts
2 slices granary bread
60 ml (4 tbsp) chopped parsley
50-75 g (2-3 oz) butter, melted
1 clove garlic, crushed
5 ml (1 tsp) coarse-grain mustard
5 ml (1 tsp) Worcestershire sauce
freshly ground black pepper

Sauce:
15 ml (1 tbsp) olive oil
1 onion, chopped
2 large mushrooms, chopped
300 ml (½ pint) brown beef stock
120 ml (4 fl oz) red wine
15 ml (1 tbsp) sherry
salt and freshly ground black pepper

To Serve:
25 g (1 oz) butter
50 g (2 oz) wild mushrooms, or shiitake
squeeze of lemon juice

1 Begin by making the sauce. Heat the olive oil in a pan, add the onion and mushrooms and cook until golden brown. Pour on the stock and red wine and bring to the boil. Simmer until reduced to a shiny sauce consistency. Strain into a clean pan and add the sherry. Season well. Set aside until ready to serve.

2 To prepare the herb crust, grill the bacon until crispy; let cool, then chop finely in a food processor. Place in a large shallow dish. Finely chop the nuts in the food processor; add to the bacon. Whizz the bread in the processor to make fine breadcrumbs; add to the dish with the parsley. Mix the melted butter with the garlic, mustard and Worcestershire sauce. Pour onto the crumb mixture, season well with pepper and mix thoroughly. (The bacon will probably add sufficient salt.) Set aside.

3 Season the meat liberally with pepper. Heat the olive oil in a frying pan and quickly seal the meat on all sides, over a high heat. Cool a little, then brush the top and sides with beaten egg yolk. Coat with the crumb mixture, pressing it very firmly onto the meat to ensure it adheres. Place in a roasting tin and roast in a preheated oven at 190°C (375°F) mark 5 for about 30 minutes for rare meat.

4 Shortly before serving, reheat the sauce. Heat the butter in another pan and sauté the mushrooms until just softened. Add a squeeze of lemon juice and pepper to taste.

5 Leave the beef to rest for a few minutes, then carve into thick slices, allowing 2-3 per person. Arrange on warmed serving plates with the mushrooms. Pour on the sauce and serve with a Warm Spinach Salad (see page 201) and accompaniments of your choice.

Clare Askaroff

Fillet of Beef with Oriental Mushrooms

575 g (1½ lb) fillet of beef, in one piece
15 g (½ oz) dried wild ceps or porcini
40 g (1½ oz) butter
225 g (8 oz) mixed fresh mushrooms (eg shiitake, oyster and brown cap)
2 cloves garlic, crushed
30 ml (2 tbsp) rich soy sauce
7.5 ml (1½ tsp) sweet chilli sauce
45 ml (3 tbsp) black bean sauce
10 ml (2 tsp) yellow bean sauce
10 ml (2 tsp) oyster sauce
5 ml (1 tsp) five-spice powder
salt and freshly ground black pepper
2.5-5 ml (½-1 tsp) sugar

1 Put the dried mushrooms in a bowl, pour on 175 ml (6 fl oz) hot water and leave to soak for 20 minutes.

2 Melt 25 g (1 oz) of the butter in a pan, add the fresh mushrooms and garlic and cook over a medium heat for 3-4 minutes. Drain the soaked mushrooms, reserving the liquid, add to the pan and cook for 2 minutes. Stir in the oriental sauces, then add the five-spice powder and cook for a further 1 minute. Season with salt and pepper, and add sugar to taste. Add the reserved mushroom soaking liquid and cook over a medium heat until reduced and thickened. Add 175 ml (6 fl oz) water and reduce once more, until thickened.

3 Insert a long pointed knife into one end of the beef fillet to make a slit through to the centre. Repeat from the other end – meeting in the middle – to form a cavity for the stuffing. With a slotted spoon, take some mushrooms from the sauce and use to fill the beef fillet cavity. Either sew up both ends or secure with skewers.

4 Melt the remaining butter and brush over the stuffed beef fillet. Place under a preheated medium grill for 7 minutes, turning occasionally to seal on all sides. Transfer to a baking tray and cook in a preheated oven at 180°C (350°F) mark 4 for 20 minutes for rare meat, or longer if preferred.

5 When cooked, cover the beef and leave to stand in a warm place for 5 minutes. Meanwhile, reheat the mushroom sauce. Cut the beef into thick slices and place on warmed serving plates. Pour the mushrooms and sauce over and around the beef. Serve at once, with accompaniments of your choice.

Connie Stevens

Fillet of Beef poached in St Emilion with a Confit of Shallots

450 g (1 lb) pink shallots
50 g (2 oz) unsalted butter
30 ml (2 tbsp) olive oil
1 bottle of St Emilion, or other full-bodied red wine
450 g (1 lb) fillet of beef, in one piece
1 carrot, sliced
2 pieces streaky bacon, derinded and chopped
1 thyme sprig
600 ml (1 pint) beef stock
salt and freshly ground black pepper

1 Finely slice the shallots, reserving 15 ml (1 tbsp) for later. In a small saucepan, melt 25 g (1 oz) of the butter with 15 ml (1 tbsp) of the olive oil. Add the shallots and cook until beginning to soften and turn golden. Increase the heat and add 150 ml (¼ pint) of the wine. Bring to the boil, then simmer over a very low heat for about 45 minutes until the shallots have absorbed all of the wine and are very soft.

2 Meanwhile, heat the remaining oil in a large heavy-based pan. Add the beef and seal on all sides over a high heat, then remove. Add the reserved spoonful of shallots to the pan with the carrot, bacon and thyme; fry until browned. Add half the remaining wine, bring to the boil and reduce by half. Strain into a small saucepan and reserve for the sauce.

3 Meanwhile, pour the stock and remaining wine into a large saucepan and bring to the boil. Add the beef, reduce the heat to a gentle simmer and cook for about 10-15 minutes, depending on the thickness of the meat; it should still be pink in the middle. Lift out the meat, cover with foil and rest for 15 minutes.

4 Reheat the wine reduction reserved for the sauce and add a similar amount of cooking liquid from the beef. Reduce again until a good consistency is obtained and taste for seasoning. Whisk in a knob of butter.

5 To serve, slice the beef into 12 thin rounds. Place a mound of shallots in the centre of each serving plate and arrange three slices of beef to one side. Serve with Savoy cabbage and baby carrots.

Elaine Bates

Angus Steak with Whisky and Green Peppercorn Sauce

4 Angus beef fillet steaks, each about 175-225 g (6 -8 oz)
a little olive oil
1 clove garlic, crushed
15 ml (1 tbsp) crushed black peppercorns

Green Peppercorn Sauce:
knob of butter
3 shallots, finely chopped
200 ml (7 fl oz) light beef or chicken stock
10 ml (2 tsp) Dijon mustard
10 ml (2 tsp) Worcestershire sauce
2-3 parsley sprigs
10 ml (2 tsp) green peppercorns in brine, drained
125 ml (4 fl oz) double cream or crème fraîche
15-30 ml (1-2 tbsp) whisky
salt and freshly ground black pepper

1 Rub the steaks all over with a little olive oil, the garlic and crushed black peppercorns. Set aside in a cool place.

2 To make the sauce, melt the butter in a pan, add the shallots, cover and sweat until softened. Add the stock and simmer until reduced by about half. Add the mustard, Worcestershire sauce and parsley. Transfer to a blender or food processor and work until smooth. Return the mixture to the pan and add the green peppercorns. Cook for 2-3 minutes; cover and set aside.

3 To cook the steaks, oil a cast-iron grill plate and heat to sizzling. Place the steaks on the grill plate and cook for 4-5 minutes each side according to taste, turning regularly and brushing with extra oil if they start to stick to the pan. Set aside to rest in a warm place whilst finishing the sauce.

4 Reheat the sauce, then add the cream and whisky. Cook gently for 2-3 minutes. Check the seasoning.

5 Slice each steak and fan out on warmed serving plates. Spoon over the sauce and serve immediately, accompanied by Mejadarra with Mushrooms (see page 237) and Beetroot and Preserved Lime Salad (see page 220).

Barbara Vazana

Note: If you do not have a grill pan, cook the steaks in a heavy-based frying pan or under a preheated grill, basting frequently with oil.

Fillet of Aberdeen Angus Beef with Buttered Spinach and Parsnip Chips

4 Angus beef fillet steaks, each about 125-175 g (4-6 oz) and 2 cm (¾ inch) thick
salt and freshly ground black pepper
25 g (1 oz) unsalted butter

Parsnip Chips:
oil for deep-frying
125 g (4 oz) parsnips

Buttered Spinach:
450 g (1 lb) spinach, stalks removed
25 g (1 oz) butter

1 Season the steaks with salt and pepper. Heat the butter in a cast-iron griddle pan until sizzling.

2 Meanwhile, for the chips, heat the oil in a deep-fat fryer and thinly slice the parsnips.

3 Place the steaks in the griddle pan and cook for 2-3 minutes each side, according to taste.

4 In the meantime, cook the spinach with just the water clinging to the leaves after washing and a little seasoning in a tightly covered pan for 3-4 minutes or until just wilted. Add the butter and toss to melt.

5 Whilst cooking the steaks and spinach, deep-fry the parsnips in the hot oil for about 30 seconds to 1 minute until crisp and golden brown. Drain on kitchen paper.

6 Place each steak on a warmed serving plate with a pile of parsnip chips and a mound of buttered spinach. Serve immediately, accompanied by Horseradish Bubble and Squeak (see page 225).

Amanda Farnese

Fillet Steaks in Black Bean Sauce

4 Aberdeen Angus fillet steaks, each about 150 g (5 oz)
20 ml (4 tsp) fermented black beans
1 small garlic clove, peeled
4 cm (1½ inch) cube of fresh root ginger, peeled and roughly chopped
dash of rice wine
450 ml (15 fl oz) well-flavoured reduced beef stock
15 ml (1 tbsp) olive oil
60 ml (2 fl oz) red wine
salt and freshly ground black pepper

Ginger and Coriander Crisps:
150 g (5 oz) fresh root ginger
about 30 coriander leaves
sunflower oil for deep-frying

1 Trim the fillet steaks and set aside.

2 Rinse the fermented black beans well and pat dry with kitchen paper. Put half into a mortar. Add the garlic and ginger and pound with the pestle until smooth; the mixture should be quite dry and thick. Add a dash of rice wine and mix to a smooth paste. Warm the stock in a saucepan, then add the black bean paste. Turn off the heat and leave to infuse.

3 To make the ginger and coriander crisps, peel the ginger, cutting off any knobbly bits and trim to a good even shape. Slice extremely thinly across the diagonal to make 24-32 crisps. Rinse the coriander leaves and pat dry. Heat the oil for deep-frying to 160°C (325°F). Deep-fry the crisps in batches until golden, then drain on kitchen paper; they will crisp up as they cool. Deep-fry the coriander leaves for about 1 minute; do not overcook. Drain on kitchen paper.

4 To cook the steaks, heat the olive oil in a heavy-based pan or griddle. Add the steaks and cook for 3 minutes each side for medium rare. Remove from the pan and keep warm. Deglaze pan with the wine, then add the stock and black bean paste. Let bubble for a few moments, then strain and return to the pan. Add the whole black beans and check seasoning.

5 Carve each steak into 5mm (¼ inch) thick slices. Arrange on warmed plates and pour over the sauce. Sprinkle the ginger crisps and coriander leaves on top. Serve with accompaniments of your choice.

Gill Tunkle

Fillet of Beef stuffed with Oysters with a Claret and Oyster Sauce

575 g (1¼ lb) fillet of beef
salt and freshly ground black pepper
12 oysters
juice of 1 lemon, or to taste
30 ml (2 tbsp) olive oil

Claret and Oyster Sauce:
25 g (1 oz) butter
1 shallot, chopped
1 clove garlic, bruised
2 strips of finely pared lemon rind, each 2.5 x 1 cm (1 x ½ inch)
pinch of freshly grated nutmeg
pinch of cayenne pepper
50 g (2 oz) mushrooms, chopped
2 anchovy fillets, pounded
325 ml (11 fl oz) beef stock
375 ml (13 fl oz) claret
450 ml (¾ pint) double cream
lemon juice, to taste

To Garnish:
watercress sprigs

1 Trim the beef of all fat, then make a lengthways cut along the side of the beef, three quarters through. Open out and season with salt and pepper.

2 Open the oysters and reserve the beards and liquor. Lay about six of the oysters, overlapping along the open fillet to within 2 cm (¾ inch) of each end. (Reserve the other oysters for the sauce.) Sprinkle the oysters and fillet with lemon juice. Reshape meat to enclose oysters and tie at 2.5 cm (1 inch) intervals with string. Cover and set aside.

3 To make the sauce, melt the butter in a pan. Add the shallot, garlic, lemon rind, nutmeg and cayenne. Cook over a low heat for 2-3 minutes until the onions are soft. Add the mushrooms and cook for 1 minute. Stir in the anchovies, oyster beards and liquor. Simmer for 2 minutes.

4 Add the reserved oysters and poach gently in the liquor for 1-2 minutes or until the edges begin to curl. Remove with a slotted spoon and set aside.

5 Add the beef stock and all but 45 ml (3 tbsp) claret to the pan and reduce by half, or until the liquid is of a syrupy consistency. Add the cream and reduce again until the sauce is thick enough to coat the back of a spoon. You should have about 400 ml (14 fl oz). Strain the sauce through a fine sieve into a clean bowl and keep warm over a steamer.

6 Purée the reserved oysters in a blender or food processor with the remaining 45 ml (3 tbsp) claret. Stir into the sauce. Add lemon juice, salt and pepper to taste.

7 To cook the beef, heat the oil in a heavy-based frying pan. Season the fillet with salt and pepper, then add to the pan and sear over a high heat on all sides. Transfer to a rack over a roasting tin, containing 150 ml (¼ pint) warm water.

8 Roast in a preheated oven at 220°C (425°F) mark 7 for 15-20 minutes. Cover and leave to stand in a warm place for 20 minutes, before carving into slices.

9 To serve, spoon a little of the sauce on to each plate and arrange the beef slices on top. Garnish with watercress.

Tony Purwin

'Hong Kong' Steak Pie with Marinated Pigeon Breast

Marinated Pigeon Breasts:
4 pigeon breasts, skinned
15 ml (1 tbsp) thin honey
5 ml (1 tsp) Chinese five-spice powder
30 ml (2 tbsp) dark soy sauce
15 ml (1 tbsp) oil
10 ml (2 tsp) balsamic vinegar
5 ml (1 tsp) Tabasco sauce

Pie Filling:
350 g (12 oz) braising steak
15 ml (1 tbsp) flour
salt and freshly ground black pepper
15-30 ml (1-2 tbsp) oil
150 ml (¼ pint) water
30-45 ml (2-3 tbsp) fermented salted black beans
30-45 ml (2-3 tbsp) dry sherry
8 pickled walnuts, chopped
5-10 ml (1-2 tsp) Tabasco sauce
225 g (8 oz) button mushrooms, quartered

Pastry:
225 g (8 oz) self-raising flour
125 g (4 oz) shredded suet
150 ml (¼ pint) water (approximately)

1 Place the pigeon breasts in a shallow dish. For the marinade, mix together the remaining ingredients in a bowl, then pour over the breasts. Turn to coat, then leave to marinate for 1-2 hours (no longer or the flavour will be overpowering).

2 For the pie filling, cut the steak into strips and toss in the flour, seasoned with pepper only. Heat the oil in a heavy-based frying pan until smoking, then brown the meat in batches: cook, turning, for a few minutes until evenly browned. Transfer to a 600 ml (1 pint) pie dish or 4 individual pie dishes, using a slotted spoon.

3 Add the water, black beans, sherry and walnuts to the pan. Scrape up the sediment from the bottom of the pan and allow the mixture to come to the boil. Add the Tabasco. Taste to ensure that the flavour is sufficiently pronounced: depending on the strength of the black bean sauce you may need to add more; the Tabasco should add 'kick' without being too fiery.

4 Add the mushrooms to the meat then pour over the sauce, ensuring that the liquid covers the meat; top up with a little water if necessary.

5 To make the pastry dough, mix together the self-raising flour, suet and seasoning in a bowl. Add sufficient water to make a soft dough. Knead lightly until just smooth. Roll out to a 1 cm (½ inch) thickness and use to cover the pie dish(es).

6 Bake in a preheated oven at 180°C (350°F) mark 4 for 40 minutes to 1 hour, depending on the size of your dish.

7 About 10 minutes before serving, preheat a cast-iron griddle or cast-iron frying pan. Add the pigeon breasts and cook for 1-2 minutes on each side. Transfer the breasts to a warmed plate and leave to rest for a few minutes before carving into slices on the diagonal.

8 Serve the steak pie, cut into portions if appropriate, on warmed serving plates and arrange the pigeon breast alongside. Serve at once, with Salud's Cabbage (see page 215) and steamed mangetouts.

Mandy Ford

Veal Medallions with Onion Marmalade

4 onions, sliced
salt and freshly ground black pepper
750 ml (1¼ pints) chicken stock
22 ml (1½ tbsp) red wine vinegar
350 ml (12 fl oz) double cream
8 veal medallions, each 75 g (3 oz)
flour, for dusting
30 ml (2 tbsp) sunflower oil
50 g (2 oz) butter
250 ml (8 fl oz) port

To Garnish:
sage leaves

1 Put the onions in a medium saucepan with seasoning. Add 500 ml (16 fl oz) of the chicken stock and the vinegar. Cook, covered, over a moderate heat for about 15 minutes until the liquid is almost totally evaporated.

2 In a separate small pan, bring the cream to the boil and boil steadily to reduce to 60-75 ml (4-5 tbsp). Add the cream to the onions and bring back to the boil. Check the seasoning and remove from the heat.

3 Season the veal with salt and pepper and dust all over with flour. Heat the oil and half of the butter in a large heavy-based frying pan. Add the veal and sauté for 3-4 minutes on each side until browned, but pink inside. Remove and keep warm.

4 Pour off any remaining fat from the pan, then add the port to deglaze, scraping up any sediment from the base of the pan. Add the remaining chicken stock, bring to the boil and boil to reduce to 60-75 ml (4-5 tbsp). Gradually whisk in the remaining 25 g (1 oz) butter, a piece at a time, to yield a smooth glossy sauce.

5 To serve, gently reheat the onions and spoon a portion onto each warmed serving plate. Top with the veal and spoon on the sauce. Garnish with sage and serve with Sage Tagliatelle (see page 235) and French beans.

Holly Schade

Oxtail in Port with Root Vegetables and Hedgerow Jelly

1.5 kg (3 lb) oxtail
2 onions, sliced
150 ml (¼ pint) port
2 bay leaves
15 ml (1 tbsp) tomato purée
grated rind and juice of 1 orange
juice of 1 lime
1.2 litres (2 pints) oxtail stock (see right)
salt and freshly ground black pepper
225 g (8 oz) carrots, sliced
225 g (8 oz) parsnips, sliced
2 sticks celery, sliced
1 leek, sliced
15 ml (1 tbsp) hedgerow jelly

To Serve:
chopped parsley to garnish
Hedgerow Jelly (see right)

1 Trim the fat from the oxtail, then seal the meat in a hot heavy-based saucepan, without additional fat, on all sides. Remove and set aside. Fry the onions in the fat remaining in the pan until softened, then remove. Deglaze the pan with half of the port, stirring to scrape up the sediment.

2 Place the onions, oxtail, meat juices, bay leaves, tomato purée, fruit juices, stock and seasoning in a pressure cooker and cook for 45 minutes. Alternatively, cook in a flameproof casserole in a preheated oven at 190°C (375°F) mark 5 for 1½-2 hours.

3 If using a pressure cooker, transfer to a flameproof casserole. Mop up excess fat from the surface with absorbent kitchen paper. Add the carrots, parsnips, celery and leek with 15 ml (1 tbsp) hedgerow jelly. Add a little more stock if necessary. Cover and cook in a preheated oven at 180°C (350°F) mark 4 for about 45 minutes to 1 hour. Check the seasoning. Add the remaining port and reduce until the sauce has thickened slightly, on top of the cooker.

4 Serve sprinkled with parsley and accompanied by hedgerow jelly.

Linda Yewdall

Oxtail Stock: Use the thinner tail ends, with fat removed, to make this. Place in a large pan with a few flavouring vegetables, ie onions, leeks, carrots, and a bouquet garni. Add water to cover, bring to the boil and skim the surface. Cover and simmer gently for 2-3 hours. Alternatively cook in a pressure cooker for just 30 minutes.

Hedgerow Jelly: Chop 1 kg (2 lb) crab apples, without peeling or removing the cores. Place the crab apples and 1 kg (2 lb) sloes (stalks removed) in a preserving pan with 1.2 litres (2 pints) water. Bring slowly to the boil, then simmer for about 1 hour. Ladle the fruit and juice into a scalded jelly bag over a bowl and leave to drip through for several hours.

Measure the juice and return to the preserving pan. Add 450 g (1 lb) sugar to each 600 ml (1 pint) juice. Stir over a low heat until the sugar has dissolved, then bring to the boil. Boil rapidly until setting point is reached; this will take approximately 10 minutes. Skim any froth from the surface, then immediately pot in hot sterilised jars.

Calves Liver and Papaya with a Madeira Sauce

4 thin slices calves liver, each about 75-125 g (3-4 oz)
15 ml (1 tbsp) flour
salt and freshly ground pepper
50 g (2 oz) clarified butter
25 g (1 oz) shallots, finely chopped
150 ml (¼ pint) medium dry Madeira
150 ml (¼ pint) veal stock
50 g (2 oz) unsalted butter, chilled and diced
1 papaya, thinly sliced

1 Coat the liver lightly with flour and seasoning. Heat the clarified butter in a frying pan. When it is very hot, add the calves liver and cook over a high heat for 1 minute on each side. Transfer to a plate and keep warm.

2 Sauté the shallots in the same pan until soft, then add the Madeira and boil until reduced by half. Add the stock and boil until the sauce is a little syrupy. Pass the sauce through a sieve into a clean pan and whisk in the chilled butter, a little at a time, over a low heat. Season to taste.

3 Place the calves liver on warmed serving plates and pour over the sauce. Arrange the papaya slices around the liver and serve immediately, accompanied by a Mixed Leaf and Walnut Salad (see page 200).

Amita Baldock

Pan-fried Calves Liver with Grilled Pineapple

1 small pineapple
125 ml (4 fl oz) plum wine
125 ml (4 fl oz) Japanese rice wine vinegar
10 ml (2 tsp) olive oil
5 ml (1 tsp) unsalted butter
700 g (1½ lb) calves liver
flour, for coating

Sauce:
125 ml (4 fl oz) red wine
125 ml (4 fl oz) port
30 ml (2 tbsp) rice vinegar
60 ml (4 tbsp) veal stock
50 g (2 oz) chilled unsalted butter, in pieces
large pinch of ground cinnamon
salt and freshly ground black pepper

To Garnish:
16 chives, with flowers if possible
5 ml (1 tsp) jalapeno peppers, chopped (optional)

1 Cut the top and base off the pineapple, then cut away the skin and remove the brown 'eyes'. Cut four 1 cm (½ inch) slices from the centre of the pineapple; chop the rest, discarding the hard central core and set aside 125 g (4 oz) for the garnish. Combine the plum wine and rice vinegar in a shallow dish. Add the pineapple rings, turn to coat with the mixture and leave to marinate for 15 minutes.

2 Meanwhile prepare the sauce. Put the red wine, port and rice vinegar in a small pan and boil until reduced by half. Add the veal stock and boil to reduce until the sauce starts to thicken. Whisk in the butter, cinnamon and salt and pepper to taste until smooth. Keep warm.

3 Drain the pineapple rings and cook under a preheated hot grill, turning occasionally, until golden brown on both sides.

4 Meanwhile cut the liver into 5 mm (¼ inch) thick slices – to give 2-3 slices per serving. Drizzle with a little olive oil. Toss in flour to coat evenly. Heat the butter and remaining olive oil in a heavy-based frying pan. When it is very hot, add the liver slices and sauté over a high heat for no longer than 1 minute each side.

5 To serve, toss the chopped fresh pineapple in the sauce. Arrange the liver and grilled pineapple slices on warmed serving plates. Garnish with the chives, and peppers if using. Serve with the sauce.

David Chapman

Roast Rack of Lamb with a Rosemary and Port Sauce

For this recipe, ask your butcher to French trim the racks of lamb, removing all fat and sinews between the bones down to the 'eye' of the meat.

2 whole best ends of lamb, fat removed and French trimmed
olive oil, for cooking
sea salt and freshly ground black pepper
4 rosemary sprigs
3-4 cloves garlic, peeled

Rosemary and Port Sauce:
300 ml (½ pint) lamb stock
60 ml (4 tbsp) port
2 rosemary sprigs
50 g (2 oz) butter, chilled and diced

Croûtes:
4 slices bread
30 ml (2 tbsp) chopped parsley

1 Brush the racks of lamb with olive oil and season with salt and pepper. Heat a little olive oil in a large heavy-based frying pan and sear the meat over a high heat on all sides.

2 Lay the rosemary sprigs and garlic cloves in a roasting tin and place the lamb racks on top (reserving the juices in the pan). Roast in a preheated oven at 200°C (400°F) mark 6 for 12-14 minutes, until tender but still pink in the middle.

3 Meanwhile, make the sauce. Put the lamb stock in a saucepan with the reserved pan juices. Add the port and rosemary sprigs and boil for about 5 minutes to reduce. Lower the heat and whisk in the butter, a piece at a time, to thicken the sauce and give it a glossy finish.

4 When the lamb is cooked, cover and leave to rest in a warm place for 5 minutes. In the meantime, cut a 7.5 cm (3 inch) round from each slice of bread, using a suitable pastry cutter. Heat a thin layer of olive oil in a frying pan and shallow-fry the bread rounds until crisp and golden on both sides. Drain on kitchen paper, then dip the croûtes in chopped parsley to coat.

5 To serve, place a parsley croûte in the centre of each warmed serving plate and arrange 3 lamb cutlets on top. Surround with the sauce and garnish with rosemary. Serve with Carrots with Cumin (see page 217) and Anna Potatoes (see page 234).

Judith Elliott

Rack of Lamb in a Wine and Shallot Sauce

2 racks of lamb, each with 6 chops
30 ml (2 tbsp) olive oil
2 rosemary sprigs
2 thyme sprigs
salt and freshly ground black pepper

Wine and Shallot Sauce:
8 shallots, roughly chopped
1 thyme sprig
1 bay leaf
50 ml (2 fl oz) port
50 ml (2 fl oz) matured sherry vinegar
400 ml (14 fl oz) red wine
400 ml (14 fl oz) lamb stock
15 g (½ oz) cold unsalted butter, diced

Leek Garnish:
1 leek
groundnut oil, for frying

To Serve:
Horseradish and Ginger Rösti (see page 234)

1 First prepare the wine and shallot sauce. Combine all the ingredients, except the stock and butter, in a bowl or non-reactive pan and leave to infuse as long as time allows, but preferably overnight. Transfer to a pan if necessary and bring to the boil. Simmer until reduced by two thirds. Add the stock and reduce again by half. Strain through a fine sieve and work in the butter a piece at a time. Keep warm.

2 Heat the oil in a large frying pan until very hot. Sear each rack of lamb for 1 minute on each side and 3 minutes on its back. Transfer to a hot roasting tin, placing the rack on the reserved lamb bones. Lay a sprig of thyme and rosemary on each rack and roast in a preheated oven at 220°C (425°F) mark 7 for 12 minutes. Season.

3 To prepare the garnish, halve the leek and cut into fine julienne strips. Heat the oil to 140°C (285°F) and fry the leeks until pale golden in colour. Drain well on absorbent kitchen paper.

4 Leave the meat to rest in a warm place for a few minutes before carving into individual cutlets. Serve the cutlets on the horseradish and ginger röstis. Spoon the wine and shallot sauce around, and top with the leek garnish. Serve with a selection of baby vegetables.

Gregory Lewis

Note: The racks of lamb should be French trimmed and lean. Ask your butcher for extra lamb bones to use as a trivet for roasting the lamb.

Southdown Lamb Fillet with Garlic Sauce

600 g (1¼ lb) lamb fillet, from the loin
salt and freshly ground black pepper
14 g (½ oz) butter
4 good thyme sprigs, leaves rubbed off the stalks

Garlic Sauce:
20 large cloves garlic (unpeeled)
200 ml (7 fl oz) milk
20 g (¾ oz) butter
5 ml (1 tsp) sugar
500 ml (16 fl oz) good lamb or chicken stock
150 ml (¼ pint) crème fraîche

1 Season the lamb fillet with salt and pepper. Rub all over with the butter, then with the thyme leaves, pressing them into the meat. Leave to stand for 20 minutes or longer if possible. Place in a lightly buttered roasting tin and roast in a preheated oven at 200°C (400°F) mark 6 for 10 to 15 minutes.

2 To make the garlic sauce, put the garlic cloves in a saucepan and cover with the milk. Bring to the boil and simmer for 1 minute; drain.

3 Heat the butter in a roasting tin, add the garlic, season with salt, pepper and sugar and cook over a medium heat for 2-3 minutes, stirring constantly. Transfer to the oven and bake for 15 minutes, turning the garlic frequently.

4 Wrap 8 of the garlic cloves in foil and reserve; peel the remainder and chop finely. Place the chopped garlic in a pan with the stock and crème fraîche. Bring to the boil. Simmer until reduce to the correct consistency; you should have approximately 400 ml (14 fl oz) liquid. Pass through a sieve into a clean saucepan, pushing as much of the garlic through as possible. Adjust the seasoning.

5 Place the reserved garlic cloves in the oven to warm. Carve the lamb into thin slices and season with salt and pepper. Spoon a little sauce on to each plate and arrange the lamb in overlapping slices on the sauce. Spoon a little more sauce over the lamb and position two garlic cloves on each plate to garnish.

Vanessa Binns

Char-grilled Loin of Lamb Fillet with Glazed Turnips and a Cassis and Madeira Sauce

2 lamb loin fillets (plus reserved bones), total weight about 675 g (1½ lb)

Marinade:
180 ml (6 fl oz) red wine (eg Claret)
180 ml (6 fl oz) crème de cassis
juice of 1 lemon
1 large clove garlic, chopped
30 ml (2 tbsp) olive oil
few mixed herbs (eg bay leaf, parsley sprig, rosemary sprig)
1 tomato, chopped
salt and freshly ground black pepper

Sauce:
30 ml (2 tbsp) olive oil
reserved lamb bones
1 stick celery, with leaves
1 large carrot, chopped
1 medium onion, chopped
15 ml (1 tbsp) tomato purée
10 ml (2 tsp) Dijon mustard
50 ml (2 fl oz) Madeira
5 ml (1 tsp) redcurrant jelly
a little crème de cassis, to taste (optional)

Glazed Turnips:
4 turnips, sliced
5 ml (1 tsp) light brown sugar
30 ml (2 tbsp) crème de cassis
25 g (1 oz) butter
15 ml (1 tbsp) muscovado sugar

To Garnish:
herb sprigs
handful of blackcurrants, glazed in sugar syrup (optional)

1 Mix all the ingredients for the marinade together in a shallow dish. Add the lamb fillets and turn to coat. Cover and leave to marinate in a cool place overnight or for several hours at least.

2 The next day, remove the lamb from the marinade and set aside; reserve the marinade.

3 To prepare the sauce, heat the oil in a large saucepan. Add the lamb bones, celery, carrot and onion and fry, stirring, for a few minutes until browned; do not burn. Add the reserved marinade and 250 ml (8 fl oz) water. Bring to the boil and simmer for 30-45 minutes. Increase the heat and reduce the liquid by two thirds.

4 Meanwhile, prepare the glazed turnips. Put the turnips in a pan with 250 ml (8 fl oz) water, the light brown sugar, crème de cassis and seasoning. Bring to the boil, cover and cook for about 30 minutes until tender. Drain the turnips, adding the cooking liquor to the sauce. Add the butter and muscovado sugar to the turnips and toss over a moderate heat to glaze; keep warm.

5 When the sauce has reduced, remove from the heat and strain into another pan. Add the tomato purée, mustard, Madeira and redcurrant jelly. Check the seasoning and add a little more crème de cassis if needed; keep warm.

6 Meanwhile, preheat the grill to high (or a griddle). Place the lamb on the grill rack (or griddle) and cook for 3-5 minutes each side, until browned on the outside but still pink in the middle.

7 To serve, thinly slice the lamb and arrange alternate pieces of lamb and turnip on the serving plate. Spoon around the sauce and garnish with herbs and glazed blackcurrants if desired.

Jill O'Brien

Marinated Fillet of Lamb with a Madeira Sauce

For this recipe, you will need to prepare the stock a day in advance (see below); or up to 1 week ahead if stored in the freezer.

2 whole filleted best ends of lamb, trimmed of all fat
salt and freshly ground black pepper
knob of butter
15-30 ml (1-2 tbsp) groundnut oil

Marinade:
5 shallots, peeled and quartered
2 large rosemary sprigs
12 chives, chopped
3 cloves garlic, sliced
250 ml (8 fl oz) full rich Madeira

Madeira Sauce:
reserved Madeira from the marinade
600 ml (1 pint) homemade stock (see below)
small knob of unsalted butter

1 To marinate the lamb, lay the fillets in a long casserole dish. Sprinkle with the shallots, rosemary, chives and garlic, then pour on the Madeira. Cover and leave to marinate for at least 1½ hours, turning the meat at least once during that time.

2 Lift the meat out of the marinade and pat dry; strain and reserve the marinade. Season the meat with salt and pepper.

3 To make the sauce, put the strained marinade into a pan and simmer to reduce by half. Add the stock and reduce to the required consistency. Check the seasoning, then stir in the knob of unsalted butter.

4 To cook the lamb, heat the butter and a little groundnut oil in a heavy-based frying pan until sizzling. Add the meat and quickly seal on both sides. Turn down the heat and cook for a further 6-8 minutes, depending on the thickness of the meat. Transfer to a warmed plate, cover loosely with foil to keep warm and leave to rest for about 10 minutes.

5 To serve, carve the meat into slices. Arrange on warmed serving plates and pour on the sauce. Serve with Potatoes Dauphinoise, Roast Parsnip Cups filled with Parsnip Purée (see page 228) and Savoury Spinach with Lamb's Kidneys (see page 204).

Wendy Burnley

Homemade Stock: To make the stock, put 675 g (1½ lb) beef bones and 1.2 kg (2½ lb) lamb bones into a large roasting tin and roast in a preheated oven at 180°C (350°F) mark 4 for 30 minutes. Spread about 150 ml (¼ pint) passata over the bones and add 2 large onions, peeled; 3 leeks; 450 g (1 lb) carrots, peeled; 3 celery sticks and 3 cloves garlic, peeled. Roast for a further 45 minutes.

Using a slotted spoon, transfer the vegetables and bones to a stock pot. Add the bouquet garni and cover with water. Skim the fat off the juices in the roasting tin, then deglaze with a little boiling water and add to the stockpot. Bring to the boil and simmer for 3-4 hours, skimming off any fat and residue that rises to the surface. Strain through a large colander, then several times through a muslin-lined sieve.

Transfer the stock to a clean pan and reduce to just over 600 ml (1 pint). Pour into a jug and allow to cool, then chill in the refrigerator, until required. It will set to a solid jelly.

Fillets of Lamb wrapped in Spinach and Prosciutto

2 loin of lamb fillets, each about 225 g (8 oz)
10 ml (2 tsp) olive oil
salt and freshly ground black pepper
8-10 large spinach leaves, stalks removed
5 ml (1 tsp) French mustard
5 ml (1 tsp) Dijon mustard
2.5 ml (½ tsp) wholegrain mustard
2.5 ml (½ tsp) chopped dill
4-6 slices prosciutto or Parma ham
2-3 shallots, finely chopped
1 clove garlic, finely chopped
200 ml (7 fl oz) rosé wine
250 ml (8 fl oz) well-flavoured veal or lamb stock
2.5 ml (½ tsp) tomato purée

1 Heat the olive oil in a heavy-based pan, add the lamb fillets and seal on all sides over a high heat. Season with salt and pepper and set aside. (Don't rinse the pan).

2 Plunge the spinach leaves into a pan of boiling water, then remove immediately so as not to overcook them. Lay them out on a clean tea-towel to drain. Spread out, overlapping the leaves slightly to form two 'sheets' of spinach.

3 Mix the mustards together with the dill. Spread all but 2.5 ml (½ tsp) evenly on both sheets of spinach.

4 Place a lamb fillet on each spinach sheet and wrap the spinach around the lamb to enclose completely. Lay out the prosciutto slices, overlapping them slightly to form two 'sheets'. Place the lamb fillets on top and fold the prosciutto around each fillet to enclose. The prosciutto should adhere to itself and hold together, but if at all concerned, tie at intervals with cotton string to hold it in place. (Wrap in cling film and left to rest in a cool place until ready to cook.)

5 Roast the lamb in a preheated oven at 220°C (425°F) mark 7 for 15-20 minutes, depending on how you like your lamb. Meanwhile make the gravy. Reheat the oil remaining in the pan used to seal the lamb, add the shallots and garlic and cook until softened. Deglaze with the rosé wine, stirring to scrape up the sediment. Simmer to reduce by one third then add the stock and reduce again by about a third.

6 Strain the sauce through a conical sieve or pass through a mouli to purée the shallot and garlic. Return to the pan, add the tomato purée and if necessary, reduce to the desired consistency. Add a little of the reserved mustard mixture to taste.

7 Cover the lamb lightly with foil and let rest for at least 5 minutes.

8 To serve, slice each lamb fillet into 3 or 4 medallions, depending on size. Arrange on warmed plates and serve with the sauce and accompaniments of your choice.

Joanna Crossley

Fillet of Lamb on a Root Vegetable Plinth

1 boned loin of lamb, about 600 g (1¼ lb)
150 ml (¼ pint) port
30 ml (2 tbsp) oil
250 ml (8 fl oz) brown stock
shredded zest and juice of 1-2 lemons

Vegetable Plinth:
200 g (7 oz) carrots
200 g (7 oz) parsnips
200 g (7 oz) potatoes
200 g (7 oz) turnip
200 g (7 oz) sweet potato
2 eggs
100 ml (3½ fl oz) double cream
2 cloves garlic, crushed
30 g (1¼ oz) spring onions, finely chopped
30 g (1¼ oz) finely chopped parsley
salt and freshly ground black pepper

1 Ensure that the lamb is trimmed of all fat and sinew. Place in a shallow dish, pour the port over the meat and leave to marinate for 2 hours.

2 Meanwhile, prepare the vegetables. Cut all the root vegetables into strips, about 5 cm (2 inches) long and about 5-10 mm (¼-½ inch) in diameter. Cook in lightly salted boiling water for about 10-12 minutes. Drain and leave to cool.

3 Beat the eggs in a bowl, then mix in the cream. Add the garlic, spring onions, parsley and seasoning to taste.

4 Add the vegetable strips to the cream mixture and mix gently together, taking care not to mash or break the vegetable strips. Using a palette knife, shape the mixture into an oblong on a large greased baking tray. Bake in a preheated oven at 190°C (375°F) mark 5 for 20-25 minutes until golden.

5 Remove the meat from the marinade, reserving the marinade. Heat the oil in a heavy-based pan. When hot, add the whole piece of lamb and fry over a high heat for about 4 minutes, turning regularly to ensure that the whole surface is sealed and browned. Remove, cover and leave to rest in a warm place.

6 Add the stock, reserved marinade, lemon zest and juice to the pan. Bring almost to the boil and simmer until reduced by half. Check the seasoning.

7 To serve, cut the vegetable oblong into 4 plinths and place one on each serving plate. Cut the lamb into thick slices and arrange on top, then pour over the port and lemon gravy. Serve with Raspberried Red Cabbage (see page 213) and Stuffed Savoy Cabbage (see page 214).

Tommy Sheppard

Lamb en Croûte with a Port and Orange Sauce

25 g (1 oz) unsalted butter
2 fillets of lamb, each about 400 g (14 oz)
salt and freshly ground black pepper
18 large spinach leaves
450 g (1 lb) ready-made puff pastry
beaten egg, to glaze

Port and Orange Sauce:
150 ml (¼ pint) veal stock
150 ml (¼ pint) dry red wine
juice of 2 oranges
juice of ½ lemon
30 ml (2 tbsp) redcurrant jelly
1 shallot, finely chopped
1 clove garlic
2.5 ml (½ tsp) chopped fresh root ginger
1 thyme sprig
1 bay leaf
60 ml (4 tbsp) ruby port
65 g (2½ oz) unsalted butter, chilled and diced
salt and freshly ground pepper

1 Heat the butter in a frying pan, add the lamb fillets and cook over a high heat for 2 minutes, turning to seal on all sides. Remove from the pan, season with salt and pepper and allow to cool.

2 Blanch the spinach leaves in boiling water for 5-7 seconds only, refresh in cold water, then drain. Lay out the spinach leaves in two lines, the same length as the lamb fillets. Lay a lamb fillet on each line of spinach and wrap the spinach leaves around each piece of lamb to enclose.

3 Cut the pastry in half. Roll out each piece to a rectangle and place a spinach-wrapped fillet in the centre. Brush the edges of the pastry with beaten egg and wrap each fillet in pastry, pressing the edges to seal. Place seam-side down on a baking sheet and leave to rest at room temperature for about 30 minutes.

4 Meanwhile to make the sauce, put all the ingredients, except the port, butter and seasoning, in a pan. Bring to the boil and boil to reduce by three quarters, skimming occasionally. Strain through a fine sieve, then return to the pan and reheat. Add the port and simmer for a few minutes.

5 To cook the lamb, brush the pastry with beaten egg and bake in a preheated oven at 200°C (400°F) mark 6 for 15-20 minutes, until the pastry is crisp and golden brown.

6 To finish the sauce, whisk in the butter a piece at a time on and off the heat, making sure each piece is thoroughly incorporated before adding the next. Season with salt and pepper to taste.

7 To serve, cut the lamb into slices and arrange on warmed serving plates. Spoon on the sauce and serve at once, with vegetables of your choice.

Richard Kuch

Best End of Lamb with Roasted Beetroot and Garlic

2 best ends of neck of lamb
350-450 g (¾-1 lb) extra lamb bones, chopped up
salt and freshly ground black pepper
3-4 rosemary sprigs
15 g (½ oz) butter, softened
3-4 thyme sprigs, leaves only

Beetroot Jus:
1 raw beetroot, cut into small pieces
12 black peppercorns
6 cloves
2 bay leaves
5 ml (1 tsp) wine vinegar
5 ml (1 tsp) caster sugar

Roasted Beetroot and Garlic:
4-6 raw baby beetroots (unpeeled but washed)
60 ml (4 tbsp) extra-virgin olive oil
150 ml (¼ pint) milk
8 garlic cloves, unpeeled
8 shallots, peeled
4 thyme sprigs
30 ml (2 tbsp) caster sugar
15 ml (1 tbsp) sherry vinegar

To Finish Sauce:
50 g (2 oz) cold unsalted butter, diced

1 First make the beetroot jus. Place all the ingredients in a pan with 300 ml (½ pint) cold water and bring to the boil. Lower the heat and simmer for 20 minutes. Cool, then strain. If necessary, make up to 150 ml (¼ pint) with cold water. Set aside until required for the sauce.

2 Season the lamb bones liberally, then place in a roasting tin with the rosemary sprigs. Roast in the oven at 200°C (400°F) mark 6 for 30-45 minutes.

3 Meanwhile, rub the meat all over with the softened butter. Season liberally with salt and pepper and press the thyme leaves into the meat. Leave to stand for a while.

4 Cut the beetroot into quarters, place in a roasting tin and drizzle with 30 ml (2 tbsp) olive oil. Roast in the oven for 10 minutes. Meanwhile bring the milk to the boil, add the garlic and cook for 1 minute. Drain and skin the garlic cloves. Add to the roasting tin containing the beetroot. Add the shallots, thyme and remaining 30 ml (2 tbsp) olive oil. Season generously with salt and pepper, baste well and return to the oven for 20 minutes.

5 Stand the meat on top of the lamb bones and roast in the oven for 10-15 minutes. Transfer the meat to a warmed dish, cover with foil and leave to rest in a warm place.

6 Sprinkle the roasted vegetables with the sugar and sherry vinegar. Place on the hob and allow to sizzle for about 1 minute to caramelise. Transfer to a warmed serving dish with a slotted spoon. Keep warm. Deglaze the roasting tin with half of the beetroot jus.

6 Remove the lamb bones from their roasting tin and deglaze the tin with the remaining beetroot jus. Strain the liquids from both roasting tins into a saucepan. Boil to reduce a little, then whisk in the butter a little at a time until the sauce is glossy and a little thicker. Adjust the seasoning.

7 Carve the meat into thick slices and arrange on warmed serving plates. Surround with the caramelised vegetables. Pour on the sauce and serve with accompaniments of your choice.

Clare Askaroff

Walnut-coated Best End of Lamb

2 best ends of lamb, preferably Manx Lochtan
a little extra-virgin olive oil
beaten egg yolk, for brushing

Coating:
100-175 g (4-6 oz) walnut halves
50 g (2 oz) brown sugar
15 ml (1 tbsp) chopped parsley

Sauce:
600 ml (1 pint) gamey lamb stock (see right)
15 ml (1 tbsp) good malty real ale
salt and freshly ground black pepper
knob of butter, to thicken

To Garnish:
3-4 firm pickled walnuts
flat-leaved parsley

1 To prepare the lamb, scrape the ribs until they are completely clean to avoid any scraps of tissue burning.

2 Put all the ingredients for the coating in a food processor and process until the mixture resembles fine crumbs, then spread out on a large plate.

3 Heat a little olive oil in a frying pan and sear the lamb joints on all sides, then place on the trivet of extra bones (or on a metal trivet) in a roasting tin. Roast in a preheated oven at 220°C (425°F) mark 7 for 8-10 minutes, then remove and brush the meat (not the rib bones) with egg yolk. Holding the rib bones, dip the meat in the walnut mixture to coat evenly. Put back on the trivet and roast for a further 8-10 minutes (depending on the size of the joint and how pink you like your lamb).

4 While the lamb is cooking, reduce the lamb stock by boiling until it is thick enough to coat the back of a spoon. Just before serving, add the ale and season well with salt and pepper. Remove from the heat and whisk in the butter. Keep warm.

5 Cover the lamb with foil and leave to rest for 5 minutes, then carve into cutlets. Arrange these on hot serving plates, spoon the sauce over the meat and garnish with sliced pickled walnuts and parsley.

Brian Tompkins

Note: Get your butcher to French trim the lamb and, if possible, ask for some extra lamb bones to use as a trivet for roasting the lamb.

Gamey Lamb Stock: Prepare this in advance. You will need 1 kg (2 lb) 'gamey' lamb bones, or include a pheasant carcass if using a domestic breed of lamb. Place in a roasting tin with 1 onion, quartered; 1 carrot, quartered lengthways; 1 leek, roughly chopped; and 2 tomatoes, halved. Roast at 200°C (400°F) mark 6 for about 15 minutes until well browned.

Transfer the bones and vegetables to a large saucepan and add 5 pints (3 litres) water, salt and a bouquet garni. Bring to the boil and simmer gently for 3-4 hours, skimming from time to time. Strain through a fine sieve and allow to cool. Chill, then remove any fat from the surface. Return to a clean pan and reduce to about 600 ml (1 pint) by boiling to concentrate the flavour.

Pan-fried Fillet of Lamb with Roasted Aubergine and Garlic, Couscous and Caramelised Plum Tomatoes

1 best end of lamb fillet, about 600 g (1¼ lb)
60 ml (4 tbsp) olive oil (not extra-virgin)
few rosemary sprigs, leaves only
salt and freshly ground black pepper

Roasted Aubergine and Garlic:
1 long, thin aubergine, thinly sliced
8 cloves garlic
olive oil, for drizzling

Caramelised Plum Tomatoes:
4 plum tomatoes, quartered lengthwise
30 ml (2 tbsp) extra-virgin olive oil
7.5 ml (1½ tsp) caster sugar
15 ml (1 tbsp) balsamic vinegar
150 ml (¼ pint) jellied lamb stock

Couscous:
15 ml (1 tbsp) olive oil
pinch of freshly grated nutmeg
pinch each of ground cinnamon, coriander, cumin and ginger
4 shallots, sliced into rounds
225 g (8 oz) couscous
150 ml (¼ pint) hot jellied lamb stock
300 ml (½ pint) boiling water
15 ml (1 tbsp) roasted garlic-flavoured olive oil (see note)
15 ml (1 tbsp) chopped flat-leaf parsley
15-30 ml (1-2 tbsp) skinned pistachio nuts

1 First prepare the roasted aubergine and garlic. Sprinkle the aubergine slices with salt. Place in a colander, cover with a saucer and weight down. Leave to degorge for 30 minutes. Blanch the garlic cloves in a pan of boiling water for 5 minutes. Rinse the aubergine slices and pat dry. Place on an oiled baking tray with the garlic cloves and sprinkle liberally with olive oil. Roast in a preheated oven at 175°C (335°F) mark 3½ for 45 minutes.

2 For the caramelised tomatoes, heat the olive oil in a frying pan. Add the tomatoes and sizzle for about 3 minutes, then add the sugar and balsamic vinegar. Simmer for about 5-10 minutes until the tomatoes are just cooked, but still holding their shape. Remove from the pan with a slotted spoon; set aside in a warm place. Add the lamb stock to the pan and boil to reduce by about half. Season and reserve this jus.

3 For the couscous, heat the 15 ml (1 tbsp) olive oil in a heavy-based frying pan with the spices. As soon as the spices begin to release their aroma, add the shallots and fry until softened but not browned. Put the couscous into a bowl. In a measuring jug, mix the lamb stock and boiling water together and add the 15 ml (1 tbsp) roasted garlic olive oil. Pour this liquid over the couscous, cover and let stand for 5 minutes. Transfer the plumped up couscous to a steamer and steam over boiling water for 20 minutes.

4 To cook the lamb, heat the olive oil in a heavy-based frying pan over a high heat. Add the lamb with the rosemary leaves and cook for 7-8 minutes until browned and crispy on the outside, but still pink inside. Season with salt and pepper to taste. Reheat the shallots, add the parsley and pistachio nuts, then mix with the couscous.

5 Slice the lamb and arrange on a bed of roasted aubergine and garlic, with the caramelised tomatoes and couscous. Drizzle the jus over the tomatoes and serve at once.

Charlotte Bircher

Note: You can buy olive oil flavoured with roasted garlic, or make your own by infusing roasted garlic cloves in olive oil.

Rosette of Welsh Lamb with Pistou Sauce

2 fillets of Welsh lamb, each about 225-300 g (8-10 oz)
25 g (1 oz) butter
15 ml (1 tbsp) olive oil
salt and freshly ground black pepper

Pistou Sauce:
handful of basil leaves
12 stems of parsley
30 ml (2 tbsp) pine nuts
1 clove garlic
300 ml (½ pint) well-flavoured lamb stock
125 g (4 oz) butter

Vegetables:
4 carrots
½ swede
1 leek
unsalted butter, for cooking
2 potatoes
5 ml (1 tsp) freshly grated nutmeg

To Garnish:
basil sprigs

1 To make the pistou sauce, blanch the herbs in boiling water for 15 seconds, then refresh in iced water. Drain and chop finely. Press through a sieve. Toast the pine nuts, then grind with the garlic. Place the stock, butter, herbs and garlic mixture in a saucepan. Bring to the boil and reduce by half; keep warm.

2 To prepare the vegetables, 'turn' the carrots and swede by cutting into classic barrel shapes of uniform size. Cook in boiling salted water until tender; drain and keep warm. Cut the leek into julienne strips. Sweat the leek in a pan with a knob of butter until tender.

3 To prepare the potato rösti, grate the potatoes and mix with the nutmeg and seasoning. Melt 40 g (1½ oz) butter in a heavy-based frying pan. Set four 7.5 cm (3 inch) metal rings in the pan. Divide the potato mixture evenly between the rings, pressing well down. Cook over a moderate heat for about 5 minutes until the underside is crisp and golden brown. Turn and cook the other side until crispy. Drain on kitchen paper.

4 Season the lamb fillets with salt and pepper. Heat the butter and olive oil in a heavy-based frying pan, add the lamb fillets and fry, turning frequently, for 5-6 minutes depending on thickness; they should still be pink inside. Remove from the pan, cover and leave to rest in a warm place for 5 minutes.

5 To serve, cut the lamb into noisettes. Position a rösti on each serving plate and top with leek julienne. Arrange the noisettes on top. Surround with the pistou sauce and vegetables. Garnish with basil.

Gareth Richards

Rosettes of Lamb with a Potato and Parsnip Rösti Crust and a Wine and Redcurrant Sauce

175 g (6 oz) potato, such as Maris Piper
2 parsnips
2 whole best end of lamb fillets, trimmed of all fat and sinew
2 garlic cloves, crushed
salt and freshly ground black pepper
plain flour, for dusting
2 egg yolks
15 ml (1 tbsp) vegetable oil
25 g (1 oz) unsalted butter

Sauce:
25 g (1 oz) shallots, chopped
275 ml (9 fl oz) Cabernet Sauvignon
250 ml (8 fl oz) lamb stock
2 rosemary sprigs
30-45 ml (2-3 tbsp) redcurrant jelly
5 ml (1 tsp) cornflour, mixed with a little water (optional)

To Garnish:
redcurrants
rosemary sprigs

1 Peel and halve the potato and parsnips. Par-boil in water for about 7 minutes. Drain and cool.

2 Cut each lamb fillet into 4-6 rosettes, depending on size. Rub all over with the crushed garlic. Season with salt and pepper and dust with flour; set aside.

3 To prepare the rösti crust, grate the potatoes and parsnips into a bowl (avoiding the 'woody' centre of the parsnips). Add the egg yolks and seasoning; mix well. Place a spoonful of the rösti mixture on each lamb rosette and press down firmly. Refrigerate until required.

4 Heat the oil and butter in a heavy-based frying pan and fry the lamb rosettes in batches, on both sides until golden brown. Transfer the lamb to a baking tray and cook in a preheated oven at 200°C (400°F) mark 6 for about 8-10 minutes, until browned on the outside but still pink in the middle; keep warm.

5 Meanwhile make the sauce. Pour off most of the fat from the frying pan, add the shallots and sweat until softened. Add the wine and let bubble until reduced by half. Add the stock, rosemary sprigs and redcurrant jelly to taste. Reduce to the desired consistency, adding the cornflour to thicken if necessary. Check the seasoning and pass through a fine sieve.

6 Remove the string from the lamb and arrange on warmed serving plates. Garnish with the redcurrants and rosemary. Serve accompanied by Parsnip Crisps (see page 226), Glazed Baby Carrots (see page 218) and Caramelised Shallots (see page 220).

Louise Halfhide

Noisettes of Lamb with Thyme and Red Wine

2 lamb fillets, each about 225-300 g (8-10 oz)
hazelnut oil, for brushing
handful of thyme sprigs
25 g (1 oz) butter
30 ml (2 tbsp) olive oil
salt and freshly ground pepper
150 ml (¼ pint) good red wine
300 ml (½ pint) strong lamb stock

1 Rub the lamb fillets with hazelnut oil and thyme. Place in a shallow dish, cover and leave to marinate for 1-2 hours.

2 Heat half of the butter and the olive oil in a heavy-based frying pan. Lightly season the lamb and fry, turning frequently, for 5-6 minutes depending on thickness. Remove from the pan and leave to rest in a low oven while making the sauce.

3 Add the red wine to the pan with a few thyme sprigs, stirring to deglaze. Add the lamb stock and reduce until syrupy. Stir in the remaining butter and check the seasoning. Strain through a muslin-lined sieve.

4 To serve, cut the lamb into noisettes; they should be pink inside. Arrange on individual serving plates and spoon the sauce around the noisettes. Serve accompanied by pasta, and spinach flavoured with nutmeg.

Sue Lawrence

Medallions of Lamb with Redcurrant and Port Sauce

1.2 kg (2½ lb) best end of lamb, boned (plus reserved bones)
salt and freshly ground black pepper
30 ml (2 tbsp) olive oil

Sauce:
300 ml (½ pint) lamb stock (made from the reserved bones)
150 ml (¼ pint) ruby port
125 g (4 oz) redcurrant jelly
juice of 1 orange
5 ml (1 tsp) arrowroot (optional)

To Garnish:
redcurrants (optional)

1 Trim the lamb if necessary and season with salt and pepper.

2 To make the sauce, pour the lamb stock into a saucepan and bring to the boil. Boil steadily until reduced by about half. Add the port and boil to reduce further. Whisk in the redcurrant jelly until amalgamated, then add the orange juice. The sauce should be thick enough to lightly coat the back of a spoon. If it requires thickening, mix the arrowroot with a little water, stir into the sauce and cook, stirring, for 1-2 minutes until thickened and translucent. Set aside.

3 Heat the oil in a heavy-based pan until hot, then add the lamb and quickly seal until browned on all sides. Transfer the meat to an ovenproof tin and cook in a preheated oven at 230°C (450°F) mark 8 for 15-20 minutes. Wrap in foil and leave to rest in a warm place for 5-10 minutes.

4 To serve, carve the lamb into slices and arrange on warmed serving plates. Garnish with redcurrants if desired.

Jenni Guy

Fillet of Lamb with Tarragon Marsala Sauce

2 lamb (loin) fillets, each about 225 g (8 oz)
15 g (½ oz) unsalted butter
20-30 rashers sweet-cured streaky bacon, derinded
125 g (4 oz) spinach leaves
30-45 ml (2-3 tbsp) tarragon mustard

Sauce:
300 ml (½ pint) lamb stock
15 g (½ oz) chopped tarragon
150 ml (¼ pint) Marsala
15-30 ml (1-2 tbsp) redcurrant jelly
15 ml (1 tbsp) crème fraîche or mascarpone

To Garnish:
tarragon sprigs

1 Melt the butter in a frying pan, add the lamb fillets and brown evenly; remove and drain.

2 Stretch the bacon rashers with the back of a knife. Arrange them overlapping on a board to form 2 sheets (the same length as the lamb fillets). Blanch the spinach leaves in boiling water for 30 seconds, plunge into cold water to refresh, then drain thoroughly. Spread a thin layer of mustard over the bacon. Arrange the spinach leaves in a layer on top.

3 Place a lamb fillet at one end of each spinach and bacon 'sheet', then roll up. Wrap loosely in foil and set aside until required.

4 Place the lamb parcels in a roasting tin and cook in a preheated oven at 190°C (375°F) mark 5 for 20-25 minutes, according to taste.

5 Meanwhile, prepare the sauce. Put the stock in a pan with half of the chopped tarragon and boil to reduce by half. Add the Marsala and, again, reduce by half. Strain through a fine sieve into a clean pan, pressing the tarragon with the back of a wooden spoon to extract the juices.

6 Allow the cooked lamb to rest for 5 minutes before carving. Add the juices from the roasting tin to the sauce. Add the redcurrant jelly and heat, stirring, to dissolve. Whisk in the crème fraîche or mascarpone and reduce to the desired consistency. Stir in the remaining tarragon.

7 To serve, cut each lamb fillet into 6 slices. Arrange 3 slices on each warmed serving plate and surround with the sauce. Garnish with tarragon and serve with accompaniments of your choice.

Gillian Humphrey

Lamb with Pumpkin Risotto

450 g (1 lb) boned loin of lamb
coarse sea salt and freshly ground black pepper
30 ml (2 tbsp) extra-virgin olive oil
45-60 ml (3-4 tbsp) red or white wine
45-60 ml (3-4 tbsp) lamb stock

Pumpkin Risotto:
90 ml (6 tbsp) extra-virgin olive oil
2 onions, chopped
2 cloves garlic, chopped
2 large red chillis, deseeded and chopped
300 g (10 oz) Arborio rice
250 ml (8 fl oz) white wine (eg Australian Semilion Chardonnay)
5 ml (1 tsp) turmeric
about 1.2 litres (2 pints) chicken stock
250 g (9 oz) butternut squash or pumpkin, finely chopped
100 g (3½ oz) goat's cheese, cut into small pieces
100 g (3½ oz) pine nuts, toasted

1 First prepare the risotto. Heat the olive oil in a frying pan, add the onions and garlic and fry until softened. Stir in the chopped chillis. Add the rice and cook for 2-3 minutes, then add the wine and stir gently until the liquid is absorbed. Stir in the turmeric.

2 Gradually start adding the chicken stock, stirring constantly over a low heat. Continue adding the stock, a ladleful at a time, as each addition is absorbed. Once half the stock has been absorbed, add the pumpkin. Continue to stir in the stock until the rice is plump and tender but still retains a bite. The maximum cooking time is 30 minutes; you may not need to use all of the stock.

3 When the risotto is nearly ready, cook the lamb. Season the meat with the pepper. Heat the oil in a frying pan, add the lamb and fry over a very high heat for 2-3 minutes each side. Transfer to a warmed dish and allow to stand briefly before carving. Meanwhile, deglaze the pan with the wine and stock, stirring to scrape up the sediment.

4 When the risotto is cooked, stir in the goat's cheese, turn off the heat and cover the pan to encourage the cheese to melt.

5 To serve, season the meat with salt and pepper and slice thinly. Fold most of the pine nuts into the risotto. Spoon the risotto onto warmed serving plates and arrange the lamb slices alongside. Moisten the meat with a little of the deglazed pan juices. Sprinkle the remaining pine nuts over the risotto and serve at once, accompanied by a Chicory and Watercress Salad (see page 201).

Alison Fiander

Grilled Fillet of Lamb with Spiced Couscous

4 best-end of neck lamb fillets, each about 200 g (7 oz)
salt and freshly ground black pepper

Marinade:
60 ml (4 tbsp) olive oil
30 ml (2 tbsp) lemon juice
30 ml (2 tbsp) coriander seeds, crushed

Couscous:
1 medium aubergine, finely diced
90 ml (6 tbsp) olive oil
2.5 ml (½ tsp) ground cumin
1 onion, finely chopped
1 clove garlic, finely chopped
10 ml (2 tsp) ground mixed spice
250 ml (9 fl oz) tomato juice
200 g (7 oz) couscous
1 courgette, finely diced
finely grated zest of 2 lemons
1 bunch coriander, leaves finely chopped (stalks reserved)

For the Jus:
600 ml (1 pint) lamb stock
reserved coriander stalks

1 Lay the lamb fillets in a shallow dish and drizzle over the olive oil and lemon juice. Turn the fillets to coat with the mixture, then sprinkle with the crushed coriander seeds and season with salt and pepper. Cover and leave to marinate in a cool place for 1-2 hours.

2 For the couscous, put the diced aubergine in a small baking tin, drizzle over 60 ml (4 tbsp) of the olive oil and sprinkle with the ground cumin. Season with salt and pepper to taste. Roast in a preheated oven at 200°C (400°F) mark 6 for about 12-15 minutes until lightly browned.

3 Meanwhile, heat the remaining olive oil in a large saucepan, add the onion and fry until softened and golden brown. Add the garlic and mixed spice and fry for a few seconds more. Pour in the tomato juice and bring to the boil.

4 Add the couscous, roasted aubergine, courgette and grated lemon zest. Toss well and season with salt and pepper to taste. Cover and leave to stand in a warm place for at least 15 minutes for the couscous to soften.

5 Meanwhile, preheat a ridged griddle pan, add the lamb fillets and cook over a medium-high heat for about 15-20 minutes, until tender but still pink in the middle. Cover and leave to rest in a warm place for 10 minutes before carving.

6 In the meantime make the jus. Bring the stock to the boil in a pan and reduce by half. Add the coriander stalks and leave to infuse for 10 minutes. Strain through a fine sieve and reheat.

7 To serve, carve each lamb fillet into 5 or 6 slices. Add the chopped coriander to the couscous and fork through. Pile some couscous into the centre of each warmed serving plate and arrange the lamb around it. Spoon over the jus and serve at once.

Neil Haidar

Note: During the summer, this lamb is exceptionally good cooked over a charcoal barbecue.

Moroccan Couscous with Pumpkin

700 g (1½ lb) lamb (shoulder and knuckle)
4 large Spanish onions
225 g (8 oz) unsalted butter
1 chicken quarter
2.5 ml (½ tsp) turmeric
5 ml (1 tsp) ground ginger
2 pinches of pulverised saffron
10 ml (2 tsp) freshly ground pepper
salt
1.75 litres (3 pints) light lamb stock
450 g (1 lb) couscous
425 g (15 oz) can chick peas, drained
450 g (1 lb) carrots, cut into chunks
700 g (1½ lb) pumpkin, cut into chunks
175 g (6 oz) raisins
60 ml (4 tbsp) sugar
1 cinnamon stick

To Serve:
dash of rosewater
sprinkling of ground cinnamon
chopped coriander leaves
harissa sauce (see note)

1 Cut the lamb into 4 or 5 steaks. Halve the onions and slice lengthwise. Heat half of the butter in a large heavy-based saucepan or cooking pot. Add the lamb, chicken, onions, turmeric, ginger, saffron, pepper and salt and fry gently for 3-4 minutes, until lightly coloured. Add the stock, bring to the boil and simmer, covered, for 1 hour.

2 Meanwhile, empty the couscous on to a baking tray. Pour on about 600 ml (1 pint) water, then immediately strain off the water. Leave the moistened couscous to swell for 20 minutes, raking it with your fingers after about 10 minutes to separate the grains.

3 Place a tight-fitting steamer over the stew pan, making sure it stands well clear of the stew. Put the couscous into the steamer, and steam uncovered over the simmering stew for 20 minutes.

4 Return the couscous to the baking tray and sprinkle with a cup of cold salted water, containing 5 ml (1 tsp) salt. Let swell for 15 minutes, occasionally sifting with your hands to break up any lumps.

5 In the meantime, rub the chick peas to remove the skins, then add to the stew with the carrots, pumpkin, raisins and sugar. Return to a simmer and cook for at least a further 30 minutes. Replace the couscous in the steamer and steam over the stew for about 30 minutes. A few minutes before the end of the cooking time, add the cinnamon to the stew.

6 To serve, toss the couscous in the remaining 125 g (4 oz) butter and stir out any lumps. Sprinkle with rosewater and cinnamon. Spread the couscous on 4 warmed plates, making a well in the centre. Divide the meat into pieces and place in the centre of the plates. Ladle the stew over the meat and couscous and sprinkle with chopped coriander. Serve with harissa sauce.

Nicole Sochor

Note: Harissa sauce is a spicy Moroccan condiment – available from delicatessens.

Saddle of Jacob Lamb with a Black Pudding Stuffing

1 boned saddle of lamb, about 575 g (1¼ lb)

Stuffing:
50 g (2 oz) skinless chicken breast fillet
1 egg
175 g (6 oz) black pudding
1 rosemary sprig, leaves only, finely chopped
salt and freshly ground black pepper

Sauce:
150 ml (¼ pint) blackberry wine, or fruity red wine
300 ml (½ pint) good lamb stock
8 blackberries, squashed
4 peppercorns
5 ml (1 tsp) blackberry jelly
few knobs of butter

Caramelised Apple:
1 Granny Smith apple
25 g (1 oz) unsalted butter
1 large pinch of caster sugar

To Garnish:
16 blackberries

1 To make the stuffing, process the chicken meat with the egg in a food processor until smooth, then add the black pudding and process until fairly smooth. Add the rosemary and process until evenly mixed.

2 Spread the stuffing into the boned saddle, roll up and tie at 2.5 cm (1 inch) intervals with cotton string. Keep in a cool place until ready to cook. Place in a roasting tin and cook in a preheated oven at 180°C (350°F) mark 4 for 40 minutes. Remove from the oven, cover loosely with foil and leave to rest in a warm place for 10-15 minutes.

3 Meanwhile make the sauce. Simmer the blackberry wine until reduced by half. Add the lamb stock and reduce again by half. Add the squashed blackberries and the peppercorns. Leave to infuse for 10 minutes. Add the blackberry jelly and stir until melted. Strain, return to the pan and whisk in the butter to finish the sauce.

4 To caramelise the apple, peel the apple and cut into wedges. Melt the butter with the sugar in a small frying pan, then add the apple and cook quickly over a high heat until golden brown.

5 To serve, carve the lamb into 2 cm (¾ inch) slices and arrange on warmed serving plates. Garnish with the caramelised apple and blackberries and carefully spoon the sauce around. Serve at once, with vegetable purées.

Marion MacFarlane

Note: Jacob lamb is an ancient breed; the meat is lean with a superb 'gamey' taste and texture. You can of course use traditional Scottish lamb instead.

Braised Lamb Shanks

8 small or 4 medium lamb shanks
45 ml (3 tbsp) olive oil
1 onion, chopped
4 cloves garlic, crushed
50 g (2 oz) tomato purée
2 carrots, sliced
125 g (4 oz) canned chopped tomatoes
350 ml (12 fl oz) red wine
350 ml (12 fl oz) lamb stock
5 ml (1 tsp) finely chopped rosemary leaves
5 ml (1 tsp) finely chopped thyme leaves
2.5 ml (½ tsp) allspice
salt and freshly ground black pepper
5-10 ml (1-2 tsp) arrowroot, mixed with a little water
thyme sprigs, to garnish

1 Heat half of the olive oil in a heavy flameproof casserole. Add the onion and sauté for 3-4 minutes until soft. Add the garlic and cook for a further 2 minutes. Add the tomato purée, carrots, tomatoes, wine, stock, herbs, allspice and seasoning. Bring to the boil.

2 Meanwhile, heat the remaining olive oil in a heavy-based frying pan and brown the lamb shanks on all sides. Add the lamb to the casserole, cover and cook in a preheated oven at 180°C (350°F) mark 4 for 1½-2 hours, stirring from time to time, until the meat comes away from the bone easily. Lower the oven temperature to 110°C (225°F) mark ¼.

3 Lift the lamb shanks out of the casserole and place in an ovenproof dish; keep warm in the oven. Strain the sauce into a saucepan and boil steadily until reduced by about half. Add the arrowroot to thicken the sauce slightly if necessary, and heat, stirring, until thickened.

4 Place the lamb on warmed serving plates and pour on the sauce. Garnish with thyme and serve with minted carrots and Colcannon (see page 216).

Holly Schade

Devilled Pork Tenderloin in a Port Sauce

14 prunes (preferably Agen), stoned
600 ml (1 pint) port
2 pork tenderloins, each 225-300 g (8-10 oz)
25 g (1 oz) butter
salt and freshly ground black pepper
12 rashers rindless streaky bacon (dry-cure)
30 ml (2 tbsp) olive oil

Sauce:
reserved port (see recipe)
2 shallots, peeled
300 ml (½ pint) reduced homemade chicken stock
15 g (½ oz) unsalted butter, in pieces

1 Put the prunes in a bowl with the port and leave to soak for 1 hour. Remove the prunes with a slotted spoon, reserving the port.

2 To prepare the pork, split each tenderloin lengthways with a sharp knife, without cutting all the way through. Open out and put a row of 7 prunes down the middle of each tenderloin. Bring up the sides of the meat to form a sausage and secure temporarily with cocktail sticks; smear with the butter and season with salt and pepper.

3 Place a line of 6 bacon rashers close together on the work surface. Lay the pork on top of the bacon and bring the rashers over the top of the pork, crossing over if necessary. Repeat with the other piece of pork. Cut 12 pieces of string slightly longer than the bacon rashers and tie the meat at regular intervals to secure the bacon.

4 Put the olive oil in a roasting tin and heat in a preheated oven at 200°C (400°F) mark 6. Add the pork tenderloins, turning quickly to brown. Bake in the oven for 45 minutes or until cooked through and brown.

5 Meanwhile, make the sauce. Set aside 45 ml (3 tbsp) of the port. Put the rest in a pan with the shallots and simmer over a low heat until reduced to one third of the original volume. Strain through a fine sieve and discard the shallots. Heat the reduced stock and add to the port; if necessary strain the sauce through a fine sieve again to obtain a smooth consistency. Add the reserved port and whisk in the butter.

6 After cooking, leave the pork to rest in a warm place for 10 minutes, then carve into 1 cm (½ inch) thick slices. Serve with the port sauce, garlic roast potatoes and seasonal vegetables.

Nicola Kidd

Pork wrapped in Spinach and Bacon with a Mushroom Stuffing

575 g (1¼ lb) pork tenderloin
450 g (1 lb) spinach (about 30 leaves)
20 g (¾ oz) dried porcini mushrooms
45 ml (3 tbsp) olive oil
1 clove garlic, crushed
10 ml (2 tsp) dried sage
175 g (6 oz) chestnut mushrooms, chopped
salt and freshly ground black pepper
12 thin-cut rashers unsmoked streaky bacon

1 Cut the pork tenderloin into 6-8 strips of even length and cut each strip in half.

2 Blanch the spinach leaves in a microwave with just the water clinging to the leaves after washing for 30 seconds. Alternatively cook in a saucepan for 30 seconds to 1 minute until softened. Drain thoroughly. Wrap the pork tenderloin strips in the spinach leaves, ensuring that each strip is completely covered.

3 Soak the porcini mushrooms in hot water to cover for 10 minutes. Drain, reserving the soaking liquid. Pass the liquid through a fine sieve to remove any grit.

4 Heat the olive oil in a frying pan with the garlic and sage. Add the chestnut mushrooms and porcini, together with 45-60 ml (3-4 tbsp) of the liquid. Add a further 45-60 ml (3-4 tbsp) liquid, then reduce the mixture until there is little liquid remaining and the mushrooms are cooked. Season with salt and pepper to taste. Transfer the mixture to a food processor and process until it is the consistency of a paté.

5 Lay 6 rashers of bacon side by side on a clean surface, overlapping them slightly to form a 'sheet'. Spread a quarter of the mushroom mixture across the middle and place 3-4 of the spinach-wrapped pork pieces horizontally across the bacon on top of the mushroom mixture. Spread another quarter of the mushroom mixture on top of the pork. Wrap the bacon pieces around the pork and place on an oiled baking tray, join-side down.

6 Repeat the process with the remaining bacon, pork and mushroom mixture so that you have 2 bacon-wrapped 'joints' on the baking tray. Roast in a preheated oven at 200°C (400°F) mark 6 for 20-25 minutes or until the bacon is cooked and crispy.

7 Remove from the oven and cut into slices, using a sharp knife. Carefully transfer to warmed serving plates, using a fish slice. Serve accompanied by Parsnip Purée with Parmesan (see page 227), broccoli and spinach.

Charlotte Bircher

Stuffed Pork Tenderloin with a Rosemary and Garlic Crust, served with a Madeira Sauce

900 g (2 lb) pork tenderloin (fillet)
12 fresh dates, stoned

Crust:
1 small bunch of rosemary
3 cloves garlic, chopped
50 g (2 oz) breadcrumbs
5 ml (1 tsp) salt
2.5 ml (½ tsp) freshly ground black pepper
50 g (2 oz) butter, melted

Sauce:
100 g (3½ oz) butter, diced
1 onion, chopped
50 ml (3½ tbsp) Madeira
350 ml (12 fl oz) chicken stock

To Garnish:
fresh dates
rosemary sprigs

1 Trim any excess fat and sinew from the meat. Make an incision in the side of the fillet and fill with the dates.

2 To make the crust, strip the rosemary leaves from their stems and chop them finely; reserve half of the rosemary for the sauce. Place the other half of the rosemary leaves in the food processor with the garlic, breadcrumbs, salt, pepper and half of the melted butter. Process until evenly mixed, adding a little more melted butter if the mixture seems dry.

3 Pat the crust mixture thickly over the pork and drizzle the remaining melted butter over the top. Roast in a preheated oven at 160°C (325°F) mark 3 for 45 minutes or until the juices run clear, when the thickest part of the meat is pierced with a fine skewer.

4 To make the sauce, heat 15 g (½ oz) of the butter in a saucepan and sauté the onion until softened, but not coloured. Add the Madeira, reserved rosemary and chicken stock. Reduce by half. Whisk in the butter cubes, one by one, making sure each piece is thoroughly incorporated before adding the next. Strain the sauce through a sieve and keep warm.

5 To serve, slice the pork and arrange on warmed serving plates. Garnish with fresh dates and rosemary. Serve with the Madeira sauce and vegetables in season.

Richard Kuch

Fillet of Pork with Prunes

For this recipe you will need to soak the prunes overnight.

12 prunes
450 ml (¾ pint) dry white wine
700 g (1½ lb) pork fillet
plain flour, for coating
salt and freshly ground black pepper
50 g (2 oz) salted butter (approximately)
30 ml (2 tbsp) olive oil
30 ml (2 tbsp) redcurrant jelly
175 ml (6 fl oz) double cream
sage leaves, to garnish

1 Rinse the prunes under cold running water, then place in a small bowl and pour on 300 ml (½ pint) of the wine. Cover and leave to soak overnight.

2 Transfer the prunes and soaking liquid to a small pan and simmer for 10-15 minutes. Remove from the heat; keep warm.

3 Meanwhile, trim the pork fillet and cut on the diagonal into 2.5 cm (1 inch) thick pieces. Lay on a board and flatten slightly with a rolling pin or meat mallet. Season the flour with salt and pepper and spread on a plate. Toss the pork pieces in the flour to coat, shaking off excess.

4 Heat the butter and oil in a frying pan. Brown the pieces of pork a few at a time; remove with a slotted spoon and set aside. Add more butter to the pan as you fry the later batches, if needed.

5 Return all the browned meat to the pan. Add the rest of the wine and let bubble for a few minutes. Lower the heat and simmer, covered, for 20 minutes until tender.

6 Lift out the pork with a slotted spoon, place in a covered dish and keep warm. Drain the prunes, adding the soaking wine to the frying pan. Boil until reduced, then add the redcurrant jelly and stir until dissolved. Add the cream and reduce until the sauce is thick enough to thinly coat the back of the spoon. Add the cooked prunes.

7 Arrange the pork slices on warmed serving plates and surround with the sauce. Serve immediately, garnished with sage leaves and accompanied by Creamed Polenta (see page 236) and Broccoli with Crisp Pancetta (see page 206).

Judith Elliott

Note: To add gloss to the sauce whisk in a few knobs of butter before adding prunes.

Spiced Pork Tenderloin

4 pork tenderloin fillets

Marinade:

60 ml (4 tbsp) chopped parsley
30 ml (2 tbsp) Mexican chilli powder
6 cloves garlic, crushed
15 ml (1 tbsp) cumin seeds
15 ml (1 tbsp) ground coriander
5 ml (1 tsp) ground cinnamon
200 ml (7 fl oz) red wine
30 ml (2 tbsp) red wine vinegar
generous pinch each of chopped oregano, basil and thyme

Sauce:

225 g (8 oz) butter
3 tomatoes, chopped
generous pinch of sugar
salt and freshly ground black pepper

1 Using the tip of a knife, make pinpricks in the pork fillets all over. Mix together the ingredients for the marinade in a shallow dish, then add the pork and turn to coat with the mixture. Leave to marinate for at least 1 hour, then drain, reserving the marinade for the sauce.

2 Place the pork fillets on a baking tray and cook on the top shelf of a preheated oven at 190°C (375°F) mark 5 for about 30 minutes.

3 To make the sauce, melt the butter in a saucepan, then add the reserved marinade, 500 ml (16 fl oz) water, tomatoes and sugar. Bring to a simmer and reduce until the sauce is slightly thickened and rich brown in colour; about 20 minutes. Adjust the seasoning.

4 Slice the pork fillets and arrange on warmed individual plates. Spoon over the sauce. Serve immediately with cardamom-flavoured rice.

Rose Gibson

Pan-fried Tenderloin of Tamworth Pork with a Prune and Armagnac Sauce

2 pork tenderloins (preferably Tamworth), about 350 g (12 oz)
salt and freshly ground black pepper
16 prunes (preferably Agen prunes)
600 ml (1 pint) good homemade chicken stock
15 g (½ oz) clarified butter, for frying
120 ml (4 fl oz) Armagnac or brandy
150 ml (¼ pint) double cream

1 Season the pork tenderloins with salt and pepper. Put the prunes and stock in a pan and boil gently to reduce to just over 300 ml (½ pint). Remove the prunes with a slotted spoon and set aside half of them for the garnish. Remove the stones from the rest and pass through a sieve to form a purée, reserve the prune purée and stock.

2 Heat the clarified butter in a pan, add the pork tenderloins and sear over a high heat, turning to seal on all sides. Either transfer to a roasting tin and cook in a preheated oven at 225°C (425°F) mark 7 for about 10 minutes, depending on size, or continue to fry the pork in the pan, stirring frequently, until just cooked through but still moist.

3 Just before the tenderloins are fully cooked, pour on the Armagnac and set alight, shaking the pan to release the sediment on the base of the pan. When the flames die down, remove the pork from the pan, wrap in foil and leave to rest in a warm place for 5 minutes.

4 Add the reserved stock to the pan and boil vigorously until reduced to 150 ml (¼ pint). Stir in the prune purée to thicken the sauce and season with salt and pepper to taste.

5 Bring the cream to the boil in a separate pan and reduce by half. Add a tablespoonful of the purée sauce to impart colour.

6 To serve, slice the pork and arrange on warmed serving plates on a pool of prune sauce. Pour on a little of the cream sauce and garnish with the reserved prunes. Serve immediately, with vegetable accompaniments of your choice.

Brian Tompkins

Pork Fillet with Redcurrant and Port Sauce

2 pork fillets, trimmed
25 g (1 oz) butter
2 shallots, finely chopped
15-30 ml (1-2 tbsp) finely chopped sage
15 red pepper berries, crushed
pinch of ground mace
salt and freshly ground pepper
12 rashers streaky bacon, rinds removed

Sauce:
1 shallot, finely chopped
15 g (½ oz) butter
125 ml (4 fl oz) port
30 ml (2 tbsp) redcurrants
15 ml (1 tbsp) redcurrant jelly
squeeze of lemon juice (optional)

1 Cut a slice through each pork fillet, two thirds of the way along the length, so that you have two long pieces and two short pieces. Slit each piece horizontally, but do not cut right through the meat, so that you can open each piece of pork like a book.

2 Heat the butter in a pan and cook the shallots until softened. Remove from the heat and add the sage, pepper berries, mace and a little salt.

3 Spread half the mixture on the opened surface of one long piece of pork. Position the two smaller pieces side by side on top. Cover with the rest of the shallot mixture and top with the remaining long piece of pork fillet, so that it looks like a large double-decker sandwich.

4 Stretch the bacon rashers with the back of a knife and line them up parallel and overlapping one another. Place the pork 'sandwich' on top of the bacon and wrap the bacon tightly round the pork. Place in a baking tin and cook in a preheated oven at 190°C (375°F) mark 5 for 1 hour.

5 For the sauce, cook the shallot in the butter until soft. Add the port and reduce slightly. Add the redcurrants, redcurrant jelly, salt and pepper. Adjust the flavour with lemon juice if required, then sieve.

6 To serve, cut the pork into slices and serve with the redcurrant and port sauce.

Gillian Stallard

Bacon and Parsley Dumpling on a Hot Apple, Walnut and Fennel Salad

Suet Pastry:
300 g (10 oz) self-raising flour
150 g (5 oz) shredded vegetable suet
pinch of salt
200 ml (1/3 pint) water (approximately)

Filling:
15 ml (1 tbsp) extra-virgin olive oil
200 g (7 oz) maple-cured streaky bacon, finely chopped
1 large onion, finely diced
1 large bunch flat-leaf parsley, stalks removed, finely chopped

Tarragon-scented Tomato Sauce:
30 ml (2 tbsp) extra-virgin olive oil
1 large onion, finely chopped
1 clove garlic, finely chopped
20 ml (4 tsp) tomato purée
400 g (14 oz) can plum tomatoes
few tarragon leaves, finely chopped
small bunch of basil leaves, finely chopped
dash of white wine vinegar
pinch of sugar, to taste

Hot Apple Salad:
15 g (½ oz) unsalted butter
70 g (2½ oz) walnut halves
1 large fennel bulb, finely sliced
1 Granny Smith apple, cored and sliced
1 small Cos lettuce, cored and shredded

To Garnish:
parsley sprigs

1 To prepare the pastry, combine the flour, suet and salt in a mixing bowl. Add sufficient water to make a firm dough, mixing with a round-bladed knife. Leave to rest for 15 minutes.

2 Heat the oil in a heavy-based frying pan. Add the bacon and cook, stirring, over a medium heat for 2 minutes. Add the onion and cook until softened. Remove from the heat and stir in the chopped parsley and salt and pepper to taste. Leave to cool.

3 Divide the dough into 4 even portions. Roll out each piece to a rectangle about 23 x 15 cm (9 x 6 inches). Divide the bacon mixture evenly between the 4 sheets of dough leaving a 2.5 cm (1 inch) border free along the edges. Moisten the pastry edges with water. Roll up each one from the long end, sealing the edges as you do so. Wrap loosely in cling film and refrigerate until needed. Bring the water in a steamer to the boil. Place the puddings in the steamer, and cook for approximately 1 hour.

4 To make the tomato sauce, heat the oil in a pan, add the onion and garlic and fry until softened. Stir in the tomato purée, tomatoes and herbs. Stir well and cook over a low heat for 10 minutes. (If necessary, thin the sauce with a little hot water.) Add the vinegar and season with sugar, salt and pepper to taste. Purée in a blender or food processor, then pass through a sieve. Reheat if necessary before serving.

5 Prepare the salad about 5 minutes before the dumplings will be ready. Melt the butter in a heavy-based saucepan over a medium heat. Add the walnuts and fry for 2 minutes, stirring occasionally. Add the fennel and cook for a further 2 minutes. Add the apple and cook for 1 minute. Add the chopped lettuce and cook until it is wilted. Season with salt and pepper to taste.

6 Divide the hot salad between individual plates. Arrange the halved dumplings on top. Pour the sauce around them and serve at once, garnished with parsley.

Andrew Whiteley

Accompaniments

Salad Leaves in a Herb Vinaigrette

about 100 g (3½ oz) endive (frisée or batavia)
about 100 g (3½ oz) radicchio leaves

Herb Vinaigrette:
75 ml (5 tbsp) olive oil
1 shallot, crushed
1 thyme sprig
1 basil leaf
4 rosemary sprig needles
1 chervil sprig
15 ml (1 tbsp) white wine vinegar
45 ml (3 tbsp) cold water
1.25 ml (¼ tsp) salt
1.25 ml (¼ tsp) white pepper
1.25 ml (¼ tsp) caster sugar

1 To make the herb vinaigrette, combine the olive oil, shallot and herbs together in a small saucepan. Bring to a simmer, then remove from the heat. Leave to stand for 2 hours. Strain the mixture through a fine sieve into a bowl. Whisk in the vinegar, water, salt, pepper and sugar.

2 Just before serving, toss the salad leaves in the dressing.

Chris Rand

Mixed Leaf and Walnut Salad

200 g (7 oz) mixed salad leaves, eg frisée, radicchio, endive, sorrel, lollo rosso, oakleaf, lamb's lettuce, watercress
50 g (2 oz) shelled walnuts

Dressing:
10 ml (2 tsp) sherry vinegar
10 ml (2 tsp) balsamic vinegar
45 ml (3 tbsp) walnut oil
10 ml (2 tsp) olive oil
2.5 ml (½ tsp) Dijon mustard
½ clove garlic, crushed
salt and freshly ground pepper

1 Put the salad leaves in a bowl. Briefly immerse the walnuts in boiling water to remove the skins, then drain and pat dry. Break into small pieces and add to the salad leaves.

2 Put the vinegar, oil, mustard, garlic, salt and pepper in a screw-topped jar and shake vigorously to combine.

3 Pour the dressing over the salad and toss lightly to mix. Divide between individual plates to serve.

Amita Baldock

Warm Spinach Salad

350 g (12 oz) spinach leaves
25 g (1 oz) sun-dried tomatoes in oil, drained and roughly chopped
25 g (1 oz) pecan nuts, roughly chopped
1 clove garlic, crushed
2 spring onions, sliced
15 g (½ oz) freshly grated Parmesan cheese
30 ml (2 tbsp) oil from the sun-dried tomatoes
black pepper

To Garnish:
2 parsnips
few flat-leaved parsley sprigs
groundnut oil, for deep-frying
coarse sea salt

1 To prepare the garnish, peel the parsnips and pare long thin shreds, using a zester. Mix with a few sprigs of flat-leaved parsley. Heat the oil for deep-frying, then deep-fry the parsnip shreds and parsley, in batches, for about 1 minute until crispy. Remove with a slotted spoon and drain on kitchen paper. Immediately season with freshly ground salt; keep warm.

2 Meanwhile, steam the spinach for about 4 minutes until just wilted, then chop roughly. Place in a bowl with the rest of the ingredients and mix well. Served while still warm, or at room temperature; do not refrigerate. Pile the deep-fried parsnips and parsley on top of the salad to serve.

Clare Askaroff

Note: If preferred omit the deep-fried parsnip garnish and sprinkle with crisp-fried snippets of bacon instead.

Chicory and Watercress Salad

1 bunch of watercress
2 heads of chicory

Vinaigrette:
15 ml (1 tbsp) tarragon vinegar
45 ml (3 tbsp) walnut oil
salt and freshly ground black pepper

1 Trim the watercress; rinse and drain thoroughly. Separate the chicory leaves. Put the watercress and chicory into a bowl.

2 To make the vinaigrette, put the vinegar and oil in a screw-topped jar with salt and pepper to taste. Shake vigorously to combine.

3 Pour the dressing over the salad leaves and toss lightly. Serve at once.

Alison Fiander

Tomato and Basil Salad

4 tomatoes
salt and freshly ground black pepper
30-45 ml (2-3 tbsp) finely shredded basil
30 ml (2 tbsp) red wine vinegar
60 ml (4 tbsp) olive oil
basil sprigs, to garnish

1 Slice the tomatoes, season with salt and pepper to taste and layer in a bowl with the shredded basil.

2 In a small bowl, whisk together the vinegar and oil, season and pour over the tomatoes, turning them carefully once or twice to ensure they are well coated with dressing.

3 Cover and leave at room temperature for at least 1 hour before serving to allow the flavours to develop.

Angela Geary

Thai-style Salad

125 g (4 oz) sugar snap peas
125 g (4 oz) baby sweetcorn, halved lengthways
¼ Chinese cabbage
½ red pepper, cored and deseeded
½ bunch spring onions, trimmed
2 carrots, peeled
¼ fresh pineapple, peeled and cored
125 g (4 oz) oyster mushrooms
handful (¼ cup) coriander leaves, roughly torn

Dressing:
45 ml (3 tbsp) groundnut oil
45 ml (3 tbsp) rice wine vinegar
5 ml (1 tsp) wasabi paste
5 ml (1 tsp) sugar
salt and freshly ground black pepper

1 Blanch the sugar snap peas and baby sweetcorn separately in boiling water for 1 minute. Drain and refresh under cold water; then drain thoroughly.

2 Finely shred the cabbage; finely slice the red pepper. Cut the spring onions into thin strips, on the diagonal. Pare the carrots into thin strips, using a vegetable peeler. Cut the fresh pineapple into finger-sized sticks. Combine all of these salad ingredients in a bowl.

3 Sauté the oyster mushrooms briefly in the groundnut oil for the dressing. Remove with a slotted spoon and add to the salad. Add the rest of the ingredients for the dressing to the pan and stir well. Pour over the salad, add the coriander leaves and toss well to serve.

Alison Fiander

Spinach with Nutmeg

450 g (1 lb) young spinach leaves
7.5 ml (½ tbsp) hazelnut oil
7.5 ml (½ tbsp) olive oil
15 g (½ oz) shallot, finely chopped
2 cloves garlic, crushed
freshly grated nutmeg
coarse sea salt
freshly ground pepper

1 Roughly tear the spinach leaves. Heat the hazelnut and olive oils in a pan, add the shallot and garlic and sweat for about 2 minutes.

2 Add the torn spinach leaves to the pan, with just the water clinging to their leaves after washing. Sauté briefly for about 2 minutes, then season liberally with nutmeg, salt and pepper. Serve immediately.

Sue Lawrence

Spinach Purée

450 g (1 lb) young spinach leaves
1 small clove garlic
60 ml (2 fl oz) double cream
knob of butter
freshly grated nutmeg
salt and freshly ground black pepper

1 Remove the stalks and tough central veins from the spinach, then wash thoroughly. Cook the spinach in a covered pan with just the water clinging to the leaves after washing, and the garlic until just wilted. Drain in a sieve or colander, pressing out excess water.

2 Transfer to a food processor or blender and chop finely. Add the cream, butter, and nutmeg. Season with salt and pepper to taste. Serve piping hot.

Marion MacFarlane

Savoury Spinach with Lamb's Kidneys

225 g (8 oz) spinach leaves
salt and freshly ground black pepper
15 g (½ oz) butter
5 shallots, finely chopped
1 plump clove garlic, crushed
5 ml (1 tsp) dried marjoram
2 lamb's kidneys, cored and finely chopped
small bunch of chives, chopped

1 Preheat a heavy-based frying pan, add the spinach with just the water clinging to the leaves after washing and a little salt. Cook, stirring, for 1-2 minutes, then drain thoroughly in a sieve, pressing out excess moisture. Set aside.

2 Melt the butter in the frying pan, add the shallots and garlic and sauté until softened, but not brown. Add the marjoram and chopped kidneys and cook for 4-5 minutes, until the kidney is cooked.

3 Add the chives, spinach and pepper to taste. Stir well, heat through and check the seasoning. Serve at once.

Wendy Burnley

Spinach and Cucumber Ribbons

1 cucumber
450 g (1 lb) large spinach leaves

1 Using a swivel vegetable peeler, pare ribbons from the length of the cucumber, rotating the cucumber as you do so. Roll the cucumber ribbons into nest shapes.

2 Wash the spinach and drain thoroughly. Stack the leaves in piles, then roll them up and slice into fine ribbons, using a sharp knife. Form into nest shapes.

3 Bring the water to the boil in the base of a steamer. Put the cucumber and spinach nests in the steamer and steam for 4-5 minutes until the spinach has just wilted. Serve at once.

Mandy Ford

Glazed Green Beans

225 g (8 oz) fine green beans, trimmed
salt and freshly ground black pepper
15 g (½ oz) butter
30 ml (2 tbsp) water

1 Add the beans to a large pan of boiling salted water and cook for 2-3 minutes. Drain and refresh under cold running water. Place in a bowl of cold water and set aside.

2 When ready to serve, drain the beans. Melt the butter with the 30 ml (2 tbsp) of water, a pinch of salt and a few turns of pepper. Add the beans, bring to the boil, cover and cook for 1 minute.

3 Remove the lid and cook for a further 1 minute until the beans are glazed. Taste and adjust the seasoning. Serve at once.

Chumki Banerjee

Stir-fried Broccoli with Ginger

450 g (1 lb) broccoli
salt
30 ml (2 tbsp) corn oil
1 clove garlic, thinly sliced
2.5 cm (1 inch) piece fresh root ginger, finely shredded
2.5 ml (½ tsp) sesame oil

1 Separate the broccoli spears into florets and cut the base of the stems diagonally to neaten. Blanch in a saucepan of boiling salted water for 30 seconds. Drain and refresh in cold water; drain thoroughly.

2 Heat the oil in a wok or frying pan, add the garlic and ginger and stir-fry for 30 seconds. Add the broccoli and stir-fry for 2 minutes.

3 Sprinkle over the sesame oil and stir-fry for 30 seconds only. Serve immediately.

Betsy Anderson

Broccoli with Crisp Pancetta

450 g (1 lb) broccoli, cut into florets
6-8 slices of pancetta, cut into 1 cm (½ inch) squares
30 ml (2 tbsp) olive oil
50 g (2 oz) pine nuts

1 Par-cook the broccoli in a steamer over boiling water for about 3-4 minutes until almost cooked but still quite crunchy; take care to avoid overcooking.

2 In the meantime, dry-fry the pancetta in a heavy-based frying pan until crisp; remove and set aside. Add the olive oil to the frying pan and fry the pine nuts until golden brown; remove with a slotted spoon.

3 Drain the broccoli, add to the frying pan and stir-fry for 2-3 minutes. Add the pine nuts and toss to mix. Transfer to a warmed serving dish and top with the crispy pancetta.

Judith Elliot

Broccoli Timbales

450 g (1 lb) broccoli, cut into florets (including stalks)
90 ml (3 fl oz) double cream
1 egg (size 2)
2.5 ml (½ tsp) freshly grated nutmeg
salt and freshly ground black pepper

1 Place the broccoli in a steamer over boiling water, cover and steam for about 5 minutes until *just* tender and still bright green. Refresh in cold water; drain thoroughly.

2 Put the broccoli in a food processor or blender with the cream, egg, nutmeg, and salt and pepper to taste. Process until smooth.

3 Divide the mixture evenly between four greased individual 150 ml (¼ pint) metal pudding basins or dariole moulds. Cook in a preheated oven at 180°C (350°F) mark 4 for 20 minutes.

4 Turn out onto warmed plates and serve at once.

Charlotte Bircher

Leeks with Warm Vinaigrette

4 medium leeks

Vinaigrette:
5 ml (1 tsp) Dijon mustard
15 ml (1 tbsp) blueberry vinegar
coarse sea salt
freshly ground pepper
45-75 ml (3-5 tbsp) olive oil

1 Cut the leeks diagonally into slices and steam over boiling water for 2 minutes, until cooked but still crunchy. Drain.

2 For the vinaigrette, mix together the mustard, vinegar and seasoning to taste. Whisk in enough olive oil to give a thick emulsion.

3 Toss the leeks in the vinaigrette and serve immediately.

Sue Lawrence

Buttered Leeks with Tarragon

450 g (1 lb) young leeks
50-75 g (2-3 oz) butter
1 large bunch of tarragon
salt and freshly ground black pepper

1 Trim the leeks and cut into 7.5 cm (3 inch) lengths. Cut each piece lengthways into 4 slices and wash thoroughly. Drain and pat dry with kitchen paper. Tie half of the tarragon into a bunch with cotton string.

2 Melt the butter in a saucepan. Add the leeks and tarragon bunch to the pan and stir well. Cover and cook over a low heat, shaking the pan occasionally, for 10 minutes or until the leeks are tender but still retain their colour. Meanwhile, strip the remaining tarragon leaves from their stalks and chop finely.

3 Just before serving, discard the bunch of tarragon. Add the chopped tarragon to the leeks, stir and season with salt and pepper to taste. Serve immediately.

Patti Hall

Three-colour Vegetable Stir-fry

1 red pepper, halved, cored and seeded
1 green pepper, halved, cored and seeded
1 carrot, peeled
15 ml (1 tbsp) sesame oil
salt and freshly ground black pepper

1 Thinly slice each vegetable into strips.

2 Heat the oil in a wok or frying pan and add the vegetables, with salt and pepper to taste. Fry over a high heat, stirring constantly for about 3-4 minutes until the vegetables are tender, but not soft. Serve immediately.

Noriko Anzai-Jackson

Medley of Green Vegetables with a Dill Dressing

125 g (4 oz) fine green beans
125 g (4 oz) sugar snap peas or mangetouts
125 g (4 oz) courgettes
125 g (4 oz) broccoli florets
salt
15 g (½ oz) slightly salted butter
10 ml (2 tsp) lemon juice
freshly ground mixed peppercorns
30 ml (2 tbsp) chopped fresh dill

1 Trim the beans and sugar snap peas. Trim the courgettes and thinly slice lengthwise, using a swivel vegetable peeler, to form fine ribbons. Divide the broccoli into small even-sized florets.

2 Cook the broccoli in a large pan of boiling salted water for 1 minute. Add the beans and sugar snap peas and cook for 2 minutes. Add the courgette ribbons and, as soon as the water returns to the boil, remove the pan from the heat. Drain the vegetables in a colander and refresh with cold water.

3 Melt the butter in a large frying pan over a moderate heat until sizzling. Add the vegetables and cook, shaking the pan constantly, for 1 minute. Add the lemon juice and freshly ground peppercorns to taste. Stir in the dill and serve at once.

Elizabeth Truscott

Mediterranean Vegetables

1 aubergine
sea salt and freshly ground black pepper
3 courgettes
1 onion
1 green pepper, cored and deseeded
1 red pepper, cored and deseeded
1 yellow pepper, cored and deseeded
4 plum tomatoes
olive oil, for frying
1 clove garlic, chopped

1 Cut the aubergine into 5 mm (¼ inch) slices and layer in a colander, sprinkling with salt. Place a small plate on top and weight down. Leave to drain.

2 Slice the remaining vegetables to about the same thickness as the aubergine. Heat a little olive oil in a heavy-based frying pan and sauté the onion and garlic until almost soft; remove from the pan and set aside.

3 Rinse the aubergine slices under cold running water and pat dry. Heat a little more olive oil in the pan, add the aubergines and fry on both sides until golden brown.

4 Blanch the courgettes and peppers in boiling water, or microwave on high for 1-2 minutes until softened.

5 Position four 7.5 cm (3 inch) metal ring moulds on a baking tray. Layer the vegetables in the moulds, starting with the aubergine slices and finishing with the tomato slices. Drizzle a generous 5 ml (1 tsp) olive oil on top of each one. Bake in a preheated oven at 190°C (375°F) mark 5 for about 25 minutes.

6 Carefully lift onto warmed serving plates, using a fish slice, and remove the metal rings. Serve at once.

Joanna Crossley

Gâteaux of Vegetables

2 carrots, peeled and cut into pieces
salt and freshly ground black pepper
2.5 ml (½ tsp) sugar
25 g (1 oz) unsalted butter, plus a knob
200 g (7 oz) spinach, thoroughly washed and drained
1 clove garlic, crushed
20 ml (4 tsp) olive oil
2 tomatoes, peeled, seeded and chopped
2 courgettes, thinly sliced
1 large parsnip, peeled and sliced
2 basil leaves, shredded

1 Cook the carrots in a little salted water, with the sugar added, until tender. Drain and chop finely or purée in a food processor with a knob of butter.

2 Melt 15 g (½ oz) butter in a pan. Remove any coarse stalks from the spinach, then add to the pan with the garlic. Cook over a fairly high heat for a few minutes until the spinach is tender and excess moisture has evaporated. Drain on absorbent kitchen paper.

3 Heat half the olive oil in a pan, add the chopped tomatoes and cook for a few minutes until soft. Fry the courgettes in the remaining olive oil for about 2 minutes until softened.

4 Parboil the parsnips in salted water for 2-3 minutes. Drain and refresh in cold water. Dry on absorbent kitchen paper, then grate. Mix with the remaining 15 g (½ oz) butter and cook gently until lightly coloured.

5 Line 4 loose-based 10 cm (4 inch) moulds with foil and pierce the foil in several places. Adjust the seasoning of the vegetables to taste.

6 To assemble each gâteau, spoon a portion of spinach into the base of each mould and press down well. Add a layer of carrot and press down. Place the courgette slices around the edge, slightly overlapping them to form a well. Add the chopped basil to the tomato and spoon into the well. Fill the moulds to the top with parsnip, pressing down well.

7 Reheat the gâteaux in a steamer, then turn out before serving.

Gregory Lewis

Baby Vegetables en Papillote

For these you will need 4 sheets of greaseproof paper and 8 wooden clothes pegs.

12 baby carrots
8 cauliflower florets
12 baby corn cobs
12 mangetouts
8 broccoli florets
salt and freshly ground black pepper
5 bouquet garnis, tied with string

Herb Butter:
125 g (4 oz) butter, softened
10-15 ml (2-3 tsp) herbs
5-10 ml (1-2 tsp) lemon juice

1 First make the herb butter. Put the butter, herbs and lemon juice in a bowl and mix well. Season with salt and pepper to taste. Set aside.

2 Bring a large pan of water to the boil. Add the carrots and cauliflower and parboil for about 3 minutes, then remove with a slotted spoon.

3 Place a bamboo steamer over the pan of boiling water and place all of the vegetables in the steamer, together with one of the herb bouquets. Cover and steam the vegetables for 6 minutes. Remove the steamer from the heat.

4 Distribute the vegetables evenly between 4 buttered sheets of greaseproof paper, placing them in the centre of the paper. Sprinkle with a little salt and top each portion with a spoonful of the herb butter. Bring the two ends of the paper together, then roll down leaving enough space for air to circulate. Twist the two open ends and secure with wooden clothes pegs.

5 Place in a microwave oven and cook on high for 30 seconds. Serve the vegetables in their paper packets. Garnish each serving with a bouquet of herbs.

Betsy Anderson

Note: Reheating the vegetables by microwave ensures that they retain their bright colours. Alternatively you could return to the steamer to heat through.

Cheese and Sesame Tuile filled with Baby Vegetables

These very delicate savoury biscuits are rolled into cones and filled with steamed tiny vegetables.

Tuiles:

30 ml (2 tbsp) grated red Leicester cheese
15 ml (1 tbsp) softened butter
35 ml (2½ tbsp) plain flour
2.5 ml (½ tsp) paprika
1.25 ml (¼ tsp) cayenne pepper
large pinch of salt
30 ml (2 tbsp) milk (approximately), to mix
35 ml (2½ tbsp) sesame seeds

Vegetable Filling:

8-12 baby carrots
4-8 baby leeks
4-8 baby parsnips
12 green beans
tiny herb sprigs (eg parsley, dill)

1 To make the tuiles, beat the cheese and butter together in a bowl until evenly mixed. Add the flour, paprika, cayenne and salt, then mix in enough milk to make a soft dough. Stir in the sesame seeds.

2 Spread 4 thin rounds of the mixture, about 12 cm (5 inches) in diameter, on a baking sheet lined with non-stick baking parchment. Bake in a preheated oven at 200°C (400°F) mark 6 for 10-12 minutes until the edges are lightly browned.

3 Leave to cool for a minute or two on the baking sheet then, while still warm and pliable, shape around cream horn cones and leave to cool.

4 Steam the baby vegetables until just tender. Fill the tuiles with the hot vegetables, adding a few herb sprigs. Serve at once.

Marian Freeman

Aubergine Crisps

oil for deep-frying
1 aubergine
salt and freshly ground black pepper

1 Heat the oil in a deep-fat fryer to 160°C (325°F).

2 Meanwhile, cut the aubergine into very fine slices and pat dry on kitchen paper.

3 Deep-fry the aubergine slices in the hot oil in small batches until crisp and golden; remove and drain on kitchen paper. Keep hot while frying the remainder. Season with salt and pepper to taste. Serve at once.

Liz Franklin

Raspberried Red Cabbage

400 g (14 oz) red cabbage, cored
100 ml (3½ fl oz) water
15 ml (1 tbsp) lemon juice
50 ml (2 fl oz) raspberry vinegar
25 g (1 oz) sugar
pinch of salt
25 g (1 oz) butter

1 Place the red cabbage in a saucepan with the water, lemon juice, raspberry vinegar, sugar and salt. Bring to the boil and simmer for about 15 minutes until just tender.

2 Remove the lid and allow to bubble until any excess liquid has evaporated.

3 Add the butter to the cabbage and toss before serving.

Tommy Sheppard

Braised Cabbage Rolls

40 ml (2½ tbsp) vegetable oil
1 garlic clove, finely chopped
1 shallot, finely chopped
100 g (3½ oz) smoked bacon, derinded and diced
1 baby white cabbage, cored and finely shredded
300 ml (½ pint) chicken stock
4 large Savoy cabbage leaves

1 Heat the oil in a large pan, add the garlic, shallot and bacon and fry until the bacon is golden. Add the cabbage and sweat until most of the liquid has evaporated. Add the stock and bring to the boil. Simmer over a low heat for 25-30 minutes until tender.

2 Meanwhile, blanch the 4 large Savoy cabbage leaves in boiling salted water until pliable. Drain thoroughly and cut out any tough central veins; lay the leaves flat on a clean surface.

3 Drain off any excess liquid from the braised cabbage, then place a generous spoonful at one end of each Savoy leaf. Roll up, folding in the edges to seal. Place, seam-side down, in a warmed ovenproof dish. Warm through in the oven just prior to serving.

James Hurd

Stuffed Savoy Cabbage

1 large Savoy cabbage
25 g (1 oz) butter
50 g (2 oz) chopped walnuts
freshly grated nutmeg
salt and freshly ground black pepper

1 Discard any damaged or discoloured leaves from the cabbage, then select the 4 best, largest, outer leaves. Blanch these in a large pan of boiling salted water for 2 minutes until pliable. Lift out the leaves, using a slotted spoon and reserve the liquid. Immediately rinse the blanched leaves under cold water to prevent further cooking. Drain and pat dry with kitchen paper.

2 Finely shred the white heart of the cabbage and blanch in the reserved liquid for about 1 minute. Drain, reserving the liquid, and mix the cabbage with the butter, walnuts and nutmeg. Season with salt and pepper to taste.

3 Lay the blanched whole green leaves out on a clean surface and place a large spoonful of the shredded cabbage mixture in the centre of each one. Wrap the leaves around the filling to form parcels.

4 Bring the reserved cooking water to the boil in the base of a steamer. Place the cabbage parcels in the steamer and steam for 5-10 minutes. Serve at once.

Tommy Sheppard

Salud's Cabbage

125 g (4 oz) rindless streaky bacon, finely diced
15 ml (1 tbsp) oil
2 cloves garlic, finely sliced
¼ firm green or white cabbage, cored and very finely shredded
15 ml (1 tbsp) light soy sauce

1 Dry-fry the bacon in a deep frying pan or wok until crispy, then remove with a slotted spoon and drain on kitchen paper.

2 Add the oil to the pan and heat, then add the garlic and cook until golden brown. Add the cabbage to the pan and stir to coat with the oil. Cook, stirring continuously, until the cabbage just begins to wilt.

3 Add the soy sauce and cook for 1-2 minutes; do not allow the cabbage to become too soft.

4 To serve, scatter the bacon pieces over the cabbage.

Mandy Ford

Braised Red Cabbage

10 ml (2 tsp) olive oil
15 g (½ oz) butter
50 g (2 oz) unsmoked bacon, derinded and chopped
1 onion, chopped
2 cloves garlic, crushed
450 g (1 lb) red cabbage, sliced
1 cooking apple
300 ml (½ pint) mixed red wine and stock
pinch of cloves
freshly grated nutmeg
1.25 ml (¼ tsp) salt
freshly ground pepper

1 Heat the oil and butter in a large pan and sauté the bacon, onion and garlic until softened. Add the red cabbage and cook, stirring, for 10 minutes.

2 Peel, core and chop the apple. Add to the cabbage with the remaining ingredients and bring to the boil.

3 Transfer to an ovenproof dish, cover and cook in a preheated oven at 160°C (325°F) mark 3 for 2-3 hours until tender.

Sue Lawrence

Colcannon

6 medium potatoes
1 green cabbage, cored and chopped
185 ml (6 fl oz) double cream
75 g (3 oz) butter
2 cloves garlic, crushed
salt and freshly ground black pepper

1 Peel and quarter the potatoes, then cook in boiling salted water until tender. Drain well and mash with the cream, using a potato ricer or masher.

2 Meanwhile, steam the cabbage for 5 minutes. Heat the butter in a large heavy-based saucepan and sauté the garlic for about 2 minutes until softened. Add the cabbage and cook for about 5 minutes until soft.

3 Purée the cabbage in a food processor, then add to the creamed potato and mash well. Season with salt and pepper to taste. Serve hot.

Holly Schade

Braised Celery Hearts

2 heads of celery
5 ml (1 tsp) chopped thyme
salt and freshly ground black pepper

1 Discard the outer celery stalks, then cut off the top half of the remaining stalks. Halve each celery heart, then place in a single layer in a saucepan.

2 Pour on sufficient cold water to cover. Add the thyme and salt and pepper. Cook gently for about 15 minutes; the celery should still be slightly crunchy. Drain and serve.

Elaine Bates

Celeriac with Coriander

1 celeriac root, about 675 g (1½ lb)
juice of 1 lemon
salt and freshly ground black pepper
25-50 g (1-2 oz) butter
30 ml (2 tbsp) soured cream
10 ml (2 tsp) coarse-grain mustard
1 spring onion, finely chopped
30-45 ml (2-3 tbsp) chopped coriander leaves

1 Peel the celeriac and cut into chunks. Quickly immerse in a bowl of cold water with the lemon juice added to prevent discolouration.

2 Cook the celeriac in boiling salted water for 10-15 minutes until tender; drain well.

3 Roughly mash the celeriac with the butter. Add all the rest of the ingredients and season liberally with salt and pepper. Stir well and serve piping hot.

Clare Askaroff

Carrots with Cumin

700 g (1½ lb) carrots
50 g (2 oz) butter
10 ml (2 tsp) cumin seeds, lightly crushed
juice of 1 lemon
salt and freshly ground black pepper

1 Peel and grate the carrots.

2 Melt the butter in a saucepan, add the cumin and fry gently for 2 minutes.

3 Add the carrots and lemon juice to the pan. Cover and simmer gently for 10-15 minutes. Season with salt and pepper to taste before serving.

Judith Elliott

Carrots with Fresh Ginger

350 g (12 oz) carrots, cut into matchsticks
salt and freshly ground black pepper
15 g (½ oz) butter
15 g (½ oz) fresh root ginger, peeled and finely chopped
15 ml (1 tbsp) sugar

1 Cook the carrots in boiling salted water for 5-10 minutes until just tender. Drain, then plunge into a bowl of cold water to refresh.

2 Drain the carrots thoroughly and return to the pan with the butter, ginger and sugar. Stir over a low heat until the carrots are well coated with the mixture. Cover and simmer for 2 minutes, then check the seasoning and serve.

Judi Geisler

Glazed Baby Carrots

25 g (1 oz) unsalted butter
12 baby carrots, trimmed with a little green left on if possible
25 g (1 oz) caster sugar
salt and freshly ground black pepper

1 Melt the butter in a pan, and add the carrots and sugar. Cook for 2-3 minutes.

2 Half-cover with water, put a lid on the pan and simmer for about 5 minutes until cooked, but still firm. Season lightly and keep warm until ready to serve.

Louise Halfhide

Lemon-glazed Carrot Ribbons

4 carrots, peeled
25 g (1 oz) unsalted butter
15 ml (1 tbsp) caster sugar
grated zest of ½ lemon
salt and freshly ground black pepper
1 small lemon balm sprig, finely chopped

1 Using a swivel potato peeler, pare the carrots into long thin ribbons. Blanch in a large pan of boiling water for 15 seconds; drain thoroughly.

2 Heat the butter and sugar in a saucepan until very hot. Add the carrots and stir-fry for 2 minutes. Add the lemon zest and season with salt and pepper to taste.

3 Add the chopped lemon balm and toss to mix. Serve immediately.

Andrew Whiteley

Tiered Shredded Vegetable Crowns

180 g (6 oz) courgettes
180 g (6 oz) carrot
180 g (6 oz) parsnip
180 g (6 oz) broccoli
salt and freshly ground black pepper
20 ml (4 tsp) butter
5-10 ml (1-2 tsp) chopped parsley

To Garnish:
herb sprigs

1 Finely shred or grate the courgettes, carrot and parsnip (keeping them separate). Divide the broccoli into small florets. Season each of the vegetables with salt and pepper.

2 Place 5 ml (1 tsp) butter in the bottom of each of 4 ramekins and sprinkle with the chopped parsley. Arrange the broccoli florets on top of and around the butter. Cover with the courgettes, followed by the carrot and finally the parsnip.

3 Cover each ramekin with foil, place in a steamer over boiling water and steam for approximately 5 minutes until just tender. (Alternatively cover the ramekins with cling film and microwave on high for about 1½ minutes.)

4 To serve, uncover the ramekins and invert onto warmed serving plates. Turn the vegetable crowns the right way up and garnish with herbs. Serve at once.

Glen Tabor

Note: The vegetable crowns will hold their shape once turned out.

Caramelised Shallots

16 shallots or button onions, peeled
150 ml (¼ pint) lamb stock
25 g (1 oz) unsalted butter
25 g (1 oz) caster sugar
salt and freshly ground black pepper

1 Put the shallots into a heavy-based pan and cover with the stock. Bring to the boil, lower the heat and simmer for 10 minutes; drain well.

2 Melt the butter in the clean, dry pan, then add the shallots, sugar and seasoning. Cover and cook, stirring occasionally, for about 10 minutes until tender and glazed. Keep warm.

Louise Halfhide

Beetroot and Preserved Lime Salad

4 smallish beetroot, freshly boiled and peeled
2 preserved lime quarters (see below), plus a little of the oil
2 spring onions, trimmed and chopped
5 ml (1 tsp) ground cumin
30 ml (2 tbsp) freshly chopped parsley
scant 15 ml (1 tbsp) olive oil
5 ml (1 tsp) caster sugar
10 ml (1 tsp) raspberry vinegar
freshly ground black pepper

1 Cut the beetroot into cubes and finely slice the preserved lime quarters.

2 Mix all the other ingredients together in a bowl. Add the beetroot and lime slices, toss to mix, cover and set aside to allow the flavours to develop for 1 hour before serving.

Barbara Vazana

Preserved Limes: To prepare these, scrub 500 g (1¼ lb) limes, then cut into quarters and put into a colander. Sprinkle generously with sea salt, and leave for at least 24 hours to soften. Pack the limes into a sterilised pickling jar. Add 4 dried red chillies, then add sufficient corn oil to cover. Seal tightly and set aside in a cool place for about 3 weeks.

Mashed Turnips with Crispy Shallots

700 g (1½ lb) turnips, peeled and diced
50 g (2 oz) butter, plus 15 ml (1 tbsp)
6 large shallots, thinly sliced
150 ml (¼ pint) double cream
pinch of freshly grated nutmeg
salt and freshly ground black pepper
15 ml (1 tbsp) finely chopped parsley

1 Cook the turnips in a pan of simmering water for about 10 minutes until tender. Drain and purée in a food processor.

2 Melt 50 g (2 oz) butter in a heavy-based pan and gently sauté the shallots until golden brown and crisp; this may take at least 15 minutes. Drain on kitchen paper and keep warm.

3 Put the cream and 15 ml (1 tbsp) butter in a saucepan and bring to the boil. Add the turnips and stir briskly. Season generously with the nutmeg, salt and pepper, then stir in the parsley. Serve at once, topped with the crispy shallots.

Sophie Buchmann

Turnip, Potato and Walnut Purée

350 g (12 oz) turnip, peeled and chopped
125 g (4 oz) potato, peeled and chopped
75 g (3 oz) butter
25 g (1 oz) walnuts, chopped
freshly grated nutmeg
salt and freshly ground black pepper

1 Cook the turnip and potato in boiling salted water until tender. Drain and purée in a food processor or blender with the butter.

2 Return to the pan and add the walnuts and nutmeg, salt and pepper to taste. Reheat gently to serve if necessary.

Marion MacFarlane

Swede Purée

100 g (3½ oz) butter
200 g (7 oz) onions, coarsely chopped
650 g (1½ lb) swede, peeled and chopped
250 ml (8 fl oz) chicken stock
salt and freshly ground black pepper

1 Melt the butter in a heavy-based saucepan, add the onions and cook gently until soft. Add the swede and the stock and bring to the boil. Turn the heat down to very low and cover the pan with a sheet of greaseproof paper and a tight-fitting lid. Cook for 30 minutes.

2 Transfer the contents of the pan to a blender or food processor and work until smooth. Season with salt and pepper to taste. Reheat gently to serve if necessary.

Ashley Wilson

Spiced Butternut Squash Purée

1 small butternut squash
salt and freshly ground black pepper
freshly grated nutmeg
15-30 ml (1-2 tbsp) mascarpone cheese

1 Peel and dice the squash. Place in an ovenproof dish, cover and bake in a preheated oven at 180°C (350°F) mark 4 for about 45 minutes, until soft.

2 Mash the squash until smooth, adding salt, pepper and nutmeg to taste. Beat in the mascarpone cheese to give a creamy texture. Serve piping hot.

Gillian Humphrey

Butternut Squash Balls

45 ml (3 tbsp) olive oil
15 ml (1 tbsp) dried sage
1 large clove garlic, crushed
1 large butternut squash

1 Put the olive oil in a small bowl, add the sage and garlic and set aside to infuse.

2 Cut the squash in half lengthwise. Scoop out and discard the seeds. Using a melon baller, scoop out the flesh into balls, shaping as many as possible.

3 Put the squash balls in an ovenproof dish, add the oil mixture and turn to coat. Bake in a preheated oven at 180°C (350°F) mark 4 for 35 minutes or until tender.

Charlotte Bircher

Root Vegetable Purée

225 g (8 oz) peeled parsnips
225 g (8 oz) peeled celeriac
225 g (8 oz) peeled carrots
large knob of butter
salt and freshly ground black pepper

1 Cook the vegetables in boiling salted water until tender. Drain, then work to a purée, using a food mill or masher.

2 Return to a low heat and heat through. Add the butter and season well to serve.

James Hurd

Clapshot with Fresh Herbs

450 g (1 lb) potatoes
350 g (12 oz) swede
salt
25 g (1 oz) butter
25 ml (1 fl oz) virgin olive oil
15 ml (1 tbsp) finely chopped chives
15 ml (1 tbsp) finely chopped parsley
10 ml (2 tsp) finely chopped celery or lovage leaves
freshly grated nutmeg, to taste

1 Cut the potatoes and swede into 2.5 cm (1 inch) cubes. Place in a saucepan and add water to cover. Bring to the boil and cook until soft.

2 Drain the vegetables thoroughly and mash until smooth. Add the butter, olive oil, herbs and celery leaves. Sprinkle with grated nutmeg to serve.

Marion MacFarlane

Sweet Potato Latkes

1 large sweet potato, about 225 g (8 oz)
2 large potatoes, each about 225 g (8 oz)
2 eggs, beaten
50 g (2 oz) plain flour, sifted
15 ml (1 tbsp) chopped onion
salt and freshly ground black pepper
50 ml (2 fl oz) oil

1 Peel all of the potatoes and immerse them in a bowl of cold water. Leave to soak for 1 hour. Drain and coarsely grate the potatoes. Add the eggs, flour and chopped onion. Mix thoroughly, seasoning with salt and pepper.

2 Heat the oil in a frying pan until it is quite hot. Place tablespoonfuls of the mixture in the pan, spacing them apart. Cook on one side for about 5 minutes until crisp and brown underneath, then turn and cook the other side for approximately 5 minutes until cooked through and brown and crispy on both sides. Serve piping hot.

Jill O'Brien

Horseradish Bubble and Squeak

125 g (4 oz) Brussels sprouts
125 g (4 oz) cabbage
65 g (2½ oz) unsalted butter
1 large onion, thinly sliced
1 clove garlic, crushed
450 g (1 lb) cooked potato
salt and freshly ground black pepper
7.5 ml (1½ tsp) grated fresh horseradish or 15 ml (1 tbsp) horseradish cream

1 Cook the Brussels sprouts and cabbage in boiling salted water until tender; drain well.

2 Meanwhile, melt 15 g (½ oz) butter in a pan, add the onion and garlic, and cook gently for 4-5 minutes until softened.

3 Mash the potato, cabbage and sprouts together in a bowl, then add the onion and mix to a firm texture. Season with salt and pepper and add the horseradish.

4 Divide the mixture between four 10 cm (4 inch) pastry cutters, pressing well down. Melt the remaining butter in a large frying pan. Carefully transfer the cutters to the frying pan and cook for 4-5 minutes.

5 Remove the cutters and carefully transfer the bubble and squeak cakes to a preheated grill. Cook until golden brown on top. Serve piping hot.

Amanda Farnese

Celeriac Rösti

1 celeriac
salt and freshly ground black pepper
25 g (1 oz) butter

1 Peel and quarter the celeriac, then grate coarsely into a bowl. Season with salt and pepper. Divide the mixture into 4 portions. Press each portion into a muffin ring or 7.5 cm (3 inch) plain metal cutter, resting on a fish slice or spatula.

2 Melt the butter in a frying pan and carefully slide the rings into the pan. Press the celeriac well down in the rings and fry for 3-4 minutes until crisp and golden brown underneath.

3 Turn the rösti, carefully remove the metal rings and cook the other side for 3-4 minutes until golden brown and cooked through. Drain on kitchen paper.

Derek Johns

Parmesan Parsnips

450 g (1 lb) parsnips, peeled and quartered
salt
60 ml (4 tbsp) olive oil
freshly grated nutmeg
125 g (4 oz) Parmesan cheese, freshly grated

1 Heat the oil in a roasting tin in a preheated oven at 180°C (350°F) mark 4. Meanwhile, parboil the parsnips in salted water for about 5 minutes. Drain and transfer to the roasting tin. Sprinkle with nutmeg and bake for 20 minutes.

2 Sprinkle with the Parmesan and bake for a further 20 minutes or until crisp and brown. Serve immediately.

Keely Smith

Parsnip Crisps

1 large parsnip (or 2 small ones)
oil for shallow-frying

1 Peel the parsnip(s) and cut in half across the middle. Pare into very thin slices, using a swivel vegetable peeler, avoiding the 'woody' centre.

2 Heat about a 2.5 cm (1 inch) depth of oil in a heavy-based deep frying pan and fry the parsnip slices in batches until crisp and golden brown. Drain on kitchen paper and keep warm until ready to serve. (They will stay crisp for up to 1 hour.)

Louise Halfhide

Parsnip Purée with Parmesan

450 g (1 lb) parsnips, roughly chopped
salt and freshly ground black pepper
90 ml (3 fl oz) single cream
75 g (3 oz) Parmesan cheese, freshly grated
50 g (2 oz) butter

1 Cook the parsnips in boiling salted water for about 10 minutes until soft.

2 Drain the parsnips and place in a food processor. Add the cream, Parmesan, butter and seasoning. Process until smooth.

3 Transfer to a warmed ovenproof serving dish. Keep warm in the oven until ready to serve if necessary.

Charlotte Bircher

Puréed Parsnip Timbales

4 small parsnips, peeled, cored and diced
60 ml (4 tbsp) double cream
salt and freshly ground white pepper
8 large outer Savoy cabbage leaves (approximately)

1 Cook the parsnips in boiling salted water until soft, then drain. Purée the parsnips, using a hand-held blender or masher. Add the cream and seasoning; mix thoroughly.

2 Blanch the cabbage leaves in a large pan of boiling water for 10 seconds to set the colour. Drain thoroughly.

3 Line 4 buttered dariole moulds with the cabbage leaves and fill with the puréed parsnip mixture. Cover tightly with foil and place in a steamer over boiling water. Cook for 5 minutes, then turn the timbales out of the dariole moulds to serve.

Andrew Whiteley

Roast Parsnip 'Cups' filled with Parsnip Purée

7 medium parsnips
30-45 ml (2-3 tbsp) groundnut oil
salt and freshly ground black pepper
15 ml (1 tbsp) double cream
5 ml (1 tsp) butter
freshly grated nutmeg

1 Cut 2 rounds from each of 6 parsnips, about 3 cm (1¼ inches) in diameter and 1 cm (½ inch) deep, reserving the remaining pieces. Peel the parsnip rounds then, using the end of a potato peeler, hollow out the centres (without cutting right through) to form little cups.

2 Heat the oil in a roasting tin. Add the parsnips and baste with the oil, then put into a preheated oven at 180°C (350°F) mark 4. Cook for about 40 minutes, until tender, turning once halfway through cooking.

3 Meanwhile, peel the remaining parsnip and reserved pieces. Remove the hard core and cut into even-sized chunks. Cook in boiling salted water until soft. Drain thoroughly and mash with the cream, butter, and pepper and nutmeg to taste. Check the seasoning. Pass through a sieve, pressing the purée through with the back of a wooden spoon; set aside.

4 Drain the roast parsnip cups of any oil, then place a spoonful of parsnip purée in each one. Return to the oven for about 5 minutes, to warm through.

Wendy Burnley

Note: If prepared in advance and cooled, you will need to warm these through in the oven for 8-10 minutes.

Parsnip and Potato Cakes

225 g (8 oz) parsnips
225 g (8 oz) floury potatoes (eg King Edward)
1 small clove garlic, crushed
15 g (½ oz) butter, plus extra if necessary
5 ml (1 tsp) dry mustard
salt and freshly ground black pepper
60 ml (4 tbsp) seasoned plain flour
2 eggs, beaten
3 slices wholemeal bread
30 ml (2 tbsp) sesame seeds
sunflower oil, for deep-frying (see note)

1 Peel the parsnips and potatoes, then cut into chunks. Cook in boiling salted water until soft.

2 Meanwhile cook the crushed garlic gently in the butter.

3 Drain the parsnips and potatoes. Mash until smooth, then beat in the garlic butter and mustard. Add a little more butter if necessary. Season well. Let cool, then chill the mixture for about 20 minutes.

4 Have ready 3 bowls: one containing the seasoned flour; one containing the beaten eggs. Process the bread to make breadcrumbs and mix with the sesame seeds in the third bowl.

5 Shape the parsnip and potato mixture into 10 small balls. Roll each ball first in the flour, then in the beaten egg, then finally in breadcrumbs. Place on a plate and chill until needed.

6 Just before serving, heat the oil for deep-frying in a suitable pan. Deep-fry the parsnip and potato balls in batches until golden brown. Drain on kitchen paper and serve piping hot.

Clare Askaroff

Potato and Courgette Soufflés

1 courgette
225 g (8 oz) cooked peeled potato
40 g (1½ oz) butter
150 ml (¼ pint) water
35 g (1¼ oz) plain flour
1 egg, beaten
salt and freshly ground black pepper
oil for deep-frying

1 Grate the courgette, then press between two sheets of kitchen paper to absorb as much moisture as possible.

2 Meanwhile, mash the cooked potato with a third of the butter. Heat the remaining butter in a saucepan with the water until the butter has melted and the liquid is almost boiling. Remove the pan from the heat, immediately add the flour and beat into the liquid. Gradually add the egg, beating to form a glossy, elastic paste. Stir in the courgette and mashed potato, and season with salt and pepper to taste.

3 Transfer the mixture to a piping bag fitted with a large plain nozzle. Pipe small balls of the mixture onto a sheet of greaseproof paper.

4 Heat the oil in a deep-fat fryer to 190°C (375°F). Cook the potato and courgette balls in batches of up to six. Gently slide into the hot oil and cook for 4-5 minutes until puffed up and golden. Drain on kitchen paper and keep hot while cooking the remainder. Serve immediately.

Claire Ketteman

Potato and Wild Mushroom Bake

60 g (2 oz) butter
750 g (1½-1¾ lb) old potatoes, peeled and thinly sliced
185 g (6 oz) mixed wild mushrooms, sliced (see note)
salt and freshly ground black pepper
freshly grated nutmeg
90 ml (3 fl oz) thick double cream

To Garnish:
herb sprigs

1 Line a loose-bottomed 20-23 cm (8-9 inch) cake tin with foil, then grease it with a little of the butter.

2 Layer the potato and mushroom slices in the tin, seasoning each layer with salt, pepper and nutmeg. Dot each layer with butter. Finish with a layer of potato slices.

3 Pour over the cream, cover with foil and bake in a preheated oven at 190°C (375°F) mark 5 for 1 hour. Remove the foil and bake for a further 30 minutes until the top is crisp and golden brown. Garnish with herbs to serve.

Glen Tabor

Note: If wild mushrooms are unavailable, cultivated varieties can be used. However, large flat mushrooms will discolour the potatoes.

Individual Potato and Mushroom Cakes

250 g (9 oz) potatoes, peeled
7 g (¼ oz) dried mushrooms
450 g (1 lb) cultivated mushrooms
30 ml (2 tbsp) butter
30 ml (2 tbsp) oil
185 ml (6 fl oz) double cream
1 clove garlic, chopped
salt and freshly ground black pepper
butter, for greasing

1 Cut the potatoes into 3 mm (⅛ inch) slices and immerse in a bowl of cold water. Soak the dried mushrooms in sufficient hot water to cover for 20 minutes. Drain well. Cut the cultivated mushrooms into 3 mm (⅛ inch) slices.

2 Heat the butter and oil in a pan and sauté the cultivated mushrooms to soften. Add the soaked mushrooms and sauté for 1 minute, then add the cream and garlic and reduce until most of the liquid has evaporated. Season with salt and pepper to taste.

3 Drain the potatoes and dry well. Melt a knob of butter in the base of each of 4 ramekins. Arrange half of the potatoes in the ramekins in overlapping spirals. Cover with a layer of mushrooms, then top with the remaining potatoes. Dot with butter and bake in a preheated oven at 200°C (400°F) mark 6 for 25-30 minutes. Unmould to serve.

Martha Spencer

French Potato Cake

30 ml (2 tbsp) butter or duck fat
600 g (1¼ lb) potatoes, peeled and thinly sliced
2.5 ml (½ tsp) salt
freshly ground pepper
15 g (½ oz) butter, plus extra for greasing
2 garlic cloves, finely chopped
30 ml (2 tbsp) finely chopped parsley

1 Heat the fat in a heavy-based frying pan and fry the potatoes, partially covered, until lightly browned, about 25 minutes. Season with salt and pepper.

2 Pack the potatoes into a buttered shallow tart tin or individual flan tins, pressing down firmly. Bake in a preheated oven at 200°C (400°F) mark 6 for about 20 minutes, or until brown and slightly puffy.

3 Drizzle butter around the edge of the tin, loosen the potato cake and carefully turn out. Cut into wedges and sprinkle with the garlic and parsley to serve.

Orlando Murrin

Sautéed Potatoes

8 small potatoes
50 g (2 oz) clarified butter
salt and freshly ground black pepper

1 Peel and finely slice the potatoes, immersing them in a bowl of cold water as you do so, to prevent discolouration. Rinse well and pat dry on a clean tea-towel.

2 Heat the clarified butter in a large heavy-based frying pan. Add the potatoes and cook for 20-30 minutes, shaking the pan from time to time to ensure they cook evenly. The cooked potatoes should be slightly crisp. Season with salt and pepper to taste during cooking.

3 Arrange a mound of sautéed potatoes on each warmed serving plate to serve.

Juliette Boisseau-Hardman

Note: Once cooked the potatoes can be kept warm in a preheated oven at 150°C (300°F) mark 2 until ready to serve.

Potatoes Dauphinoise

25 g (1 oz) butter
1 small onion, thinly sliced
1 clove garlic, crushed
450 g (1 lb) King Edward potatoes, peeled and thinly sliced
150 ml (¼ pint) double cream
a little milk
salt and freshly ground black pepper

1 Melt half of the butter in a saucepan, add the onion and garlic and cook until soft.

2 Grease a suitable dish with the remaining butter. Layer a third of the potatoes in the base of the dish. Cover with half of the onion and garlic, then pour on half of the cream and milk; season liberally. Repeat these layers and finish with a layer of potatoes.

3 Cover the dish with foil and bake in a preheated oven at 180°C (350°F) mark 4 for 45 minutes. Remove the foil and bake for a further 15 minutes until brown. Serve immediately.

Keely Smith

Potatoes Lyonnaise

900 g (2 lb) waxy potatoes
200 g (7 oz) Gruyère cheese, grated
1½ cloves garlic, finely chopped
salt and freshly ground black pepper
600 ml (1 pint) double cream

1 Peel and thinly slice the potatoes and pat dry with kitchen paper. Layer the potatoes in a large well-buttered gratin dish, sprinkling each layer with the cheese, garlic and seasoning.

2 Heat the cream until almost boiling, then pour over the potatoes. Bake in a preheated oven at 190°C (375°F) for about 1½ hours until the potatoes are tender. If the top browns too quickly during baking, cover with foil.

James Hurd

Stoved New Potatoes

16-20 new potatoes, depending on size
30 ml (2 tbsp) water
salt and freshly ground black pepper
40 g (1½ oz) unsalted butter, diced

1 Peel the potatoes and place in a single layer in a heavy-based pan (one which has a tight-fitting lid). Add the water and seasoning. Dot the butter onto the potatoes.

2 Cover the pan with a double layer of foil, then position the lid to ensure a very tight fit. Cook over a very low heat for 45 minutes to 1 hour, until tender, shaking the pan from time to time to prevent the potatoes sticking.

Chumki Banerjee

Potato Rösti

4 large potatoes
1 medium sweet potato (orange-fleshed)
1 onion, finely chopped
salt and freshly ground black pepper
15 ml (1 tbsp) lemon juice
50 g (2 oz) butter, melted
15 ml (1 tbsp) clarified butter, for cooking

1 Peel all of the potatoes, cut into quarters and cook in boiling water for 5 minutes. Drain and rinse under cold water. Allow to cool for 15 minutes.

2 Grate the cooled potatoes and place in a bowl with the onion, seasoning, lemon juice and melted butter. Mix thoroughly.

3 Heat the clarified butter in a heavy-based frying pan. Place heaped spoonfuls of the potato mixture in the pan and shape into rounds, about 7.5 cm (3 inches) in diameter. Cook over a moderate heat for about 5 minutes, pressing down firmly with a spatula to hold their shape. Turn the rösti over and cook the other side until golden brown and crisp. Drain on kitchen paper and serve at once.

Holly Schade

Horseradish and Ginger Röstis

2.5 cm (1 inch) piece fresh root ginger, grated
25 g (1 oz) fresh horseradish, grated
2 large potatoes, peeled and grated
salt and freshly ground black pepper
125 g (4 oz) butter, melted

1 Put the grated ginger in a small saucepan, add water to cover, bring to the boil and simmer for 5 minutes. Drain, refresh in cold water; drain.

2 Put the grated potato in a clean tea-towel and squeeze out all the moisture. Turn into a large bowl and add the ginger and horseradish, salt and pepper. Carefully mix well with a fork to disperse the flavourings evenly. Stir in 45 ml (3 tbsp) melted butter.

3 Heat the remaining butter in a pan until foaming. Place a greased 10 cm (4 inch) muffin ring in the pan and fill with a quarter of the potato mixture. Press down well and remove the ring. Repeat to shape a further 3 rostis. Cook on one side for approximately 5 minutes until golden.

4 Turn carefully and cook the other side. Drain on absorbent kitchen paper for a few seconds, then transfer to a wire rack to retain crispness. Reheat the röstis in a hot oven for a few minutes before serving.

Gregory Lewis

Anna Potatoes

700 g (1½ lb) potatoes
salt and freshly ground black pepper
25 g (1 oz) butter

1 Peel and thinly slice the potatoes. Layer in a greased ovenproof dish, seasoning each layer with salt and pepper.

2 Dot with butter, cover with foil and bake in a preheated oven at 190°C (375°F) mark 5 for 1 hour.

3 Remove from the oven and leave to stand for 5 minutes before serving.

Judith Elliott

Saffron Mash

Saffron imparts a wonderful yellow tone to creamy mashed potato in this simple accompaniment.

300 g (10 oz) potatoes, peeled
salt and freshly ground black pepper
pinch of saffron strands
30 ml (2 tbsp) butter
45 ml (3 tbsp) crème fraîche

1 Cook the potatoes in boiling salted water with the saffron added until tender.

2 Drain the potatoes and mash with the butter and crème fraîche. Season with salt and pepper to taste. Serve at once

Amanda Farnese

Potato Galettes

250 g (9 oz) potatoes, peeled
salt and freshly ground black pepper
75 g (3 oz) butter, melted

1 Finely grate the potatoes, season with salt and pepper and mix with the melted butter.

2 Position a 7.5 cm (3 inch) metal pastry cutter on a greased baking tray and fill with the potato mixture to a depth of 5 mm (¼ inch), pressing well down. Carefully remove the metal ring and repeat with the remaining mixture.

3 Bake in a preheated oven at 200°C (400°C) mark 6 for 10 minutes. Turn the potato galettes over and bake for a further 10 minutes or until golden and cooked through. Serve hot.

Michael Boning

Sage Tagliatelle

310 g (10½ oz) Italian "00" flour
pinch of salt
3 eggs (size 2)
3 drops of olive oil
15 ml (1 tbsp) finely chopped sage

To Serve:
butter, to taste
sage leaves, to garnish

1 To make the pasta dough, put the flour, salt, eggs, olive oil and sage in a food processor and process for about 30 seconds or until the dough forms a ball. Flatten the ball slightly with your hands, wrap in cling film and leave to rest in the refrigerator for 30 minutes.

2 Cut off about one quarter of the dough and rewrap the remainder. Flatten the piece and shape into a rectangle. Pass it through a pasta machine on its widest setting. Fold the dough and pass through the machine repeatedly, narrowing the setting by one notch each time until it passes through the second to last notch. Repeat with the remaining dough.

3 Fit the tagliatelle attachment and pass the pasta sheets through to cut the tagliatelle. Lay on clean tea-towels and leave to dry slightly, for about 5 minutes, before cooking.

4 Cook the tagliatelle in a large pan of boiling salted water for about 2 minutes until al dente (tender but firm to the bite). Drain and toss with butter to taste. Serve garnished with sage leaves.

Holly Schade

Parsley Profiteroles with Horseradish Cream

50 g (2 oz) butter
150 ml (¼ pint) water
65 g (2½ oz) plain flour
2 eggs, beaten
15 ml (1 tbsp) finely chopped parsley
pinch of salt

Horseradish Cream:
300 ml (½ pint) soured cream
30 ml (2 tbsp) grated fresh horseradish
salt and freshly ground black pepper

1 Heat the butter and water in a saucepan until the butter has melted. Bring to the boil, remove from the heat and beat in the flour to form a smooth paste. Cool slightly, then gradually add the eggs, beating all the time. Add the chopped parsley and salt.

2 Spoon 16 balls of dough on to a greased baking sheet. Bake in a preheated oven at 220°C (425°F) mark 7 for 20 minutes until golden brown and crisp. Split and pop back in the oven for a few minutes to cook the inside dough if necessary.

3 For the horseradish cream, mix the soured cream with the grated horseradish and seasoning to taste.

4 Fill the profiteroles with the horseradish cream and serve at once.

Sue Lawrence

Grilled Polenta

175 g (6 oz) polenta flour
salt
freshly grated Parmesan cheese

1 Bring 1.2 litres (2 pints) of salted water to the boil in a heavy-based saucepan. Add the polenta flour and stir vigorously for 5 minutes, to ensure that no lumps form.

2 Pour the polenta into a lightly buttered shallow baking tin, to a depth of about 2 cm (¾ inch). Allow to cool and solidify.

3 Using a 5-7.5 cm (2-3 inch) pastry cutter, cut out circles of polenta allowing 2-3 per person. Sprinkle with Parmesan and flash under a preheated grill until the cheese has melted and the polenta is heated through. Serve immediately.

Andrea Ferrari

Creamed Polenta

1 small onion, finely chopped
1 clove garlic, crushed
600 ml (1 pint) milk
300 ml (½ pint) single cream
60 ml (4 tbsp) chopped chives
60 ml (4 tbsp) chopped parsley
175 g (6 oz) quick-cook (instant) polenta
salt and freshly ground black pepper

1 Put the onion, garlic, milk and cream in a saucepan and bring to the boil. Simmer gently until the onion is soft.

2 Add the herbs, then shower in the polenta in a steady stream, stirring constantly. Beat until smooth. Cook over a low heat, stirring continuously, for 5 minutes. Season to taste. Serve at once.

Judith Elliott

Mejadarra with Mushrooms

2 large mild onions, halved lengthwise
10-15 ml (2-3 tsp) vegetable oil
2.5 ml (½ tsp) ground turmeric
5-10 ml (1-2 tsp) freshly ground cumin seeds
5-10 ml (1-2 tsp) freshly ground coriander seeds
100 g (3½ oz) large green lentils, soaked in cold water for 2-3 hours
300 ml (½ pint) beef or chicken stock
150 g (5 oz) basmati rice
salt and freshly ground black pepper
30 ml (2 tbsp) grapeseed oil (approximately)
10-12 chestnut mushrooms, sliced
handful of fresh coriander sprigs, roughly chopped

1 Finely chop one of the onion halves. Heat the vegetable oil in a pan, add the chopped onion and fry gently until softened. Add the spices and stir well. Drain the lentils and add to the pan with the stock. Bring to the boil, cover and simmer for about 20 minutes until the lentils are soft.

2 Meanwhile, put the rice in a small saucepan, cover with cold water and bring to the boil. Stir once, then lower the heat and cook for 3 minutes. Drain and rinse with cold water.

3 When the lentils are soft, add the par-boiled rice. Stir well. (Add a little water to cover if necessary.) Add salt to taste and a generous sprinkling of pepper. Bring to the boil, lower the heat, cover and cook until the liquid is absorbed and the rice is cooked.

4 Meanwhile, slice the remaining onion halves into crescent shapes. Heat the grapeseed oil in a frying pan, add the onions and fry over a medium heat until almost caramelised. Drain on kitchen paper and keep warm in the oven. Add the mushrooms to the pan, with a little more oil if necessary, and fry until tender and browned. Drain and keep warm with the onions. Stir-fry half of the coriander briefly in the remaining oil.

5 Add the rest of the coriander to the mejadarra and fork it through. Divide between warmed serving plates and top with the fried onions. Garnish with the mushrooms and fried coriander to serve.

Barbara Vazana

Wild Rice with Lemon Grass

125 g (4 oz) wild rice
25 g (1 oz) brown rice
2 lemon grass stalks
50 g (2 oz) butter
finely pared rind of 1 lemon
salt and freshly ground black pepper

1 Bring a large pan of salted water to the boil and add the wild and brown rice. Halve one stalk of lemon grass lengthways, then add to the pan with the rice. Simmer for 40 minutes, or until the rice is tender. Drain well, discarding the lemon grass.

2 Meanwhile, discard any coarse outer leaves from the other lemon grass stalk and chop very finely. Melt the butter in a pan, add the rice, lemon grass and lemon rind, and mix well. Heat through and keep warm until ready to serve.

Elaine Bates

Parsley Rice

200 g (7 oz) long-grain rice
15 g (½ oz) butter
30 ml (2 tbsp) finely chopped parsley
salt and freshly ground black pepper

1 Rinse the rice thoroughly in several changes of cold water until the water becomes clear.

2 Put the rice into a saucepan and add 400 ml (14 fl oz) water. Bring to the boil, lower the heat and simmer gently for about 15-20 minutes until the water is absorbed. Turn off the heat and leave to stand for about 15 minutes. (If using an electric rice cooker, cook according to the manufacturer's directions.)

3 Meanwhile, melt the butter in a frying pan, add the parsley with salt and pepper to taste and fry gently for 2-3 minutes.

4 Fluff up the rice, add the fried parsley and toss well.

5 Put a quarter of the rice into a warmed buttered dariole mould or cup. Press down, then turn out onto a warmed serving plate. Repeat with the other portions, then serve.

Noriko Anzai-Jackson

Desserts

Chocolate Pecan Pie

Pastry:
185 g (6½ oz) plain flour
2.5 ml (½ tsp) salt
5 ml (1 tsp) caster sugar
65 g (2½ oz) butter
25 g (1 oz) white vegetable shortening, in pieces
(2½-3 tbsp) iced water

Filling:
50 g (2 oz) plain chocolate, in pieces
50 g (2 oz) butter
4 eggs (size 1)
250 ml (8 fl oz) maple syrup
225 g (8 oz) caster sugar
5 ml (1 tsp) vanilla essence
350 g (12 oz) shelled pecan nuts, roughly chopped

To Serve:
Vanilla Ice Cream (see right)

1 To make the pastry, put the flour, salt, sugar, butter and vegetable shortening in a food processor. Process, using the pulse button, until the mixture begins to resemble breadcrumbs; do not over-mix. Transfer the mixture to a bowl and sprinkle over 40 ml (2½ tbsp) iced water. Toss with a fork, sprinkling in a little more iced water as necessary until the mixture begins to stick together. Working quickly, draw the dough together with your hands and form into a ball.

2 Roll out the pastry on a lightly floured surface and use to line a 23 cm (9 inch) fluted flan tin. Trim and crimp the edges. Chill in the refrigerator for 30 minutes.

3 Meanwhile, prepare the filling. Put the chocolate and butter in a bowl and melt together in the microwave on medium (or over a pan of simmering water). Stir until smooth, then set aside to cool.

4 Put the eggs, maple syrup, sugar and vanilla essence in a mixing bowl and beat until well combined. Stir in the chocolate mixture, then fold in the nuts. Pour into the chilled pastry case.

5 Bake in the middle of a preheated oven at 190°C (375°F) mark 5 for 50-60 minutes, or until a skewer inserted into the centre comes out only slightly fudgy. Serve warm, with the Vanilla Ice Cream.

Holly Schade

Vanilla Ice Cream

300 ml (½ pint) double cream
200 ml (7 fl oz) semi-skimmed milk
1 vanilla pod
2.5 ml (½ tsp) vanilla essence
4 egg yolks (size 1)
125 g (4 oz) caster sugar

1 Pour the cream and milk into a saucepan. Scrape the seeds from the vanilla pod into the liquid and add the vanilla essence. Slowly bring the mixture just to the boil. Meanwhile, beat the egg yolks and sugar together in a bowl until well blended. Slowly add the hot liquid, stirring constantly.

2 Return to the pan and stir over a low heat until the custard is thick enough to lightly coat the back of the wooden spoon; do not boil or it will curdle. Strain into a clean bowl and leave to cool. Transfer to an ice-cream maker and churn, according to the manufacturer's instructions, until firm.

3 If you do not have an ice-cream maker, freeze the ice cream in a suitable container, whisking 2-3 times during freezing to break down the ice crystals and ensure a smooth-textured result.

4 Serve with the Chocolate Pecan Pie.

Holly Schade

Walnut Pie with a Prune and Marsala Sauce

Pastry:
250 g (9 oz) unbleached plain flour
25 g (1 oz) icing sugar
2.5 ml (½ tsp) salt
175 g (6 oz) cold unsalted butter, diced
1 (size 2) egg, plus 1 egg yolk

Filling:
150 g (5 oz) walnuts
2 (size 2) eggs
210 g (7½ oz) vanilla-flavoured caster sugar
1 egg yolk, mixed with a little milk

Prune and Marsala Sauce:
75 g (3 oz) Agen prunes, soaked overnight in 300 ml (½ pint) water
45 ml (3 tbsp) Marsala
15 ml (1 tbsp) double cream
a little sugar, to taste

To Decorate:
icing sugar, for dusting
12 walnut halves

1 Sift the flour, icing sugar and salt into a mixing bowl. Add the butter and rub in until the mixture resembles breadcrumbs. Lightly beat the eggs and add to the flour mixture. Mix to a smooth dough, using a round-bladed knife. Wrap in cling film and leave to rest in the refrigerator for at least 30 minutes.

2 To make the filling, put the walnuts in a food processor or blender and grind to a medium fineness. Put the eggs and sugar in a mixing bowl and stir with a balloon whisk for 2 minutes, without beating. Stir in the ground walnuts.

3 Set aside one third of the pastry for the lid. Roll out the larger piece on a lightly floured surface until big enough to line an oblong loose-bottomed tart tin, measuring 36 x 11 cm (14 x 4½ inches). Line the tin with the pastry and trim the edges. (Add the trimmings to the other portion of pastry.) Fill the pastry case with the walnut mixture.

4 Roll out the reserved pastry to make a lid. Moisten the edges with a little of the egg mixture and carefully position the lid, pressing the edges together to seal. Trim off excess pastry. Make three slits in the lid and brush with the egg and milk. Bake in a preheated oven at 180°C (350°F) mark 4 for 35 minutes.

5 Meanwhile, make the sauce. Cook the prunes in the soaking water for 20 minutes or until soft. Allow to cool a little, then drain, reserving the liquor, and remove the stones. Press the flesh through a fine sieve with a wooden spoon. Put the prune pulp and Marsala in a blender and process until smooth, adding enough prune juice to make a sauce the consistency of thin cream. Pour into a small bowl and stir in the cream. Adjust the sweetness if necessary, keeping the sauce slightly tart.

6 Allow the tart to cool, then remove from the tin. Dust with icing sugar and cut into thick slices. To serve, pour a pool of sauce onto each serving plate. Place a slice of walnut pie in the centre and decorate with walnut halves.

Derek Morris

Treacle Tart with Lemon Zest and Vanilla Custard Sauce

Pastry:
175 g (6 oz) plain flour
125 g (4 oz) unsalted butter, in pieces
few drops of milk (if required)

Filling:
125 g (4 oz) fresh white breadcrumbs
finely grated zest and juice of 1 lemon
10 rounded tbsp golden syrup
2 rounded tbsp black treacle

Vanilla Custard Sauce:
300 ml (½ pint) double cream
3 egg yolks
5 ml (1 tsp) cornflour
15 ml (1 tbsp) sugar
few drops of vanilla essence

1 To make the pastry, put the flour and butter into a food processor and work to a smooth dough; the mixture should start to form a ball without any additional liquid, but it may be necessary to add a few drops of milk to bind the pastry.

2 Divide the pastry into 4 portions and use to line four individual 10 cm (4 inch) flan tins. As the pastry is very short and quite difficult to roll, you will find it easier to press the pastry directly into the tins, rather than roll it out first.

3 For the filling, put the breadcrumbs, lemon rind, syrup and treacle in a bowl and mix until evenly blended.

4 Pour the filling into the flan cases and bake in a preheated oven at 180°C (350°F) mark 4 for 30-35 minutes until set. Leave to cool slightly in the tins before removing.

5 Meanwhile, make the custard sauce. Pour the cream into a heavy-based pan and bring just to boiling point. In the meantime, beat the egg yolks, cornflour, sugar and vanilla essence together in a bowl. Pour on the hot cream, whisking constantly. Return the custard to the pan and cook over a low heat for 1-2 minutes, stirring constantly with a wooden spoon until it is thick enough to coat the back of the spoon. Do not allow to boil or it will curdle.

6 Place the treacle tarts on individual plates and serve with the custard sauce.

Amanda Farnese

Note: To make it easier to measure out the syrup, first warm the tablespoon.

Lemon Tart

Pastry:
125 g (4 oz) plain flour
pinch of salt
grated rind of 1 lemon
25 g (1 oz) icing sugar
75 g (3 oz) butter, in pieces
1 egg yolk, mixed with 15 ml (1 tbsp) iced water

Filling:
6 eggs (size 2)
225 g (8 oz) caster sugar
125 g (4 oz) unsalted butter, in pieces
grated rind of 3 lemons
150 ml (¼ pint) freshly squeezed lemon juice

To Decorate:
lemon rind shreds, blanched (optional)
icing sugar, for dusting

1 To make the pastry, put the flour, salt, lemon rind, icing sugar and butter in a food processor and process, using the pulse button, just until the mixture resembles coarse breadcrumbs. With the motor running, add the egg yolk and water, processing briefly until the mixture just holds together, but does not quite form a ball. Pull the dough together with your hands and quickly form a ball.

2 Flatten the dough then roll out between two sheets of cling film and use to line a 23 cm (9 inch) loose-bottomed flan tin. Trim edges and prick the base with a fork. Chill in the refrigerator for 30 minutes.

3 Line the pastry case with greaseproof paper and fill with baking beans or rice. Bake in a preheated oven at 200°C (400°F) mark 6 for 10 minutes. Remove the paper and beans, then return the pastry case to the oven for a further 10 minutes, to dry and cook the base. Cool on a wire rack. Lower the oven temperature to 190°C (375°F) mark 5.

4 To make the filling, place all the ingredients in a bowl over a pan of simmering water. Whisk until well blended and continue stirring until the mixture thickens slightly – just enough to coat the back of a wooden spoon. Stand the flan tin on a baking sheet. Pour the filling into the pastry case and bake for 25 minutes, or until set. Allow to cool slightly.

5 Serve warm or cold, cut into wedges, decorated with lemon rind if liked, and dusted with icing sugar. Accompany with the Crème Fraîche Ice Cream.

Holly Schade

Crème Fraîche Ice Cream

225 g (8 oz) crème fraîche
125 ml (4 fl oz) milk
45 ml (3 tbsp) lemon juice
150 g (5 oz) caster sugar

1 Put all of the ingredients in a food processor and process briefly until evenly blended and smooth. Transfer to a bowl and chill until cold, then freeze in an ice cream maker according to the manufacturer's instructions.

2 If you do not have an ice-cream maker, freeze the ice cream in a shallow container, whisking 2-3 times during freezing to break down the ice crystals and ensure an even-textured result.

3 Serve the ice cream in scoops, with the Lemon Tart.

Holly Schade

Pear and Almond Mille Feuille

80 g (3¼ oz) unsalted butter
80 g (3¼ oz) flaked almonds, toasted
90 g (3½ oz) icing sugar
1 egg (size 2)
15 ml (1 tbsp) dark rum
6 sheets of filo pastry
melted butter, for brushing
120 ml (4 fl oz) double cream
15 ml (1 tbsp) caster sugar
125 g (4 oz) mascarpone
15 ml (1 tbsp) poire William liqueur
2 ripe pears
icing sugar, for dusting

To Serve:
120 ml (4 fl oz) single cream
raspberry coulis (optional)

1 Cream the butter in a heatproof bowl until softened, then add the almonds, icing sugar and egg. Stand the bowl over a pan of simmering water and stir gently until the butter has melted and the mixture is slightly thickened. Stir in the rum, then allow to cool. Chill in the refrigerator until needed.

2 Brush the sheets of filo pastry generously with melted butter, then fold each sheet into a long strip, about 4 cm (1½ inches) wide. Cut twelve 10 cm (4 inch) lengths in total. Brush with melted butter and place on a baking sheet. Bake in a preheated oven at 200°C (400°F) mark 6 for 5-10 minutes until golden and crisp. Transfer to a wire rack to cool.

3 Whip the cream and sugar together in a bowl until it forms soft peaks. Briefly whip the mascarpone, then fold into the cream with the poire William liqueur.

4 Peel, core and slice the pears. Fold into the cream mixture.

5 Place one filo wafer in the centre of each serving plate. Cover with the chilled nut paste, then place another filo wafer on top. Cover with the cream and pear mixture, then top with the remaining filo wafers. Dust with icing sugar. Serve immediately, on a pool of cream, surrounded by a raspberry coulis if desired.

James Hurd

Pear and Almond Tart with Amaretto Ice Cream

Ice Cream:
150 ml (¼ pint) milk
2 egg yolks
110 g (4 oz) caster sugar
150 ml (¼ pint) double cream
30 ml (2 tbsp) Amaretto liqueur

Pastry:
1 egg yolk
15 ml (1 tbsp) whipping cream
40 g (1½ oz) icing sugar
few drops of vanilla essence
75 g (3 oz) unsalted butter, softened
110 g (4 oz) plain flour
15 g (½ oz) cornflour

Filling:
25 g (1 oz) unsalted butter
25 g (1 oz) icing sugar
25 g (1 oz) ground almonds
1 egg (size 3)
15 ml (1 tbsp) cream
1 ripe pear

Glaze:
50 g (2 oz) apricot jam, warmed and sieved

To Decorate:
redcurrants (or other seasonal fruit)
icing sugar, for dusting

1 To make the ice cream, pour the milk into a saucepan and slowly bring to the boil. Meanwhile, beat the egg yolks and sugar together in a bowl. Gradually pour on the milk, whisking constantly. Return the mixture to the pan and cook over a low heat, stirring constantly, until the custard begins to thicken; do not allow to boil or it will curdle. Leave until cold, then stir in the cream and Amaretto liqueur.

2 Transfer to an ice-cream maker and churn according to the manufacturer's directions. Alternatively freeze in a shallow container, whisking 2 or 3 times during freezing to break down the ice crystals and ensure an even-textured result.

3 To make the pastry, beat the egg yolk, whipping cream, icing sugar and vanilla essence together in a bowl. Mix in the softened butter. Sift in the flour and cornflour, stir well and form into a dough, using your hands, adding a little more flour to bind if necessary. Wrap in cling film and leave to rest in the refrigerator for 1 hour.

4 For the filling, mix the butter, icing sugar, ground almonds, egg and cream together in a bowl to form a smooth paste.

5 Divide the pastry into 4 portions and use to line four buttered 10 cm (4 inch) individual flan tins. (It will probably be necessary to do this with fingers as the pastry is too crumbly to roll.) Refrigerate for 10 minutes.

6 In the meantime, peel, quarter and core the pear. Slice lengthwise, leaving the stalk end intact, and fan out. Fill the pastry cases with the almond cream and lay the fanned pear quarters on top. Bake in a preheated oven at 190°C (375°F) mark 5 for 25-30 minutes.

7 Remove the tarts from the oven and while still warm brush with the warm apricot glaze. Carefully remove the tarts from their tins and place on plates. Spoon the amaretto ice cream onto the plates, and decorate with redcurrants or other fruit. Dust with icing sugar and serve at once.

Andrew Urbanek

Blackcurrant Tart with Lime Sorbet

Pastry:
150 g (5 oz) unsalted butter, diced (at room temperature)
90 g (3½ oz) icing sugar
1 egg (size 3), beaten
275 g (9 oz) plain flour

Filling:
350 g (12 oz) blackcurrants
5 ml (1 tsp) ground cinnamon
90 ml (6 tbsp) crème de cassis
60-90 ml (4-6 tbsp) soft brown sugar
2 eggs (size 1)
2 egg yolks (size 1)
250 ml (8 fl oz) whipping cream
60 ml (4 tbsp) demerara sugar
grated rind of 1 lime

Lime Sorbet:
10 limes
caster sugar (see recipe)
30 ml (2 tbsp) triple lime liquor

1 First make the pastry. Beat the butter and icing sugar together in a bowl until light and fluffy. Gradually beat in the egg. Sift in the flour and stir until the mixture comes together. Form the pastry into a ball, wrap in cling film and chill in the refrigerator, preferably overnight.

2 To make the lime sorbet, squeeze the juice from 8 limes and measure the volume of juice obtained; set aside. Measure an equal volume of caster sugar. Cut the remaining 2 limes into quarters and discard the pips. Place the lime quarters in a food processor with the sugar and process to a pulp. Add the reserved lime juice and lime liquor; process briefly. Transfer to an ice-cream machine and churn until frozen.

3 Roll out the chilled pastry as thinly as possible, and use to line an 18 cm (7 inch) loose-bottomed flan tin. Leave to rest in the refrigerator for 30 minutes. (Freeze the leftover pastry for another occasion.)

4 Line the pastry case with greaseproof paper and baking beans and bake blind in a preheated oven at 200°C (400°F) mark 6 for 10-15 minutes until firm, but not coloured. Remove the paper and beans.

5 Put the blackcurrants in a saucepan with the cinnamon and 30 ml (2 tbsp) of the crème de cassis. Sweeten to taste with the brown sugar, then turn into the part-baked pastry case.

6 In a bowl, beat together the whole eggs, egg yolks, whipping cream, demerara sugar, lime rind and remaining 60 ml (4 tbsp) crème de cassis. Pour over the blackcurrants in the pastry case.

7 Return the tart to the oven and bake for 15-20 minutes until the filling is just firm. Let stand for 5 minutes, then remove from the flan tin.

8 To serve, cut the tart into 4 portions and place on individual serving plates. Serve warm with a generous scoop of lime sorbet.

Chumki Banerjee

Note: If you do not have an ice-cream maker, freeze the sorbet in a shallow container, whisking 2 or 3 times during freezing to break down the ice crystals and ensure an even-textured result.

Grapefruit Tart with Orange Sauce and Vanilla Cream

Pastry:
200 g (7 oz) plain flour
pinch of salt
25 g (1 oz) caster sugar
100 g (3½ oz) butter, in pieces
a little water, to bind

Filling:
50 g (2 oz) butter
50 ml (2 fl oz) grapefruit juice
50 g (2 oz) caster sugar
4 eggs, beaten

Decoration:
50 g (2 oz) butter
zest of 1 grapefruit
zest of 1 orange
zest of 1 lime

Sauce:
300 ml (½ pint) orange juice
150 g (5 oz) caster sugar
50 ml (2 fl oz) Grand Marnier or other orange liqueur
few drops of vanilla essence
200 ml (7 fl oz) double cream

1 To make the pastry, sift the flour, salt and sugar into a bowl. Rub in the butter until the mixture resembles fine crumbs. Add the minimum amount of cold water to bind the pastry and form a stiff dough. Wrap in cling film and leave to rest in the refrigerator for at least 30 minutes.

2 Roll out the pastry thinly and use to line four 10 cm (4 inch) individual flan tins. Line with greaseproof paper and baking beans and bake blind in a preheated oven at 200°C (400°F) mark 6 for 15-20 minutes. Remove the paper and beans. Cool on a wire rack.

3 To prepare the filling, melt the butter in a heatproof bowl over a pan of boiling water (or a double saucepan). Add the grapefruit juice and sugar and stir until dissolved. Add the eggs and whisk over the heat until the mixture thickens. Remove the bowl from the heat and allow to cool, stirring occasionally to prevent a skin forming.

4 For the decoration, heat the butter in a small pan, add the grapefruit, orange and lime zest and fry until crisp and lightly browned. Remove from the pan and drain on kitchen paper; set aside.

5 To make the sauce, put the orange juice and sugar in a saucepan and dissolve over a low heat. Increase the heat and cook steadily until the sauce is reduced by about half, and thickened. Allow to cool slightly, then add the liqueur. Add a few drops of vanilla essence to the cream, then stir into the sauce.

6 Divide the grapefruit filling between the pastry cases, spreading it evenly.

7 To serve, pour the orange sauce around one half of each serving plate, so that it coats a semi-circle. Pour the cream onto the other half of each plate. Place the tarts in the middle and decorate with a spoonful of the fried citrus zest.

Tommy Sheppard

Note: For the decoration, use a zester to remove the rinds from the citrus fruits in fine shreds.

Raspberry Tart with Vanilla Ice Cream

Pastry:
150 g (5 oz) unsalted butter (at room temperature), diced
100 g (3½ oz) icing sugar
1 egg (size 3), beaten
250 g (9 oz) plain flour

Filling:
450 g (1 lb) raspberries
45 ml (3 tbsp) crème de framboise liqueur
icing sugar, to taste

Glaze:
90 ml (6 tbsp) good quality seedless raspberry jam
juice of ¼ lemon

Vanilla Ice Cream:
2 vanilla pods
3 egg yolks
100 g (3½ oz) caster sugar
250 ml (8 fl oz) milk
300 ml (½ pint) double cream

1 To make the pastry, beat the butter and icing sugar together in a bowl, until light and fluffy. Gradually beat in the egg. Sift the flour into the bowl. Mix until the dough comes together. Form the pastry into a ball, wrap in cling film and chill in the refrigerator for at least 1 hour, preferably overnight.

2 To make the ice cream, split the vanilla pods and scrape the seeds out into a bowl, reserving the pods. Add the egg yolks and sugar and whisk until smooth. Pour the milk into a heavy-based saucepan and add the vanilla pods. Heat slowly until just below boiling point. Discard the vanilla pods, then pour the hot milk onto the egg and sugar mixture, whisking all the time.

3 Pour the custard back into the pan and stir constantly over a moderate heat until the mixture is just thick enough to lightly coat the back of a spoon; do not allow to boil or the custard will curdle. Remove from the heat and stir in the cream. Churn in an ice-cream maker until firm.

4 Roll out the chilled pastry as thinly as possible and use to line an 18 cm (7 inch) loose-bottomed flan tin. Leave to rest in the refrigerator for 30 minutes. (Freeze leftover pastry for another occasion.) Line the flan case with greaseproof paper and baking beans and bake blind in a preheated oven at 200°C (400°F) mark 6 for 10-15 minutes until firm, but not coloured.

5 Meanwhile, prepare the filling. Put the raspberries into a bowl with the crème de framboise. Stir gently to mix, adding icing sugar to taste. Leave to steep for 15 minutes. Remove the raspberries with a slotted spoon, reserving the juice, and use to fill the part-baked pastry shell. Return to the oven for a further 15-20 minutes or until the pastry is golden brown.

6 Meanwhile prepare the glaze. Put the jam and lemon juice in a small heavy-based pan with 30 ml (2 tbsp) of the reserved juice from the raspberries. Heat, stirring, until the jam is dissolved.

7 Remove the cooked tart from the oven and brush with the warm glaze.

8 To serve, cut the tart into 4 portions and place on individual serving plates. Serve warm with a scoop of vanilla ice cream.

Chumki Banerjee

Note: If you do not have an ice-cream maker, freeze the ice cream in a shallow container, whisking 2 or 3 times during freezing to break down the ice crystals and ensure an even-textured result.

Bruléed Lime Curd Cream Tartlets with Raspberry Coulis

Pastry:
250 g (9 oz) plain flour
pinch of salt
25 g (1 oz) ground almonds
15 ml (1 tbsp) icing sugar
150 g (5 oz) chilled unsalted butter, diced
1 egg yolk

Filling:
3 eggs (size 1), plus 3 egg yolks
scant 75 g (3 oz) vanilla caster sugar
finely grated rind and juice of 3 limes
15 g (½ oz) butter
185 ml (6 fl oz) double cream
225 g (8 oz) raspberries

Raspberry Coulis:
225 g (8 oz) raspberries
50 g (2 oz) sugar
squeeze of lemon juice (optional)

To Decorate:
icing sugar, for dusting
8 mint leaves
30 ml (2 tbsp) single cream

1 Mix the flour, salt, ground almonds and icing sugar together in a bowl. Rub in the butter until the mixture resembles breadcrumbs. Add the egg yolk and about 30 ml (2 tbsp) cold water, to form a smooth dough. Wrap in cling film and place in the freezer for 20-30 minutes to chill thoroughly until firm enough to handle.

2 Roll out the pastry thinly on a lightly floured surface and use to line 4 individual loose-bottomed flan tins (see note). Line with greaseproof paper and baking beans and bake blind in a preheated oven at 200°C (400°F) mark 6 for 10 minutes. Remove paper and beans and return to the oven for 5 minutes or until the bases are cooked. Let cool in the tins, then turn out.

3 Meanwhile, make the filling. Whisk the eggs, extra yolks and sugar together in a bowl until thick and creamy. Add the lime rind and juice, and stand the bowl over a pan of simmering water for about 10 minutes, whisking occasionally. When the lime curd has thickened just enough for the whisk to leave a trail when lifted, remove the bowl from the heat. Stir in the butter and allow to cool.

4 For the raspberry coulis, put the raspberries in a shallow dish, sprinkle with the sugar and leave to macerate for about 1 hour. Press through a nylon sieve into a bowl to remove the pips. Add a squeeze of lemon juice to taste.

5 To finish the tartlets, whip the cream until thick and fold into the lime curd. Fill the tartlet cases with raspberries, reserving 4 for decoration. Cover with the lime curd and chill in the refrigerator for 30 minutes.

6 Dust the tartlets with icing sugar. Protect the edges of the pastry with foil and place under a preheated high grill to caramelise the sugar; this will take about 10 seconds. Allow to cool.

7 Place each tartlet on a large serving plate and decorate with the reserved raspberries and mint leaves. Surround with the raspberry coulis, dot with the cream and feather with a skewer. Serve at once.

Gillian Humphrey

Note: This pastry is a little difficult to roll out, so handle it as little as possible. You will have more than you need for this recipe; freeze the rest for another occasion.

Damson Tart with Meringue Topping

Pastry:
110 g (4 oz) unsalted butter
50 g (2 oz) icing sugar
1 egg yolk
110 g (4 oz) plain flour
25 g (1 oz) ground rice
pinch of salt

Filling:
450 g (1 lb) damsons
110 g (4 oz) caster sugar, or to taste
30 ml (2 tbsp) cornflour, blended with 30 ml (2 tbsp) water
2 egg yolks (size 2), beaten

Meringue Topping:
3 egg whites (size 2)
75 g (3 oz) caster sugar

1 To make the pastry, cream together the butter and icing sugar in a bowl. Mix in the egg yolk until thoroughly incorporated. Add the flour and ground rice, together with the salt. Work in using your fingertips; the mixture should start to form a ball without any additional liquid. Wrap the pastry in cling film and chill in the refrigerator for at least 30 minutes.

2 For the filling, place the damsons in a heavy-based pan. Cover and cook over a low heat until the fruit is soft. Press through a nylon sieve into a bowl to remove the tough skins and stones. Stir in the sugar. Set aside about 60 ml (4 tbsp) of the damson purée for decoration.

3 Place the rest of the damson purée in a saucepan and reheat. Add the blended cornflour and bring to the boil, stirring constantly. Cook, stirring, for 1 minute until slightly thickened. Remove from the heat and allow to cool slightly, then beat in the egg yolks. Allow to cool.

4 Meanwhile, roll out the pastry thinly and use to line four individual 10 cm (4 inch) tartlet tins or one 23 cm (9 inch) tin. Line with greaseproof paper and baking beans and bake blind in a preheated oven at 160°C (325°F) mark 3 for 10 minutes. Remove the paper and beans and allow to cool slightly. Lower the oven temperature to 150°C (300°F) mark 2.

5 In the meantime, make the meringue topping. Whisk the egg whites in a bowl until they hold stiff peaks, then whisk in half of the sugar. Gradually fold in the rest of the sugar.

6 Spread a layer of damson purée in each pastry case, then cover with the meringue; do not overfill the tarts. Cook in the oven for 20 minutes. Allow to cool.

7 Serve cold with a swirl of damson purée, thinned if necessary with a little water.

Claire Ketteman

Individual Apple Tarts with Calvados and Crème Chantilly

1 kg (2¼ lb) Cox's apples
15 g (½ oz) butter
1.25 ml (¼ tsp) ground cinnamon
50 g (2 oz) sugar
120 ml (4 fl oz) Calvados
225 g (8 oz) ready-made puff pastry
60 ml (4 tbsp) apricot jam

Crème Chantilly:
120 ml (4 fl oz) chilled whipping cream
25 g (1 oz) icing sugar

1 Set aside 4 apples. Peel, core and roughly chop the remaining apples. Place in a saucepan over a low heat with the butter. Add the cinnamon, sugar and all but 30 ml (2 tbsp) of the Calvados. Cook until the apples are soft and the mixture is reduced to a sauce, stirring occasionally. Sieve if necessary.

2 Roll out the pastry as thinly as possible on a lightly floured surface. Using a saucer as a guide, cut out 4 rounds, 1 cm (½ inch) larger than the saucer all round. Bend the edge of the pastry upwards to form a rim around each circle.

3 Spread the apple sauce over the base of the tarts. Peel, core and thinly slice the reserved apples. Arrange the apple slices over the sauce, making sure it is totally covered. Bake in a preheated oven at 230°C (450°F) mark 8 for 15 minutes. Lower the temperature to 200°C (400°F) mark 6 and bake for a further 10 minutes or until the pastry is golden brown and the apples are caramelised; make sure they do not burn.

4 Warm the apricot jam with 15 ml (1 tbsp) Calvaldos, then sieve and brush over the apple slices to glaze.

5 Prepare the crème chantilly just before serving. Whisk the cream with the icing sugar in a chilled bowl, adding the reserved 15 ml (1 tbsp) Calvados a little at a time during whisking. Take care to avoid overbeating.

6 Serve the apple tarts warm, with the crème chantilly.

Keith Kheer

Apple Streusel Pies

Pastry:
125 g (4 oz) plain flour
50 g (2 oz) unsalted butter
10 ml (2 tsp) icing sugar
1 egg yolk
15 ml (3 tsp) cold water (approximately)

Filling:
50 g (2 oz) plain flour
25 g (1 oz) unsalted butter
50 g (2 oz) caster sugar
225 g (8 oz) cooking apples
15 g (½ oz) sultanas
150 ml (¼ pint) double cream

Topping:
15 g (½ oz) caster sugar
2.5 ml (½ tsp) ground cinnamon
icing sugar, for dusting

1 To make the pastry, sift the flour into a bowl and rub in the butter until the mixture resembles fine breadcrumbs. Stir in the icing sugar. Add the egg yolk and sufficient cold water to mix to a soft dough. Wrap in cling film and chill in the refrigerator for 10-15 minutes.

2 Meanwhile, make the crumble for the filling. Sift the flour into a bowl and rub in the butter until it resembles fine bread-crumbs. Stir in the caster sugar.

3 Peel, core and thinly slice the apples. Roll out the pastry thinly and use to line four greased 10 cm (4 inch) loose-bottomed fluted flan tins. Sprinkle 10 ml (2 tsp) crumble mixture over the base of each pastry case. Divide the apples and sultanas between them arranging neatly in layers. Pour on the cream. Sprinkle the remaining crumble mixture evenly over the fruit. (You may not need to use all of it.)

4 For the topping, mix the sugar and cinnamon together and sprinkle on top of the flans. Place on a baking sheet and bake in the centre of a preheated oven at 200°C (400°F) mark 6 for 20 minutes. Lower the setting to 190°C (375°F) mark 5 and cook for a further 10 minutes.

5 Leave to stand for a few minutes, then carefully remove from the tins and place on serving plates dusted with icing sugar. Serve with the Pecan and Maple Ice Cream.

Clare Askaroff

Pecan and Maple Ice Cream

50 g (2 oz) pecan nuts
2 eggs, separated
30 ml (2 tbsp) caster sugar
150 ml (¼ pint) Jersey or double cream
30 ml (2 tbsp) maple syrup

1 Toast the pecan nuts under the grill, then chop (not too finely). Set aside a few chopped nuts for decoration.

2 In a large bowl, whisk the egg whites until very stiff. Whisk in the sugar 15 ml (1 tbsp) at a time. In another bowl, lightly whip the cream.

3 Add the cream, egg yolks, maple syrup and chopped nuts to the egg white mixture and carefully fold in.

4 Transfer the mixture to an ice-cream maker and churn for 15-20 minutes. Turn into a freezerproof container and place in the freezer until required. Unless serving within 2 hours, transfer to refrigerator 30 minutes before serving to soften. Serve sprinkled with the reserved nuts.

Clare Askaroff

Walnut and Quince Tarts

Rich Shortcrust Pastry:
125 g (4 oz) plain flour
pinch of salt
50 g (2 oz) caster sugar
50 g (2 oz) ground almonds
75 g (3 oz) unsalted butter
juice of ½ lemon
1 egg, size 3-4

Filling:
3 eggs
50 g (2 oz) light muscovado sugar
125 g (4 oz) unsalted butter, melted
125 g (4 oz) golden syrup
finely grated rind and juice of 1 lemon
225 g (8 oz) shelled walnuts (see note)

To Glaze:
30 ml (2 tbsp) quince jelly
7.5 ml (½ tbsp) quince eau-de-vie or lemon juice

Quince Cream:
225 g (8 oz) mascarpone (Italian soft cream cheese)
25 ml (5 tsp) quince jelly
15 ml (1 tbsp) quince eau-de-vie (or to taste)

1 To make the pastry, sift the flour and salt into the food processor bowl. Add the sugar and ground almonds and process briefly to mix. Add the butter, in pieces, and process until the mixture resembles fine breadcrumbs. Add the lemon juice and sufficient egg to bind, processing briefly until the dough begins to hold together. Gather the pastry into a ball, wrap in cling film and leave to rest in the refrigerator for 30 minutes or longer.

2 Roll out the pastry thinly on a lightly floured surface and use to line 4 individual 10 cm (4 inch) loose-bottomed flan tins. Line each with a disc of greaseproof paper and baking beans and bake blind at 200°C (400°F) mark 6 for 10 minutes. Remove the paper and beans and bake for a further 5 minutes.

3 Meanwhile prepare the filling. In a bowl, beat the eggs with the sugar, butter and syrup until smooth. Stir in the lemon rind and juice.

4 Divide the walnuts between the cooked pastry cases and spoon the filling mixture on top. Bake at 175°C (360°F) mark 3 for 20-25 minutes until set. Gently warm the quince jelly with the eau-de-vie or lemon juice until melted. Brush over the tarts as soon as they come out of the oven to glaze.

5 To make the quince cream, beat the mascarpone in a bowl until smooth. Gently warm the quince jelly until melted then carefully fold into the mascarpone with the eau-de-vie.

6 Serve the walnut and quince tarts warm, with the quince cream at room temperature.

Sue Lawrence

Note: Make sure you use very fresh nuts for these tarts; light amber walnuts are ideal.

Pears in Pastry Lattice with Lime Butterscotch Sauce

2 ripe, firm pears
225 g (8 oz) puff pastry
a little milk, to glaze

Sugar Syrup:
250 g (9 oz) caster sugar
25 ml (1 fl oz) lemon juice

Frangipane:
60 g (2¼ oz) unsalted butter, softened
60 g (2¼ oz) caster sugar
1 egg, beaten
60 g (2¼ oz) ground almonds
15 g (½ oz) plain flour

Sauce:
75 g (3 oz) caster sugar
50 ml (2 fl oz) liquid glucose
juice of 1 lime
250 ml (8 fl oz) double cream

To Decorate:
icing sugar, for dusting

1 To make the sugar syrup, put the sugar, lemon juice and 500 ml (16 fl oz) water in a saucepan and heat gently until the sugar is dissolved, then bring to the boil. Peel, halve and core the pears, then add to the syrup and poach for about 20 minutes until tender. Remove from the syrup and leave to cool on a plate.

2 To make the frangipane, put all the ingredients in a bowl and whisk together thoroughly using an electric whisk until smooth.

3 Roll out half of the puff pastry thinly on a lightly floured surface and cut 4 pear shapes, about 1 cm (½ inch) larger all round than the pears. Roll out the other half of the pastry, then roll with the lattice roller to make your pastry lattice.

4 Spread a small amount of frangipane on each pear-shaped piece of pastry, leaving a 1 cm (½ inch) border. Place a pear on top and brush the pastry edges with a little milk. Cut a piece of lattice pastry to fit over each pear and carefully position over the pears. Press the pastry edges together to seal and trim to neaten.

5 Place on a lightly greased baking tray and brush with milk to glaze. Cut 12 small leaves from the pastry trimmings, brush with milk and place on the baking tray. Cook in a preheated oven at 190°C (375°F) mark 5 for about 10 minutes until the pastry is crisp and golden brown.

6 To make the sauce, put the sugar and glucose in a saucepan with 25 ml (1 fl oz) water over a low heat until the sugar is dissolved. Add the lime juice and cream, bring to the boil and boil for 1 minute.

7 To serve, place a lattice pear on each warmed serving plate and decorate with the small pastry leaves. Dust with icing sugar and pour the sauce around each pear. Serve immediately.

Rachel Southall

Note: To make the pastry lattice for this dessert you will need a lattice roller. This is a plastic or perspex cylinder with 'blades' set in it. As you roll the lattice roller over the pastry it cuts slits in the pastry. When the pastry is lifted from the work surface these slits open up to form the lattice. You can buy an inexpensive lattice roller from a kitchen shop or mail order cookware supplier.

Pear Gratin with Cinnamon Ice Cream

Ice Cream:

300 ml (½ pint) milk
300 ml (½ pint) double cream
1 cinnamon stick
4 egg yolks
125 g (4 oz) sugar

Gratin:

4 ripe pears
lemon juice for sprinkling
4 egg yolks
45 ml (3 tbsp) caster sugar
100 ml (3½ fl oz) double cream, whipped
125 ml (4 fl oz) Poire Williem eau-de-vie

1 To make the ice cream, put the milk and cream in a saucepan with the cinnamon stick over a low heat. Simmer gently for 5 minutes to infuse. Remove from the heat.

2 Beat the egg yolks and sugar thoroughly to a creamy consistency, then whisk into the milk. Remove the cinnamon stick, squeezing out the juice into the mixture. Transfer to a freezerproof container and freeze for about 2 hours, until it is the consistency of ice cream.

3 For the gratin, peel, core and slice the pears, then sprinkle with lemon juice to prevent browning. Arrange in 4 small gratin dishes or on heatproof plates.

4 Beat the egg yolks and sugar together thoroughly, then fold in the whipped cream and Poire Williem. Pour the mixture over the pears, coating them completely.

5 Bake in a preheated oven at 220°C (425°F) mark 7 for 10-15 minutes. Allow to stand for 5 minutes before serving.

6 Just before serving, place a scoop of cinnamon ice cream in the centre of each pear gratin. Serve at once.

Jo Eitel

Vanilla Pears with an Almond Filling and Chocolate Sauce

175 g (6 oz) granulated sugar
juice of ½ lemon
1 vanilla pod
4 dessert pears

Almond Filling:
15 ml (1 tbsp) Grand Marnier
75 g (3 oz) white marzipan
25 g (1 oz) amaretti biscuits, crushed

Chocolate Sauce:
40 g (1½ oz) caster sugar
100 g (3½ oz) plain chocolate, chopped
20 ml (4 tsp) whipping cream
15 ml (1 tbsp) kirsch

To Decorate:
15-30 ml (1-2 tbsp) yogurt
25 g (1 oz) flaked almonds, toasted

1 Dissolve the sugar in 900 ml (1½ pints) water in a saucepan over low heat. Add the lemon juice and vanilla; bring to a simmer. Peel the pears and scoop out the cores with a melon baller, from the bases. Place the pears in the syrup. Cover with a circle of greaseproof paper and poach gently for 20-25 minutes or until tender. Leave to cool in the syrup.

2 To prepare the filling, work the Grand Marnier into the marzipan until smooth. Mix in the crushed amaretti biscuits.

3 To make the chocolate sauce, dissolve the sugar in 75 ml (5 tbsp) water in a saucepan over a low heat. Bring to the boil, then remove from the heat. Add the chocolate, stirring until dissolved, then stir in the cream and kirsch. Allow to cool.

4 Drain the pears and push a little filling into each one, through the base. Halve lengthwise and arrange on serving plates. Surround with chocolate sauce, dot with yogurt and feather with a skewer. Decorate with almonds.

Richard Kuch

Baked Bramleys with Cobnut Stuffing and Cardamom Custard

4 even-sized British Bramley cooking apples
100 g (4 oz) cobnuts or hazelnuts
100 g (4 oz) light muscovado sugar
1 egg yolk
juice of 1 orange
150 ml (¼ pint) sweet cider
knob of butter
sugar for sprinkling

Cardamom Custard:
600 ml (1 pint) full-cream milk
50 g (2 oz) sugar
6 cardamom pods
4 egg yolks, beaten

To Serve:
apple leaves and blossom to decorate (optional)

1 First make the cardamom custard. Combine the milk and sugar in a saucepan. Crush the cardamom pods and add to the pan. Heat the milk until it is almost boiling, cool slightly, then pour on to the egg yolks, stirring constantly.

2 Return to the pan and cook over a low heat, stirring continuously, until the mixture is thick enough to just coat the back of the spoon.

3 Cover the surface with a piece of greaseproof paper to prevent a skin forming and leave to infuse for about 1 hour.

4 Core the apples, retaining the stalks. Score the skin around the middle of each one.

5 Grind half of the nuts in a blender or food processor. Roughly chop the other half of the nuts and roast in a preheated oven at 180°C (350°F) mark 4 for about 10 minutes. Combine the ground and roasted nuts with the sugar, egg yolk and orange juice.

6 Stuff the apples with the nut mixture, then place in a baking dish. Pour the cider around the apples and add a knob of butter and a sprinkling of sugar. Cook in the oven for 45 minutes to 1 hour, depending on the size of the apples, basting occasionally with the juices.

7 To serve, strain the custard into a clean pan and reheat gently. Pop in the reserved stalks and smooth the wrinkled apple skins. Decorate each one with an apple leaf and some apple blossom if the season's right! Serve the baked apples in a pool of cardamom custard.

Linda Yewdell

Lavender Baked Figs on Brioche Toasts with Cassis Glacage and Blackberry Confiture

8 fresh figs
125 g (4 oz) lavender sugar

Blackberry Confiture:
60 ml (4 tbsp) caster sugar
½ glass crème de mure, or crème de cassis
30 blackberries

Cassis Glacage:
1 egg yolk
30 ml (2 tbsp) caster sugar
150 ml (¼ pint) whipping cream
15 ml (1 tbsp) cassis or blackcurrant purée (approximately)

To Serve:
8 slices brioche, each 1 cm (½ inch) thick

1 First make the confiture, dissolve the sugar in the liqueur in a pan over a low heat, then boil to reduce to a thick syrup. Add the black-berries and cook gently for about 2 minutes only, until softened but still retaining their shape. Remove the blackberries with a slotted spoon and set aside on a plate. Reserve the syrup.

2 To make the cassis glacage, whisk the egg yolk with the sugar and cream until thick, then fold in enough cassis purée to give a rich lilac colour. Set aside.

3 To prepare the syrup for the figs, put the lavender sugar (including flowers) and 100 ml (3½ fl oz) water in a pan over a low heat to dissolve sugar. Increase heat and boil to reduce the syrup slightly. Add the figs and shake the pan to coat the figs in the syrup. Transfer to an ovenproof dish, cover and place in a preheated oven at 200°C (400°F) mark 6 for 5-10 minutes to heat through. Remove from the oven and set aside.

4 Meanwhile, cut the brioche slices into rounds, then brown lightly on both sides under a hot grill.

5 To serve, pour or spread about a tablespoon of the glacage onto one side of an individual flameproof plate. Place under a very hot grill and watch carefully. First the egg will cook which sets the glacarge, then almost immediately the top will begin to brown. Remove at once before it burns. Repeat with the other servings.

6 Make a cross-cut in the top of each fig and push up from the bottom so the 'petals' open out. Place a fig on each brioche toast, next to the cassis glacage and spoon over any spare syrup. Place a spoonful of blackberry confiture syrup and a pile of blackberries on each plate. Serve immediately.

Brian Tompkins

Note: To make the lavender sugar, simply add a good handful of dried lavender flowers to a 450 g (1 lb) jar of caster sugar and leave to infuse.

Roasted Figs in Honey Butter and Orange

8-12 fresh figs
50 g (2 oz) unsalted butter
30 ml (2 tbsp) honey
finely grated rind and juice of 1 orange

Orange Cream:
150 ml (¼ pint) double cream
juice of ½ orange

To Serve:
Orange Sablés (see right)

1 Peel the figs and cut each one vertically into quarters. Melt the butter and honey in an ovenproof dish, then stir in the orange juice. Place the figs in a single layer in the dish and sprinkle over the orange rind. Cook in a preheated oven at 190°C (375°F) mark 5 for 15 minutes, basting occasionally.

2 Meanwhile, to make the orange cream, lightly whip the cream with the orange juice.

3 Transfer the figs to warmed serving plates and spoon over some of the juices. Serve warm, with the orange cream and accompanied by the Orange Sablés.

Elaine Bates

Orange Sablés

100 g (3½ oz) butter
1 egg yolk
110 g (4½ oz) plain flour
50 g (2 oz) icing sugar
finely grated rind of 1 orange
10 ml (2 tsp) orange juice (approximately)

1 Place all the ingredients, except the orange juice, in a food processor and process quickly until smooth. Add enough of the orange juice to bind the dough. Wrap in cling film and chill in the freezer for 30 minutes.

2 Roll out the dough on a lightly floured surface to a 5 mm (¼ inch) thickness and cut into 5 cm (2 inch) rounds. Place on a lightly greased baking sheet and bake in a preheated oven at 190°C (375°F) for 6-8 minutes until light golden. Cool on a wire rack.

Elaine Bates

Peppered Pineapple flambéed in Kirsch served with a Pineapple Sorbet

Pineapple Sorbet:
1 large or 2 medium pineapples, to give 675 g (1½ lb) peeled and cored weight
275 ml (9 fl oz) stock syrup (see right)
juice of ½ lemon

Pineapple Flambé:
1 medium pineapple
freshly ground black pepper
25 g (1 oz) unsalted butter
50 ml (2 fl oz) kirsch

To Decorate:
16 angelica diamonds
Spun Sugar (optional – see right)

1 To make the sorbet, top and tail the pineapple, then peel away the skin, removing the brown 'eyes'. Quarter, core and cut up into chunks. Put in a food processor with the stock syrup and lemon juice. Process until smooth and creamy, then pass through a nylon sieve into a bowl. Transfer to an ice-cream machine and churn according to the manufacturer's instructions for about 25 minutes until firm.

2 Transfer to a plastic freezerproof container, cover and place in the freezer until ready to serve. If you do not have an ice-cream maker, freeze the sorbet in a suitable container, whisking several times during freezing to break down the ice crystals and ensure an even-textured result.

3 For the pineapple flambé, put 4 large serving plates in the freezer to chill. Top and tail the pineapple, then peel away the skin, making sure you remove the brown 'eyes'. Cut into slices, about 1 cm (½ inch) thick. Cut out the central core from each slice, then sprinkle with a little black pepper. Heat the butter in a frying pan and, when hot, add the pineapple slices to heat through and colour slightly. Pour over the kirsch and immediately set alight. Once the flames have died down, the dish can be assembled.

4 To serve, place a pineapple slice in the centre of each large chilled serving plate and spoon a little of the pan juices into the hollow. Place 4 scoops or quenelles of sorbet around the plate. Position angelica diamonds in between. For an elegant presentation, top the pineapple slices with spun sugar to resemble angel's hair.

Gill Tunkle

Stock Syrup: Put 100 g (3½ oz) granulated sugar and 250 ml (8 fl oz) water in a heavy-based saucepan and dissolve over a low heat. Bring to the boil and boil steadily for 2 minutes. Cool and use as required.

Spun Sugar: Dissolve 250 g (9 oz) caster sugar in 90 ml (6 tbsp) water in a heavy-based pan over a low heat, then bring to the boil. Add 50 ml (2 fl oz) liquid glucose and cook the syrup to a pale caramel; ie until it registers 165°C (330°F) on a sugar thermometer. Take off the heat and leave to rest for 2 minutes. Hold 2 forks back to back, dip into the syrup, then quickly trickle the threads to and fro over a sheet of non-stick baking parchment to form spun sugar, or angel's hair. Use within 1 hour or keep in an airtight container with a drying agent. Do not leave in a humid atmosphere.

Serpent Cake with Oranges and Coconut Cream

Cake:
2 large sheets of filo pastry
1 egg
icing sugar, for dredging
ground cinnamon, for dusting

Filling:
225 g (8 oz) ground almonds
125 g (4 oz) icing sugar
30 ml (2 tbsp) orange flower water
15 ml (1 tbsp) water
60-90 ml (4-6 tbsp) melted butter, cooled
2.5 ml (½ tsp) almond essence
2.5 ml (½ tsp) vanilla essence
finely grated rind of ½ orange (optional)

Oranges:
2 large oranges (preferably blood oranges)
few drops of orange flower water

Coconut Cream:
25-50 g (1-2 oz) creamed coconut
150 ml (¼ pint) double cream
Cointreau, to taste

1 To make the cake filling, combine the ground almonds, icing sugar, orange flower water, water and cooled melted butter in a bowl. Add the almond and vanilla essences and, if desired, the finely grated orange zest. Mix well, knead to a smooth paste, then cover and chill.

2 Divide the chilled almond paste into 4 pieces and roll out each piece to a long sausage, 1cm (½ inch) in diameter.

3 Cut each sheet of filo pastry in half lengthwise. Lay out one pastry strip and place a filling 'sausage' along the bottom long edge. Roll up tightly. Repeat with the remaining filo and 'sausages'.

4 Line a baking sheet with non-stick baking parchment. Starting at the centre of the baking sheet, arrange the filo-covered 'sausages' in a tight spiral to resemble a coiled snake.

5 Brush with beaten egg and bake in a preheated oven at 180°C (350°F) mark 4 for about 10 minutes until the pastry is crisp and golden. Turn the filo cake over and bake for a further 10 minutes until the top is crisp and golden.

6 Transfer to a wire rack, dredge with icing sugar and decorate with fine lines of cinnamon.

7 Peel and carefully segment the oranges, over a bowl to catch the juice. Add a few drops of orange flower water and chill thoroughly.

8 Heat the coconut cream very gently until melted, adding a little water if necesary. Stir in the double cream and Cointreau to taste. Mix well; cool. The mixture may seem a bit sloppy at this stage but it will thicken on cooling.

9 Serve the serpent cake warm or cold. Slice and place on serving plates, with a fan of orange segments and a dollop of coconut cream.

Sue Longden

Raspberry and Cinnamon Torte with Raspberry Sauce

150 g (5 oz) soft margarine
150 g (5 oz) caster sugar
150 g (5 oz) ground almonds
150 g (5 oz) self-raising flour
5 ml (1 tsp) ground cinnamon
1 egg
225 g (8 oz) raspberries

Raspberry Sauce:
225 g (8 oz) raspberries
15 ml (1 tbsp) icing sugar
5 ml (1 tsp) lemon juice

To Serve:
icing sugar and ground cinnamon, for dusting
whipped cream and Greek yogurt

1 Place the margarine, caster sugar, ground almonds, flour, cinnamon and egg in a bowl. Beat thoroughly to mix.

2 Spread half of the mixture in a greased and base-lined 22 cm (8½ inch) spring-release cake tin and flatten slightly, using a fork. Sprinkle the raspberries over the mixture and dot the remaining torte mixture on top so that it almost covers the fruit.

3 Stand the tin on a baking sheet and bake in a preheated oven at 180°C (350°F) mark 4 for about 45 minutes, covering lightly with foil if the top is becoming too brown. When cooked, the torte will feel just firm and slightly springy. Leave in the tin to cool for about 1 hour.

4 Meanwhile prepare the raspberry sauce. Purée the raspberries in a food processor or blender with the icing sugar and lemon juice, then seive to remove the pips.

5 Turn out the cooled torte and dust with icing sugar sifted with cinnamon. Serve warm, accompanied by the raspberry sauce and cream mixed with yogurt.

Daphne Nelson

Caramelised Rice Pudding and Pears with a Gingered Caramel Sauce

Rice Pudding:
115 g (4½ oz) pudding rice
600 ml (1 pint) milk
½ vanilla pod, split
115 g (4½ oz) caster sugar

Poached Pears:
4 William pears
1 vanilla pod, split
125 g (4 oz) caster sugar
15 ml (1 tbsp) lemon juice
caster sugar, for sprinkling

Custard:
4 egg yolks
15 g (½ oz) caster sugar
175 ml (6 fl oz) milk
½ vanilla pod, split

Caramel:
50 g (2 oz) caster sugar

Ginger Sauce:
2.5 cm (1 inch) piece fresh root ginger, peeled and chopped
150 g (5 oz) caster sugar
40 g (1½ oz) unsalted butter

1 To make the rice pudding, blanch the rice in boiling water for 2 minutes, then drain. Put the milk and vanilla pod in a heavy-based pan and bring to the boil. Add the rice and sugar, stir well and simmer for 30 minutes. Strain through a sieve.

2 Peel and core the pears. Put them in a pan, add water to cover, then add the vanilla pod, caster sugar and lemon juice. Bring to the boil, lower the heat and gently poach the pears for 20 minutes or until tender. Leave the pears to cool in the syrup.

3 Meanwhile make the custard, whisk the egg yolks with the sugar in a bowl until pale and creamy. Put the milk and vanilla pod in a saucepan and bring to the boil. Remove from the heat and allow to cool, then whisk into the egg mixture. Strain through a sieve into a bowl and stir in the rice.

4 To prepare the caramel, put the sugar in a small pan with 30 (2 tbsp) water over a low heat until dissolved, then boil steadily until the syrup turns golden brown. Immediately pour the caramel into the base of the pudding moulds.

5 Divide the rice and custard mixture between the moulds, place in a roasting tin containing enough water to come halfway up the sides of the moulds. Bake in a preheated oven at 180°C (350°F) mark 4 for 25 minutes or until set.

6 Meanwhile to make the ginger sauce, put the ginger and sugar in a small pan with 30 ml (2 tbsp) water. Place over a low heat until the sugar is dissolved, then cook until the syrup caramelises. Carefully add the butter and a further 75-90 ml (5-6 tbsp) water a little at a time. Heat gently, stirring, then strain.

7 Cut the pears into thin slices and place on a baking sheet. Sprinkle liberally with caster sugar. Put under a very hot grill to caramelise the sugar. (Alternatively you can use a blow torch.)

8 To serve, unmould a rice pudding on to the centre of each warmed serving plate. Surround with the pear slices and gingered caramel sauce.

Alastair Hendy

Bread and Butter Pudding with Rum and Prunes

6 slices buttered bread
butter, for spreading
350 ml (12 fl oz) single cream
60 ml (4 tbsp) dark rum
few drops of vanilla essence
6 egg yolks
50 g (2 oz) caster sugar
50 g (2 oz) no-soak prunes, stoned and diced

Raspberry Coulis:
175 g (6 oz) raspberries
10 ml (2 tsp) icing sugar
10 ml (2 tsp) lemon juice
10 ml (2 tsp) orange juice

Rum Sabayon:
6 egg yolks
50 g (2 oz) caster sugar
60 ml (4 tbsp) rum
120 ml (4 fl oz) whipping cream, lightly whipped

1 Butter the bread, discard the crusts, then cut into 2.5 cm (1 inch) squares.

2 Heat the cream, rum and vanilla in a saucepan to just below boiling point, then remove from the heat. In a bowl, beat the egg yolks and sugar together until pale then gradually add the cream, whisking all the time. Strain through a fine sieve.

3 Layer the bread and prunes in 4 buttered ramekins. Pour in the cream to saturate the bread. Leave to stand for about 30 minutes.

4 Place the ramekins in a bainmarie (or roasting tin containing enough hot water to come halfway up the sides of the ramekins). Bake in a preheated oven at 180°C (350°F) mark 4 for 35-40 minutes.

5 Meanwhile to make the raspberry coulis, purée the raspberries with the icing sugar and lemon and orange juices in a blender or food processor. Pass through a sieve to remove the seeds.

6 To make the rum sabayon, put the egg yolks, sugar and rum in a large heatproof bowl over a pan of hot water and whisk until thick and creamy. Remove from the pan and whisk until cool; then fold in the whipped cream.

7 To serve, turn the bread and butter puddings out of the ramekins and place on individual serving plates with a portion of the rum sabayon. Serve accompanied by the raspberry coulis.

Michael Baxter

Cranberry and Orange Charlotte

2 oranges
225 g (8 oz) cranberries
125 g (4 oz) sugar, or to taste
6 cardamom pods, seeds only – crushed
1 brioche loaf
125 g (4 oz) unsalted butter, melted

To Serve:
icing sugar, for dusting
a little fromage frais
finely pared orange rind, shredded (simmered in sugar syrup, if preferred)

1 Finely grate the rind from 1 orange, then squeeze the juice. Peel and segment the other orange, discarding all white pith.

2 Put the cranberries and sugar in a saucepan with 150 ml (¼ pint) water. Add the grated orange rind and crushed cardamom seeds. Heat gently until the sugar is dissolved, then simmer for 10 minutes. Taste for sweetness, adding a little more sugar if necessary. Transfer half of the mixture to a blender or food processor and work until smooth, then press through a sieve into a bowl. Stir in the orange juice to make a coulis; set aside.

3 Add the orange segments to the other half of the cranberry mixture.

4 To assemble the charlottes, you will need 4 individual round tins or individual pudding moulds, about 200 ml (7 fl oz) in capacity. Cut thin slices from the brioche loaf. From these, cut 8 circles to fit the base and top of the moulds. Dip 4 brioche circles into the melted butter and fit into the base of the tins. Cut thin strips of brioche to line the sides of the tin, dip in melted butter and position around the insides of the tins. Fill with the cranberry and orange segment mixture. Dip the remaining brioche circles in butter and position on top.

5 Place on a baking sheet and bake in a preheated oven at 200°C (400°F) mark 6 for 25 minutes or until crisp and well browned. Carefully remove the charlottes from the tins.

6 Transfer to individual plates and dust with icing sugar. Surround with the coulis, dot with fromage frais and feather with a skewer. Decorate with orange rind shreds and serve immediately.

Mary Wilde

Black Cherry Clafoutis with Vanilla Ice Cream

Vanilla Ice Cream:
2 plump vanilla pods
250 ml (8 fl oz) milk
1 coffee bean, crushed
3 egg yolks (size 1)
70 g (2½ oz) caster sugar
125 ml (4 fl oz) double cream

Clafoutis:
2 eggs (size 1)
100 g (3½ oz) caster sugar
60 ml (4 tbsp) plain flour, sifted
pinch of salt
100 g (3½ oz) crème fraîche
100 ml (3½ fl oz) milk
15 ml (1 tbsp) kirsch
5 ml (1 tsp) vanilla extract
300 g (10 oz) bottled black cherries preserved in kirsch

Cherry Sauce:
375 ml (13 fl oz) red wine (preferably Syrah or Shiraz)
600 g (1 lb 5 oz) cherry compote
1-2 mint sprigs
icing sugar, to taste

1 To make the ice cream, split the vanilla pods open, scoop out the seeds and set aside. Pour the milk into a heavy-based saucepan, add the vanilla pods and coffee bean and bring slowly to the boil. Remove from the heat and set aside to infuse for 15 minutes. Meanwhile, beat the egg yolks, sugar and vanilla seeds together in a bowl until pale and creamy. Bring the milk back to the boil and pour through a sieve onto the egg mixture, stirring constantly. Return to the pan and cook over a low heat until the custard is thick enough to coat the back of a wooden spoon; about 3-5 minutes. Remove from the heat.

2 Stir the cream into the custard, allow to cool, then refrigerate for 1 hour. Transfer to an ice-cream maker and churn until thick. Turn into a freezerproof container and store in the freezer until required.

3 Butter a 22 cm (8½ inch) round ceramic baking dish for the clafoutis. Put the eggs in a bowl and whisk, using an electric beater until frothy. Add the sugar, flour, salt, crème fraîche, milk, kirsch and vanilla extract. Mix thoroughly for about 2 minutes. Allow to stand for 10 minutes.

4 Spread the cherries in a single layer in the buttered dish. Pour in the batter. Bake in a preheated oven at 200°C (400°F) mark 6 for 30-40 minutes until risen and golden.

5 Meanwhile, make the sauce. Bring the wine to the boil in a small saucepan and reduce by half. Add the cherry compote and bring to the boil. Remove from the heat, add the mint and leave to infuse for 10 minutes. Add a little icing sugar if needed; the sauce should be slightly sour.

6 Serve the clafoutis with the cherry sauce and vanilla ice cream.

Neil Haidar

Warm Chocolate and Ginger Puddings with Caramelised Pears

150 g (5 oz) quality plain chocolate (Lindt Excellence or Valrhona)
15 g (½ oz) unsalted butter
3 eggs (size 2), separated
7.5 ml (1½ tsp) chopped preserved stem ginger in syrup, drained
15 ml (1 tbsp) Calvados
45 ml (3 tbsp) caster sugar

Custard:
250 ml (8 fl oz) full-cream milk
1 vanilla pod
3 egg yolks
25 g (1 oz) caster sugar

Caramelised Pears:
1 firm, ripe pear
15 g (½ oz) clarified butter
15 ml (1 tbsp) brown sugar

1 Butter 4 ramekins and dredge with caster sugar to prevent the puddings from sticking.

2 Melt the chocolate with the butter in a heatproof bowl over a pan of hot water, then allow to cool. Stir the egg yolks, chopped ginger and Calvados into the cooled melted chocolate.

3 In a separate bowl, whisk the egg whites until they form soft peaks, then whisk in the sugar. Add a spoonful to the chocolate mixture to loosen it, then carefully fold the chocolate into the remaining whisked egg white mixture, retaining as much volume as possible.

4 Spoon the mixture into the ramekins, cover with cling film and refrigerate for at least 1½ hours.

5 Remove the cling film and place the ramekins on a baking tray. Bake in a preheated oven at 220°C (425°F) mark 7 for 15 minutes. Transfer the ramekins to a wire rack and leave to stand for 10 minutes.

6 In the meantime, make the vanilla custard. Pour the milk into a heavy-based pan, add the vanilla pod and bring to the boil. Lower the heat and simmer for about 5 minutes, then remove the pan from the heat and set aside for 5-10 minutes to infuse. Meanwhile, beat the egg yolks and sugar together in a bowl until pale and smooth. Pour on the hot milk, whisking constantly.

7 Return the custard to the pan and cook over a low heat, stirring constantly with a wooden spoon until it is thick enough to coat the back of the spoon. Do not allow to boil or it will curdle. Quickly strain the custard through a fine sieve into a cold bowl, stirring to prevent further cooking.

8 For the caramelised pear, peel, halve and core the pear, then slice lengthwise. Heat the butter in a frying pan, then add the pear slices and sugar. Cook over a high heat, turning frequently, until caramelised.

9 To serve, turn the puddings out onto warmed serving plates. Serve with the caramelised pears and vanilla custard.

Neil Haidar

Note: If preferred the custard can be made in advance, quickly cooled by standing the bowl over a large bowl filled with ice, then refrigerated until needed. Cover the surface with a piece of dampened greaseproof paper to prevent a skin forming. Warm through gently to serve.

Warm Apricot and Almond Soufflés, with Apricot and Amaretto Ice Cream

Ice Cream:
450 g (1 lb) fresh or canned apricots
100 g (4 oz) caster sugar
2 egg yolks
90 ml (3 fl oz) single cream
40 ml (1½ tbsp) Amaretto liqueur
90 ml (3 fl oz) double cream

Soufflés:
25 g (1 oz) ground almonds
finely grated zest and juice of 1 lime
75 g (3 oz) caster sugar
2 eggs (size 4 or 5), separated
90 ml (3 fl oz) double cream
25 g (1 oz) self-raising flour, sifted
1 fresh apricot, skinned, halved and stoned, or 2 canned halves, chopped
25 ml (1½ tbsp) flaked almonds

To Decorate:
15 ml (1 tbsp) flaked almonds, toasted and crushed
icing sugar, for dusting
blackcurrant sprigs
candied lime zest shreds (see note)

1 To make the ice cream, skin, halve and stone the fresh apricots if using. Roughly chop the apricots and place in a saucepan with 300 ml (½ pint) water and 25 g (1 oz) of the sugar. Bring to a simmer and cook gently until soft. Drain and press through a sieve into a bowl; let cool.

2 In a bowl, whisk the egg yolks with the remaining 75 g (3 oz) sugar until creamy. Put the single cream in a saucepan and slowly bring to the boil. Gradually pour onto the egg mixture, stirring. Let cool. Stir in the apricot purée and liqueur.

3 In another bowl, whip the double cream until it forms soft peaks, then fold into the apricot mixture until thoroughly incorporated. Transfer to an ice-cream maker and freeze according to the manufacturer's directions. (If you do not have an ice-cream maker, freeze in a shallow container, beating two or three times during freezing to break down the ice crystals and ensure an even-textured result.)

4 To prepare the soufflés, mix the ground almonds and grated lime zest together in a bowl. Beat in the sugar, egg yolks, cream and flour. Add the chopped apricot, flaked almonds and lime juice.

5 In another bowl, whisk the egg whites until soft peaks form. Stir half into the almond and apricot mixture to lighten it, then carefully fold in the rest.

6 Divide between 4 buttered individual pudding basins. Stand in a roasting tin containing enough hot water to come two-thirds of the way up the sides of the basins. Bake in a preheated oven at 180°C (350°F) mark 4 for 50-55 minutes until risen and lightly browned. If the tops appear to be browning too quickly during baking, cover with discs of greaseproof paper.

7 Turn the puddings out onto individual serving plates, sprinkle with the crushed toasted almonds and dust with icing sugar. Decorate with the blackcurrants and candied lime zest. Serve with the ice cream.

Louise Halfhide

Note: To prepare the candied lime zest, remove strips of lime zest from 1 lime, using a zester, and cut into shreds. Place in a saucepan with 150 ml (¼ pint) water and 25 g (1 oz) sugar. Heat gently until the sugar is dissolved, then simmer for 5-7 minutes. Remove with a slotted spoon and drain.

Gingerbread Soufflé

175 g (6 oz) unsalted butter
175 g (6 oz) plain flour
250 ml (8 fl oz) milk
125 ml (4 fl oz) double cream
5 egg yolks (size 2)
225 g (8 oz) soft dark brown sugar
15 ml (1 tbsp) ground ginger
5 ml (1 tsp) ground cinnamon
2.5 ml (½ tsp) ground nutmeg
1.25 ml (¼ tsp) ground cloves
30 ml (2 tbsp) crystallised ginger, diced
7 egg whites (size 2)

To Decorate:
pieces of crystallised ginger

1 Butter 4 individual soufflé dishes, about 10 cm (4 inches) in diameter.

2 Melt the butter in a heavy-based saucepan. Whisk in the flour and cook, stirring, for 1 minute. Gradually stir in the milk and cream. Cook, stirring constantly, until thickened and smooth. Remove from the heat and let cool slightly for about 1 minute.

3 Add the egg yolks, one at a time, whisking well after each addition. Whisk in the brown sugar, breaking up any lumps, and continue whisking until the mixture is smooth. Stir in the ground ginger, cinnamon, nutmeg and cloves, then stir in the crystallised ginger.

4 Whisk the egg whites in a bowl until stiff but not dry. Fold into the soufflé base and pour into the individual soufflé dishes. Bake in a preheated oven at 200°C (400°F) mark 6 for 20-25 minutes until slightly puffed and lightly golden. Place each soufflé dish on a serving plate and scatter pieces of crystallised ginger on the plate to decorate. Serve immediately.

Charlotte Bircher

Hot Passion Fruit Soufflé

2 egg yolks
150 g (5 oz) caster sugar
4 egg whites
finely grated rind of ½ lemon

Sauce:
12 passion fruit
65 g (2½ oz) caster sugar
juice of ½ lemon
juice of 1 orange

To Finish:
icing sugar, for dusting

1 First make the sauce. Cut the passion fruit in half and scoop out the pulp and seeds. Strain and reserve 30 ml (2 tbsp) juice. Put the rest of the pulp and seeds in a pan with the sugar, lemon and orange juices and 5 ml (1 tsp) water. Bring to the boil and simmer for 2 minutes. Strain through a sieve and set aside.

2 Place a roasting tin half-filled with hot water in a preheated oven at 220°C (425°F) mark 7 to heat. Grease a 12 cm (5 inch) soufflé dish with melted butter and sprinkle lightly with caster sugar.

3 In a bowl, beat the egg yolks with half of the sugar until pale and fluffy. In another bowl, whisk the egg whites with half of the remaining sugar until they start to thicken. Add the rest of the sugar and whisk to a soft peak consistency.

4 Mix 30 ml (2 tbsp) of the passion fruit syrup (not the reserved juice) with the grated lemon rind. Stir into the egg yolk mixture. Fold in one third of the whisked egg whites; lightly fold in the remainder.

5 Pour the mixture into the prepared soufflé dish and place in the roasting tin. Bake for 10-15 minutes until risen and brown.

6 To serve, add the reserved passion fruit juice to the passion fruit syrup. Heat gently to warm through. When the soufflé is ready, dust with icing sugar and serve immediately, with the warm passion fruit sauce.

Timothy Stokes

Raspberry Surprise

Whisked Sponge:
50 g (2 oz) plain flour
pinch of salt
2 eggs (size 2)
65 g (2½ oz) caster sugar

Topping:
225 g (8 oz) raspberries (fresh or frozen and defrosted)
300 ml (½ pint) soured cream
75 g (3 oz) caster sugar

To Decorate:
100 g (3½ oz) good quality plain dark chocolate
300 ml (½ pint) double cream
5 ml (1 tsp) caster sugar

1 To make the whisked sponge, line two 15 cm (6 inch) round cake tins with non-stick baking parchment. Sift the flour and salt together; set aside. Put the eggs into a mixing bowl and beat in the sugar.

2 Place the bowl over a saucepan, one-third full of boiling water, making sure the bowl does not touch the water. Using an electric hand whisk, whisk the eggs and sugar together until the mixture is thick, light in colour and significantly increased in volume; this will take at least 5 minutes. Remove the bowl from the pan. Lightly fold the flour into the mixture, using a metal spoon.

3 Divide the mixture between the prepared cake tins. Bake in a preheated oven at 190°C (375°F) mark 5 for about 20 minutes, until well risen and golden brown. Turn out and cool on a wire rack. (You will only need to use one of the sponges for this dessert, so freeze the other one for another occasion.)

4 Line four individual 7.5-10 cm (3-4 inch) round tins with non-stick baking parchment. Slice the sponge horizontally into two layers, then cut into smaller pieces and use to cover the base of the tins. Scatter the raspberries over the sponge, reserving a few for decoration.

5 Stir the soured cream and sugar together, then pour over the raspberries. Bake in a preheated oven at 180°C (350°F) mark 4 for 25 minutes until set. Allow to cool in the tins.

6 Meanwhile make the chocolate scrolls. Break the chocolate into pieces and place in a small bowl over a pan of hot water until melted. Stir until smooth, then pour onto a clean flat surface, preferably a marble slab, and allow to cool and set. Hold a long-bladed knife in both hands and push the blade away from you along the surface of the chocolate to shave off long scrolls.

7 To finish, carefully remove the desserts from their tins and place on individual serving plates. Whip the double cream with the 5 ml (1 tsp) caster sugar and spread over the top of the desserts. Decorate with the dark chocolate scrolls and reserved raspberries.

Alison Fiander

Individual Summer Puddings with a Raspberry Coulis

175 g (6 oz) caster sugar
350 ml (12 fl oz) water
1 vanilla pod
225 g (8 oz) raspberries
icing sugar, to taste
450 g (1 lb) mixed summer berries (eg strawberries, raspberries, blackberries, redcurrants), thawed if frozen
1 day-old thin sliced white loaf, crusts removed

To Decorate:
fresh berries
mint leaves

To Serve:
crème fraîche

1 Line four 150-175 ml (5-6 fl oz) individual pudding moulds with cling film, leaving a generous overhang. Place the sugar, water and vanilla pod in a saucepan. Heat slowly, stirring occasionally until the sugar has dissolved; set aside to infuse and cool slightly.

2 Crush the raspberries in a bowl, using a potato masher. Press through a fine nylon sieve into another bowl to remove the seeds. Add half of the puréed raspberries to the syrup with the berries. Heat gently for no longer than 5 minutes until the softest berries are just cooked. Remove from the heat.

3 Sweeten the rest of the raspberries with a little icing sugar to taste and set aside for the coulis.

4 Cut 4 rounds of bread to fit the base of the moulds, and 4 rounds to fit the tops. Shape the rest of the bread to fit the sides.

5 Remove the berries from the syrup with a slotted spoon and place in a bowl; set aside. Dip the shaped bread into the syrup to soak through, then use to line the base and sides of the moulds, reserving the 4 rounds for the tops.

6 Spoon the berries into the moulds so they are slightly overfilled. Position the tops and press down gently. Fold over the cling film to cover each pudding. Chill in the refrigerator for 1½-2 hours.

7 To serve, unmould each pudding on to a serving plate. Spoon the reserved raspberry coulis alongside. Decorate with fresh berries and mint. Serve with a generous spoonful of crème fraîche.

Simon Jackson

Japonais with Brandy Cream and Espresso Sauce

Meringue:
4 egg whites (size 3)
150 g (5 oz) caster sugar
100 g (3½ oz) roasted almonds, finely ground
25 g (1 oz) cornflour
50 g (2 oz) icing sugar, sifted

Praline:
50 g (2 oz) sugar
50 g (2 oz) whole almonds, roasted

Brandy Cream:
30 ml (2 tbsp) crab apple jelly (or other fairly sharp fruit jelly)
50 g (2 oz) white marzipan, in small pieces
90 ml (3 fl oz) brandy
150 ml (¼ pint) whipping cream

Espresso Sauce:
30 ml (2 tbsp) unsalted butter
45 ml (3 tbsp) golden caster sugar
75 ml (5 tbsp) whipping cream
45 ml (3 tbsp) freshly made strong espresso coffee

1 For the meringue, whisk the egg whites in a large bowl until firm peaks form, then whisk in the caster sugar, a little at a time. When all the sugar has been added, the meringue should be glossy and stand in firm peaks. Gently fold in the ground almonds, cornflour and icing sugar.

2 Line two 30 x 20 cm (12 x 8 inch) Swiss roll tins with non-stick baking parchment and divide the meringue between the tins, spreading it gently and evenly. Bake in a preheated oven at 180°C (350°F) mark 4 for about 30 minutes until golden and just firm. Invert onto a wire rack, carefully peel off the lining paper and leave to cool.

3 To make the praline, place the sugar and almonds in a heavy-based pan over a low heat until the sugar melts and turns nut brown. Immediately remove from heat and pour into a shallow oiled baking tin. Let cool until set hard, then break into pieces. Reserve a few caramel shreds for decoration. Grind the rest of the praline in a food processor or blender; set aside.

4 To prepare the brandy cream, melt the jelly in a small pan. Take off the heat and beat in the marzipan, a piece at a time, until smooth. Beat in the brandy and leave to cool in the refrigerator. Whip the cream, then gently fold in the brandy mixture.

5 To make the espresso sauce, melt the butter in a small heavy-based pan. Add the sugar and stir over a low heat until dissolved. Add the cream, bring to the boil and boil steadily for 5 minutes. Add the coffee and boil again until the sauce is a light syrupy consistency. Take off the heat and allow to cool to room temperature. If the sauce thickens too much on cooling, stir in a little more coffee to thin.

6 When the meringue is completely cold, transfer to a board and cut out twelve 9 cm (3½ inch) rounds, using a sharp metal cutter. To assemble the japonais, for each serving sandwich 3 meringue rounds together with brandy cream, making sure the cream extends to the edge of the rounds. Smooth the sides and spread a little cream on the top.

7 To finish, cut 3 strips of greaseproof paper about 5 mm (¼ inch) wide and lay parallel on top of each tower. Sprinkle with crushed praline, then carefully lift off the strips of paper to leave a pattern. Place on large serving plates with a spoonful of espresso sauce. Decorate with shreds of caramel.

Marian Freeman

Chocolate and Orange Squares with a Dark Chocolate Coating and Piquant Orange Sauce

Chocolate Sponge:
80 g (3 oz) unsalted butter
65 g (2½ oz) caster sugar
1½ egg yolks
40 g (1½ oz) plain chocolate, melted
30 ml (2 tbsp) double cream
80 g (3 oz) self-raising flour, sifted
0.75 ml (⅛ tsp) baking powder
1½ egg whites

Chocolate Sauce:
25 ml (5 tsp) double cream
10 g (⅓ oz) unsalted butter
55 g (2 oz) dark plain chocolate, broken into small pieces

Orange Sauce:
juice and grated zest of 2 oranges
juice of ⅓ lemon
55 g (2 oz) caster sugar
5 ml (1 tsp) cornflour, mixed with 15 ml (1 tbsp) cold water
20 g (¾ oz) unsalted butter
20 ml (4 tsp) malt whisky

To Assemble:
40 ml (2½ tbsp) orange marmalade
few julienne strips of orange zest, to decorate

1 For the chocolate sponge, line a 12 cm (5 inch) square tin with non-stick baking parchment. Beat the butter and caster sugar together in a large bowl until light and fluffy. Add the egg yolks, melted chocolate, double cream, flour and baking powder and mix thoroughly. In a separate bowl, whisk the egg whites until they form soft peaks, then carefully fold into the cake mixture. Pour into the prepared tin and bake in a preheated oven at 180°C (350°F) mark 4 for about 20 minutes until cooked. Turn out onto a wire rack to cool.

2 For the chocolate sauce, put the cream and butter in a small saucepan and bring to the boil. Remove from the heat, immediately add the chocolate and stir until melted. Keep warm.

3 For the orange sauce, put the orange juice and zest, and the lemon juice into a saucepan. Add the sugar, stir until dissolved, then bring to the boil. Remove from the heat and stir in the blended cornflour. Return to the heat and cook, stirring constantly, until the sauce is thickened. Cook for a further 1 minute. Stir in the butter, then the whisky. Taste and add a little more sugar if necessary. Remove from the heat.

4 To assemble the dessert, trim the edges of the sponge, then cut into four 5 cm (2 inch) squares. Slice each square horizontally into three layers and sandwich together with the marmalade. Place each square in the centre of a serving plate. Pour on the chocolate sauce to coat the top of the sponge and drizzle slightly over the edges. Pour the orange sauce around the chocolate squares. Decorate with orange zest julienne and serve immediately.

Andrew Whiteley

Lemon Genoese with a Lemon Cream Filling and Lemon Curd Sauce

Lemon Curd Sauce:
grated rind and juice of 1 lemon
25 g (1 oz) unsalted butter
50 g (2 oz) caster sugar
1 egg, beaten
20 ml (4 tsp) lemon liqueur

Genoese Sponge:
1½ eggs (size 3), beaten
35 g (1¼ oz) caster sugar
grated zest of 1 lemon
35 g (1¼ oz) plain flour, sifted
10 g (⅓ oz) unsalted butter, melted and cooled until only just warm

Lemon Cream Filling:
juice of ½ lemon
1 gelatine leaf
100 ml (3½ fl oz) crème fraîche
50 g (2 oz) caster sugar

To Decorate:
25 g (1 oz) plain dark chocolate
blanched lemon zest shreds

1 First make the lemon curd sauce. Put the lemon rind and juice, butter and caster sugar in a heatproof bowl over a pan of hot water until melted. Stir to mix thoroughly, then add the egg and stir with a wooden spoon until the mixture is thick enough to coat the back of the spoon. Remove from the heat and add the lemon liqueur. Set aside.

2 To make the sponge, whisk the eggs and sugar together in a large bowl over a pan of hot water, until the mixture is pale and thick enough to leave a ribbon trail when the beaters are lifted. Remove the bowl from the pan and continue whisking until the mixture is cool. Whisk in the grated lemon zest. Lightly fold in the flour. Pour in the butter around the edge of the bowl, and carefully fold in. Immediately pour into four lined ramekin dishes, 7.5 cm (3 inches) in diameter. Cook in a preheated oven at 190°C (375°F) mark 5 for approximately 5-8 minutes, until risen and just firm. Turn out onto a wire rack to cool.

3 For the lemon cream filling, warm the lemon juice, add the gelatine leaf and leave to soften. Mix the crème fraîche and sugar together in a bowl. Pass the gelatine and lemon juice mixture through a sieve into the bowl and mix thoroughly with the sweetened crème fraîche. Set aside to cool and thicken.

4 For the decoration, melt the chocolate in a heatproof bowl over a pan of hot water. Place the melted chocolate in a greaseproof paper piping bag and pipe a circle, about 6 cm (2½ inches) in diameter, on one side of each serving plate.

5 Using a 5 cm (2 inch) pastry cutter, cut out the centre of each sponge, then trim off ¾ cm (½ inch) from the base of these centres and discard. Dip the sponge centres into the lemon liqueur, then replace within the sponge rings.

6 Fill the sponge centres with lemon cream filling and decorate with lemon zest shreds. Carefully position a sponge on each plate next to the chocolate ring and fill the rings with the lemon curd sauce. Serve immediately.

Andrew Whiteley

Orange, Almond and Polenta Cake with Caramel Sauce

200 g (7 oz) unsalted butter
180 g (6 oz) caster sugar
200 g (7 oz) ground almonds
5 ml (1 tsp) vanilla extract
3 large eggs (size 1)
finely grated zest of 3 oranges
juice of ½ orange
100 g (3½ oz) polenta
3.75 ml (¾ tsp) baking powder

Caramel Sauce:
100 g (3½ oz) caster sugar
200 ml (7 fl oz) double cream

To Serve:
crème fraîche

1 Butter and flour a 20 cm (8 inch) loose-bottomed cake tin.

2 Cream the butter and sugar together in a bowl, using an electric mixer, until pale and fluffy. Stir in the ground almonds and vanilla, then beat in the eggs, one at a time. Add the orange zest and juice, polenta and baking powder; mix thoroughly.

3 Pour into the prepared cake tin and bake in a preheated oven at 160°C (325°F) mark 3 for 50 minutes to 1 hour, until set. Allow to cool slightly, then remove from the tin and transfer to a wire rack to cool.

4 To make the caramel sauce, melt the sugar in a small heavy-based pan over a gentle heat, then increase the heat and cook to a deep caramel. Remove from heat and whisk in the cream, taking care as the hot caramel will splutter. Reheat if necessary.

5 Serve the polenta cake warm or cool, with the caramel sauce and crème fraîche.

Neil Haidar

Italian Rice Creams with Cranberry Purée

600 ml (1 pint) milk
50 g (2 oz) caster sugar
1.25 ml (¼ tsp) freshly grated nutmeg
4 strips lemon zest
50 g (2 oz) Arborio rice
90 ml (3 fl oz) whipping cream
1 gelatine leaf
1 egg yolk (size 4 or 5)
15 g (½ oz) butter
1-2 drops of vanilla extract

Cranberry Purée:
225 g (8 oz) cranberries
40 g (1½ oz) caster sugar (approximately)

To Decorate:
mint leaves

1 Pour the milk into a saucepan. Add the sugar, nutmeg and lemon zest, stir well and bring to a simmer.

2 Add the rice and stir again. Turn the heat down to its lowest setting, cover and simmer for 40-50 minutes, stirring occasionally.

3 About 10 minutes before the end of the cooking time, pour the cream into a jug and add the gelatine leaf. Leave to soften.

4 When the rice is ready, add the egg yolk, butter and vanilla extract. Heat through, stirring, for 2 minutes. Take off the heat, add the cream mixture and stir until the gelatine is dissolved.

5 Pour the mixture into greased individual ring moulds or ramekin dishes and leave to cool completely. Cover with cling film and chill in the refrigerator for at least 1½ hours until set.

6 To make the cranberry purée, put the cranberries and sugar in a saucepan and cook gently until soft. Taste and add a little more sugar if required. Transfer to a blender or food processor and work until smooth. Pass through a sieve into a bowl, cover and chill until required.

7 To serve, run a palette knife around the edge of each rice cream and turn out onto a serving plate; it may be necessary to give the mould a firm shake. Spoon the cranberry purée around the rice creams and decorate with mint leaves.

Judith Elliott

Chilled Bread and Butter Pudding with Fruits and a Bramble Coulis

10 slices white bread (from 1 large medium sliced loaf)
175 g (6 oz) butter
1 apple
grated zest and juice of ½ lemon
50 g (2 oz) sultanas
50 g (2 oz) dried apricots, chopped
300 ml (½ pint) double cream
300 ml (½ pint) milk
1 large vanilla pod
8 free-range egg yolks (size 2)
125 g (4 oz) caster sugar
freshly grated nutmeg
ground cinnamon, for sprinkling
30 ml (2 tbsp) thin honey

Bramble Coulis:
225 g (8 oz) blackberries
icing sugar, to taste

To Decorate:
mint leaves
few blackberries

1 Remove the crusts from the bread and lightly butter both sides. Line the base and sides of a 450 g (1 lb) loaf tin with buttered greaseproof paper. Line the base and sides of the tin with the buttered bread, cutting the slices to fit.

2 Peel, core and thinly slice the apple; place in a bowl of cold water acidulated with the lemon juice to prevent discolouration.

3 Mix the sultanas, chopped apricots and lemon zest together in a bowl.

4 To make the custard, put the cream and milk in a saucepan with the vanilla pod and slowly bring to the boil. Meanwhile, whisk the egg yolks and sugar together in a bowl. Gradually pour on the milk mixture, whisking all the time. Pour about three-quarters of the custard into a jug and flavour with a pinch of nutmeg. (Cover the rest of the custard and set aside.)

5 Sprinkle a thin even layer of the dried fruit mixture in the tin and cover with a single layer of apple slices. Lightly sprinkle with ground cinnamon. Cover with a layer of bread and butter, then pour on some of the nutmeg-flavoured custard. Repeat these until the tin is full, finishing with a layer of bread and butter. Pour on the rest of the nutmeg-flavoured custard.

6 Place the loaf tin in a roasting tin containing a 4 cm (1½ inch) depth of hot water. Bake in a preheated oven at 180°C (350°F) mark 4 for 30 minutes, then remove the foil and smear the honey on top of the pudding. Bake for a further 15 minutes or until a skewer inserted into the middle comes out clean.

7 Transfer the loaf tin to a tray of cold water to cool, then chill in the refrigerator.

8 Stand the bowl of reserved custard over a pan of hot water and stir until it is the consistency of double cream; allow to cool.

9 For the bramble coulis, press the blackberries through a nylon sieve into a bowl and sweeten with icing sugar to taste.

10 Cut the chilled bread and butter pudding into 1 cm (½ inch) thick slices and arrange on individual serving plates. Spoon the bramble coulis to one side and the vanilla custard around the other side of the plate. Decorate with blackberries and mint sprigs to serve.

Timothy Hobbs

Panna Cotta with Berries

Panna Cotta:
450 ml (¾ pint) double cream
2 vanilla pods, split
3 gelatine leaves, in smaller pieces
175 ml (6 fl oz) milk
50 g (2 oz) caster sugar

Hazelnut Biscuits:
50 g (2 oz) hazelnuts, chopped and toasted
50 g (2 oz) caster sugar
150 g (6 oz) plain flour
100 g (4 oz) butter, diced

Berries:
300 g (10 oz) raspberries
caster sugar, to taste
dash of crème de framboise liqueur, to taste
125 g (4 oz) each blackberries, redcurrants and blueberries (or other summer berries)

1 For the panna cotta, put the cream in a saucepan with the vanilla pods and bring slowly to the boil. Remove from the heat and set aside to infuse. Meanwhile, soften the gelatine leaves in the milk for 10 minutes. Add the sugar, milk and gelatine to the warm cream and stir until dissolved. Set over a bowl of ice to cool. When the mixture begins to thicken slightly, pass through a muslin-lined sieve into a bowl, then divide between 4 individual moulds. Leave to set in the refrigerator.

2 To make the biscuits, finely grind the hazelnuts in a food processor. Add the sugar, flour and butter and process to a smooth dough. Wrap in cling film and rest in the refrigerator for 20 minutes.

3 Roll out the biscuit dough between 2 sheets of non-stick baking parchment until *very* thin. Trim to a large square and carefully lift (between the sheets of parchment) onto a baking sheet. Position a baking sheet on top and weight down to ensure a fine, crisp result. Bake in a preheated oven at 180°C (350°F) mark 4 for about 10 minutes. While still warm, cut out 4 rounds, using a cutter the same size or slightly smaller than the rim of the panna cotta moulds. Transfer to a wire rack to cool.

4 Purée 225 g (8 oz) of the raspberries in a food processor, adding sugar to taste. Pass through a nylon sieve into a bowl, then add the framboise to taste. Gently fold in all of the berries.

5 To serve, position a biscuit on each serving plate. Dip the panna cotta moulds briefly into hot water, then turn out onto the biscuit bases. Serve with the berries.

Liz Franklin

Ricotta Hearts with Pistachios and Kirsch served with Raspberry and Mango Purées

225 g (8 oz) ricotta cheese
60 ml (4 tbsp) icing sugar, sifted
1.25 ml (¼ tsp) vanilla extract
30 ml (2 tbsp) pistachio nuts, chopped
30 ml (2 tbsp) kirsch
150 ml (¼ pint) double cream
450 g (1 lb) raspberries, hulled
1 large ripe mango
4 mint sprigs, to decorate

1 Line 4 heart-shaped moulds with dampened squares of muslin, which are large enough to overhang the sides.

2 Pass the ricotta cheese through a sieve into a bowl and beat until light and fluffy, then beat in 30 ml (2 tbsp) icing sugar and the vanilla extract. Fold in the pistachio nuts and kirsch, until evenly blended. Whip the double cream until thick, then fold into the cheese mixture.

3 Fill the lined moulds with the cheese mixture, piling it into a slight dome in the centre. Fold the muslin over the top to enclose and chill for at least 1 hour.

4 Set aside 4 raspberries for decoration. Using the back of a ladle, press the remaining raspberries through a sieve into a bowl to remove the seeds. Stir in 15 ml (1 tbsp) icing sugar.

5 Peel, halve and stone the mango, then press the flesh through a sieve into a bowl. Add the remaining 15 ml (1 tbsp) icing sugar and stir well.

6 To serve, unmould each cheese dessert on to a flat dessert plate and carefully remove the muslin. Drizzle spoonfuls of raspberry purée around each cheese heart, followed by spoonfuls of mango purée. Using the tip of a knife, feather the fruit purées together decoratively. Top each cheese heart with a halved raspberry and a mint sprig to decorate. Serve immediately.

Tony Purwin

Pink Gin Syllabub with an Angostura Sauce

Syllabub:
5 ml (1 tsp) freshly ground mixed spice (cinnamon, juniper, allspice, nutmeg and clove)
105 ml (7 tbsp) gin
grated rind and juice of 1 lemon
15 ml (1 tbsp) angostura bitters
50 g (2 oz) caster sugar
1 drop of red food colouring
300 ml (½ pint) double cream

Angostura Sauce:
grated rind and juice of 1 lemon
150 g (5 oz) caster sugar
45 ml (3 tbsp) angostura bitters
45 ml (3 tbsp) water

Candied Lemon Zest:
finely pared rind of 1 lemon
25 g (1 oz) caster sugar
15 ml (1 tbsp) warm water
10 ml (2 tsp) grenadine

To Decorate:
mint sprigs

1 To make the syllabub, put the ground spice, gin, lemon rind and juice, angostura bitters and sugar in a bowl. Stir until the sugar is dissolved, then cover and leave to stand for 20 minutes. Strain into a mixing bowl and add the red colouring. Whisk, using an electric beater, then slowly add the cream in a steady stream, whisking constantly. As soon as the cream starts to thicken stop whisking, otherwise it will separate. Cover and chill in the refrigerator.

2 Meanwhile prepare the candied lemon zest. Cut the finely pared lemon rind into fine shreds, using a sharp knife. Blanch briefly in boiling water and drain. Dissolve the sugar in the water in a small pan over a low heat, then add the grenadine and bring to the boil. Add the lemon zest shreds and simmer for 10-15 minutes until candied. Remove the pink zests with a slotted spoon and spread out on a plate to cool.

3 To make the angostura sauce, put the lemon rind and juice in a saucepan with the sugar, water and angostura bitters. Place over a low heat until the sugar is dissolved, then bring to the boil and cook gently until you have a blush pink syrup with an aromatic lemon flavour. Strain and check the consistency: the sauce should just coat the back of a spoon; if too thick, add a drop or two of hot water.

4 To serve, pool a thin layer of the angostura sauce on each serving plate. Using two spoons dipped in hot water, quickly shape the syllabub into quenelles and arrange three on each plate, radiating from the centre. Decorate with the candied zests and mint sprigs. Serve immediately.

Roger Hemming

Rhubarb and Elderflower Syllabub with Shortbread Hearts

6 stalks rhubarb
60 ml (2 fl oz) elderflower wine
50 g (2 oz) caster sugar
5 ml (1 tsp) ground ginger
10 ml (2 tsp) arrowroot

Syllabub:
300 ml (½ pint) double cream
90 ml (6 tbsp) elderflower wine
squeeze of lemon juice
50 g (2 oz) caster sugar
5 ml (1 tsp) brandy

Shortbread:
50 g (2 oz) butter
50 g (2 oz) caster sugar
few drops of vanilla essence
50 g (2 oz) plain flour
25 g (1 oz) self-raising flour
icing sugar, for dusting

1 Cut the rhubarb into 2.5 cm (1 inch) pieces and place in a heavy-based saucepan with the wine, sugar and ginger. Bring to the boil, lower the heat and simmer until tender. Mix the arrowroot with a little cold water until smooth, then stir into the rhubarb mixture. Heat, stirring, until slightly thickened. Allow to cool.

2 Spoon the rhubarb into the base of 4 tall glasses, reserving 45 ml (3 tbsp) of the mixture for the syllabub.

3 To make the syllabub, whip the cream until thick, then whisk in the wine, lemon juice, sugar and brandy. Stir in the reserved rhubarb mixture and spoon in to the glasses. Chill until required.

4 To make the shortbread, cream the butter with the sugar and vanilla essence. Stir in the plain and self-raising flours. Knead lightly. Shape the dough into a ball and leave to rest for 30 minutes.

5 Roll out thinly and cut out heart shapes, using a suitable cutter. Bake in a preheated oven at 180°C (350°F) mark 4 for 10 minutes until pale golden. Immediately transfer to a wire rack and dust with icing sugar. Allow to cool.

6 Serve the syllabub dessert with the shortbread hearts.

Sarah Giles

Citrus Crème with Fresh Orange Segments and a Grand Marnier Sauce

Caramel:
175 g (6 oz) caster sugar
100 ml (3½ fl oz) water

Citrus Crèmes:
200 ml (7 fl oz) double cream
90 ml (3 fl oz) milk
1 vanilla pod
3 eggs (size 2)
3 egg yolks (size 2)
125 g (4 oz) caster sugar
grated zest and juice of 2 lemons

Sauce:
15 ml (1 tbsp) liquid glucose
10 ml (2 tsp) sugar
grated zest of 1 orange
30 ml (2 tbsp) Grand Marnier
15 ml (1 tbsp) concentrated orange juice

To Serve:
1 orange, peeled and segmented
mint leaves
Tuiles (see right)

1 Butter 4 ramekins or other heatproof moulds with butter and sprinkle with caster sugar.

2 To make the caramel, put the sugar and half of the water into a heavy-based saucepan and heat slowly until the sugar is melted. Increase the heat and bring to the boil. Boil rapidly, brushing down the sides of the pan with a damp pastry brush to remove sugar crystals which might burn. Once the syrup reaches a dark caramel colour, immediately remove from the heat and carefully pour in the rest of the water, (protecting your hand as it will splutter). Pour a thin layer of caramel into each of 4 buttered individual ramekin moulds. (You won't need to use all of the caramel.)

3 To prepare the citrus crèmes, heat the cream, milk and vanilla pod together in a saucepan until just bubbling. Remove from the heat and leave to infuse. Meanwhile, whisk the eggs, extra egg yolks, sugar, lemon zest and juice together in a bowl until pale and smooth. Pour on the infused milk, whisking constantly until smooth. Strain through a muslin-lined sieve into a jug.

4 Divide the crème between the moulds. Stand them in a roasting tin containing enough water to come three quarters of the way up the sides of the moulds. Cover the moulds with foil and bake in a preheated oven at 170°C (325°F) mark 3 for 40 minutes until set. Remove the moulds from the roasting tin and allow to cool, then chill in the refrigerator for 1-2 hours, or until required.

5 Meanwhile, make the orange sauce. Melt the liquid glucose and sugar in a saucepan, add the orange zest, then the Grand Marnier. Flame the Grand Marnier then, when the flames die down, add the

orange juice. Simmer to reduce to the required consistency.

6 To serve, unmould a crème onto the centre of each serving plate. Surround with the Grand Marnier sauce and decorate with fresh orange segments and mint leaves. Serve with the tuiles.

Liz Franklin

Tuiles

50 g (2 oz) icing sugar
15 g (½ oz) plain flour
40 g (1½ oz) butter
1 egg white (size 2)

To Finish:
icing sugar for dusting

1 To make the tuiles, mix all the ingredients together in a bowl until smooth, then leave to stand for 30 minutes.

2 Spoon the mixture into neat oval shapes on baking sheets lined with non-stick baking parchment, spreading it evenly.

3 Cook in a preheated oven at 150°C (300°F) mark 2 for 6-8 minutes until pale golden in colour. Whilst still warm and pliable, remove with a palette knife and place over a rolling pin. Leave to cool, then carefully remove and store the tuiles in an airtight tin to keep them crisp.

4 Dust with icing sugar to serve.

Liz Franklin

Chilled Zabaglione with a hint of Orange

4 egg yolks
50 g (2 oz) caster sugar
150 ml (¼ pint) Marsala
30 ml (2 tbsp) Cointreau, Grand Marnier or other orange liqueur
finely pared strip of orange zest
90 ml (6 tbsp) double cream

1 Whisk the egg yolks and sugar in a bowl until pale and frothy. Whisk in the Marsala and orange liqueur. Add the orange zest.

2 Place the bowl over a saucepan of simmering water and whisk the mixture, using a balloon whisk, for 10-15 minutes until thickened. Remove the bowl from the heat and cool slightly, whisking occasionally. Discard the orange zest.

3 Lightly whip the cream, then fold into the slightly cooled zabaglione and pour into individual glasses. Chill before serving, with sponge biscuits.

Amita Baldock

Floating Lemon Islands

For this dessert, you will need to prepare the sponge, lemon curd and vanilla custard in advance. Allow them to cool, then make the Italian meringue and construct the 'islands'.

Sponge:
2 eggs (size 2)
50 g (2 oz) caster sugar
50 g (2 oz) self-raising flour, sifted

Lemon Curd:
125 g (4 oz) caster sugar
finely grated rind and juice of 1 lemon
50 g (2 oz) unsalted butter, diced
1 egg, beaten (plus one extra yolk – optional)

Vanilla Custard:
1 vanilla pod, or 2.5 ml (½ tsp) vanilla essence
600 ml (1 pint) single cream
40 g (1½ oz) caster sugar
4 egg yolks (size 2)

Italian Meringue:
125 g (4 oz) caster sugar
75 ml (5 tbsp) water
2 egg whites (size 2)

Lemon Syrup:
30 ml (2 tbsp) caster sugar
30 ml (2 tbsp) water
15 ml (1 tbsp) lemon juice
30 ml (2 tbsp) dry sherry

To Decorate:
candied lemon peel
angelica pieces

1 To make the sponge, whisk the eggs and sugar together in a bowl over a pan of simmering water, until the mixture is very pale and creamy, and thick enough to leave a ribbon trail on the surface when you lift the whisk. Remove the bowl from the pan. Carefully fold in the flour.

2 Pour the sponge mixture into a greased and floured 25 x 15 cm (10 x 6 inch) Swiss roll tin and use a palette knife to spread the mixture out as evenly as possible. Bake in a preheated oven at 230°C (450°F) mark 8 for 5 minutes only; the sponge should be pale golden brown. Leave in the tin to cool.

3 To make the lemon curd, put the sugar, lemon rind and juice into a saucepan and heat gently until the sugar is dissolved. Add the butter and stir until just melted. Add the egg and cook over a *very* low heat, stirring constantly, until the mixture thickens; do not allow to boil. Pour into a bowl and allow to cool.

4 To make the custard, slit open the vanilla pod and scrape out the seeds; discard or reserve for flavouring another dish. Put the cream, sugar and vanilla pod into a saucepan and slowly bring almost to the boil. Remove from the heat and leave to infuse for 5 minutes, stirring occasionally. Meanwhile put the egg yolks into a large bowl and break them up with a fork. Bring the infused cream to the boil, then strain onto the eggs, stirring all the time. Pour the mixture back through the strainer into the saucepan.

5 Cook, stirring, over a very gentle heat until the custard thickens enough to lightly coat the back of the wooden spoon; do not allow to boil or it will curdle. Immediately take the pan off the heat and pour the custard into a clean bowl.

6 To make the meringue, put the sugar and water in a heavy-based saucepan and heat gently until dissolved. Increase the heat and boil the syrup steadily until it reaches the 'hard ball' stage, ie it registers 120°C (248°F) on a sugar thermometer (see note). Meanwhile, whisk the egg whites in a bowl until they form stiff peaks. Gradually pour on the syrup, whisking all the time. Continue to whisk for 3-5 minutes until the meringue is completely cool and very stiff.

7 To make the lemon syrup, put the sugar, water and lemon juice in a small pan and heat gently until the sugar is dissolved, then bring to the boil and boil until reduced to about 30 ml (2 tbsp). Remove from the heat and mix with the sherry.

8 Using a 7.5 cm (3 inch) plain circular cutter, cut 4 rounds from the sponge cake. Moisten the sponge rounds thoroughly with the lemon syrup. Spread each one generously with lemon curd. Pile the meringue on top of each one and neaten with a palette knife. Decorate with candied lemon peel and angelica.

9 Divide the custard between 4 soup plates. Decorate the edge of the custard with four blobs of lemon curd, running a toothpick through each to make a heart-shape. Now, using a palette knife, carefully lift an island to float on each dish of custard. Serve at once.

Mandy Ford

Note: To test the syrup for the 'hard-ball' stage, drop a little of it into a cup of cold water. It should immediately form a firm, pliable ball.

Blackberry and Cassis Fool

450 g (1 lb) blackberries
175 g (6 oz) sugar
60 ml (4 tbsp) water
60 ml (4 tbsp) crème de cassis
300 ml (½ pint) double cream, chilled
icing sugar, for dusting

1 Set aside 4 good blackberries for decoration.

2 Put the rest of the blackberries in a saucepan with the sugar and water. Cover and cook gently for 20 minutes or until the fruit is pulpy. Leave to cool for about 10 minutes, then sieve to remove the blackberry pips.

3 Pour the cassis into 4 individual glasses or a large serving bowl and chill.

4 Whip the cream until stiff peaks form, then fold in the blackberry purée until evenly combined. Carefully spoon the mixture into the serving glasses or bowl, keeping the cassis at the bottom. Chill for at least 1 hour.

5 Decorate with the reserved fruit and dust with icing sugar. Serve with crisp dessert biscuits.

Tricia Humber

Half-baked Chocolate Mousse with a Coffee Grain Sauce

Chocolate Mousse:
200 g (7 oz) plain chocolate, in pieces
50 g (2 oz) unsalted butter
2 eggs (size 2)
15 ml (1 tbsp) caster sugar
15 ml (1 tbsp) plain flour

Coffee Grain Sauce:
3 egg yolks (size 2)
25 g (1 oz) sugar
300 ml (½ pint) milk
15 ml (1 tbsp) medium-grind coffee grains

To Serve:
175 ml (6 fl oz) double cream
icing sugar, for dusting
chocolate-coated coffee beans, to decorate (optional)

1 First make the coffee grain sauce. Lightly whisk the egg yolks and sugar together in a bowl. Meanwhile, pour the milk into a pan, add the coffee grains and slowly bring almost to the boil. Pour onto the egg mixture, whisking constantly, then strain into the top of a double boiler (or into a small heavy-based pan). Cook, stirring, over a low heat, until thickened enough to lightly coat the back of a wooden spoon; do not allow to boil or the sauce will curdle. Remove from the heat and leave to cool slightly.

2 Grease 4 individual loose-bottomed fluted flan dishes, about 7.5 cm (3 inches) in diameter, with unsalted butter.

3 Melt the chocolate with the butter in a heatproof bowl over a pan of simmering water. Let cool slightly.

4 Whisk the eggs and sugar together in a bowl, using an electric beater, for 5-10 minutes until doubled in volume, thick, creamy and almost white in colour. Sift the flour over the mixture and lightly fold in.

5 Fold the cooled melted chocolate into the mixture, then divide between the prepared tins.

6 Bake in a preheated oven at 200°C (400°F) mark 6 for 7 minutes until the edges have a cake-like texture, while the middle is still a little undercooked. The perfect result is a little cake-like chocolate mousse which is gooey inside! Leave in the tins for 10-15 minutes to cool slightly.

7 To serve, pour the coffee sauce around one side of each serving plate and pour the cream around the other side. Using a fork or a skewer, feather the sauces together, to create a pattern. Carefully remove each mousse from the tin and, using a palette knife, position on the sauce. Sprinkle with icing sugar and decorate with chocolate coffee beans if desired. Serve at once, while the mousses are warm.

Charlotte Bircher

Note: Take care when removing the half-baked mousses from the flan tins as they are fragile.

Chocolate Mousse with Raspberry and Cassis Sauce

Chocolate Mousse:
60 g (2 oz) plain chocolate, in pieces
40 g (1½ oz) white chocolate, in pieces
200 ml (7 fl oz) double cream
2 egg whites

Raspberry Sauce:
200 g (7 oz) raspberries
60 ml (4 tbsp) crème de cassis

To Serve:
fresh raspberries

1 To prepare the mousse, melt the plain and white chocolate separately in bowls over pans of hot water. Allow to cool slightly.

2 In another bowl, whip the cream until it forms soft peaks. Transfer two thirds of the whipped cream to another bowl and carefully fold the cooled melted plain chocolate into it. Fold the white chocolate into the smaller portion of cream.

3 In a clean bowl, whisk the egg whites until firm peaks form. Gently fold two thirds into the plain chocolate mixture, and one third into the white chocolate mixture. Lightly fold the two mixtures together to create a marbled effect.

4 Divide the mousse between 4 individual moulds. Chill in the refrigerator until set.

5 To make the sauce, put the raspberries into a food processor and work to a purée, then pass through a nylon sieve into a bowl to remove the pips. Stir in the crème de cassis.

6 Turn out the mousses onto individual serving plates and add a generous swirl of the sauce. Decorate with fresh raspberries to serve.

Noriko Anzai-Jackson

Dark Chocolate Leaves layered with White Chocolate Mousse on a Vanilla Sauce

White Chocolate Mousse:
1 gelatine leaf
240 g (8¼ oz) white chocolate
2 egg yolks
200 ml (7 fl oz) double cream, lightly whipped

Crème Anglaise:
250 ml (8 fl oz) milk
3 egg yolks
45 ml (3 tbsp) vanilla sugar

Chocolate Leaves:
125 g (4 oz) best-quality dark chocolate

Chocolate Sauce:
45 ml (3 tbsp) milk
50 g (2 oz) dark chocolate, grated

To Decorate:
8 Cape gooseberries

1 To make the white chocolate mousse, soak the gelatine in a little cold water until soft. Meanwhile, grate the white chocolate into a bowl. Squeeze the excess water from the gelatine, then carefully melt it in 30 ml (2 tbsp) water. Pour the melted gelatine on to the chocolate and stir over a bowl of hot water until it has melted. Allow to cool, but not set.

2 Mix the egg yolks into the cooled chocolate, then fold in the lightly whipped cream. Transfer to a suitable shallow rectangular dish and refrigerate until needed.

3 To make the crème anglaise, pour the milk into a saucepan and slowly bring to a simmer over a medium heat. In a bowl, whisk the egg yolks and vanilla sugar together until light and thick. Gradually whisk in half of the hot milk, then add to the remaining milk in the saucepan and mix well. Cook over a medium heat, stirring constantly, until the sauce thickens slightly. Do not allow to boil. Pour into a clean bowl and allow to cool.

4 To make the chocolate leaves, dampen a baking sheet with water and line it with non-stick baking parchment. Melt the chocolate in a bowl over a pan of hot water, then spread very thinly on the lined baking sheet. Allow to set, then cut into 4 cm (1½ inch) squares or shapes as desired.

5 To make the chocolate sauce for feathering, place the milk in a saucepan. Add the chocolate and bring to the boil, stirring constantly until the chocolate has melted and the sauce is smooth and shiny.

6 To serve, spoon the vanilla sauce on to serving plates and feather with the chocolate sauce. Layer the chocolate leaves with white mousse, then arrange in the centre of each plate. Peel back the papery skins from the Cape gooseberries and use to decorate the dessert. Serve immediately.

Vanessa Binns

Bitter Chocolate Marquise with Cloudberry Sauce

200 g (7 oz) quality bitter chocolate (Valrhona)
15 ml (1 tbsp) strong black coffee
30-45 ml (2-3 tbsp) cloudberry liqueur, or framboise eau-de-vie
125 g (4 oz) unsalted butter, softened
125 g (4 oz) caster sugar
30 ml (2 tbsp) cocoa powder
3 egg yolks
300 ml (½ pint) double cream

Cloudberry Sauce:
450 g (1 lb) cloudberries (see note)
15 ml (1 tbsp) cloudberry liqueur, or framboise eau-de-vie
125-175 g (4-6 oz) caster sugar, to taste

To Decorate:
handful of cloudberries

1 Break the chocolate into a heatproof bowl and add the coffee and liqueur. Place over a pan of hot water until melted. Allow to cool.

2 In a bowl, beat the butter with half of the sugar until light and fluffy. Fold in the cocoa powder. In another bowl, whisk the egg yolks with the remaining sugar until pale. Lightly whip the cream.

3 Beat the cooled chocolate into the butter and cocoa mixture, then stir into the beaten egg yolk mixture. Lightly fold in the cream.

4 Line 4 small ramekins with cling film. Pour in the chocolate mixture and tap the ramekins to level. Cover and chill for 1½-2 hours until set.

5 Meanwhile, prepare the cloudberry sauce. Purée the cloudberries with the liqueur and sugar to taste in a blender or food processor. Sieve to remove all the pips.

6 To serve, invert the marquise on to individual plates, covered with a pool of cloudberry sauce. Cut out a tiny wedge of each marquise to reveal the texture. Decorate with a few fresh cloudberries.

Sue Lawrence

Note: If you are not lucky enough to find cloudberries, raspberries make a perfectly good substitute.

White Chocolate Mousse with Strawberries

100 g (3½ oz) bar white chocolate
40 g (1½ oz) butter
1½ egg yolks
5 egg whites
30-45 ml (2-3 tbsp) whipping cream

Shortbread:
50 g (2 oz) butter
25 g (1 oz) caster sugar
125 g (4 oz) plain flour

To Serve:
125 g (4 oz) strawberries
8-10 lychees
75 ml (5 tbsp) Amaretto liqueur

1 Melt the chocolate with the butter in a bain-marie (or heatproof bowl over a pan of simmering water). Take off the heat and stir in the egg yolks. Whisk the egg whites until stiff and fold into the chocolate mixture, a spoonful at a time. Whip the cream until soft peaks form, then fold into the mousse. Leave to set.

2 To make the shortbread, cream the butter and sugar together until light and fluffy. Using your fingers, work in the flour to a soft dough. Be careful not to make it too short or the shortbread will crumble. Lightly roll out to a 5 mm (¼ inch) thickness and cut out rounds, or any shape you like. Place on a lightly greased baking sheet and bake in a preheated oven at 180°C (350°C) mark 4 for 10-15 minutes until golden. Cool on a wire rack.

3 Meanwhile, soak the fruit in the liqueur for 20 minutes or longer, depending on how alcoholic you wish it to be! Drain.

4 Divide the fruit between individual glasses. Top with the chocolate mousse and decorate with the shortbread to serve.

Melanie Jappy

Cold Lemon Soufflé with a Lemon and Lime Sauce

Lemon Soufflé:
15 g (½ oz) sachet gelatine
finely grated rind and juice of 1½ lemons
2 eggs, separated
125 g (4 oz) caster sugar
150 ml (¼ pint) double cream

Lemon and Lime Sauce:
125 g (4 oz) caster sugar
finely pared zest and juice of 1 lemon
finely pared zest and juice of 1 lime
5 ml (1 tsp) arrowroot

To Serve:
Brandy Snap Baskets (see right)

1 For the soufflé, sprinkle the gelatine over 30 ml (2 tbsp) cold water in a cup. Put the lemon rind and juice in a large bowl with the egg yolks and sugar. Stand the bowl over a pan of simmering water and whisk until the mixture turns pale and starts to thicken. Remove the bowl from the pan.

2 Stand the cup of gelatine in the saucepan of hot water until it has dissolved, then add to the egg yolk mixture, stirring well.

3 In a separate bowl, whip the cream until soft peaks form. In another bowl, whisk the egg whites until stiff. Allow the egg yolk mixture to cool, stirring occasionally, then fold in the cream, followed by the egg whites. Pour into individual moulds and chill for at least 1½ hours.

4 Meanwhile, make the sauce. Put the sugar and 120 ml (4 fl oz) water in a small pan and heat gently, stirring to help dissolve the sugar. Add the lemon and lime zests and simmer gently for 15 minutes. Mix the arrowroot with the lemon juice and half of the lime juice. Add to the pan and stir until it returns to a simmer. Remove from the heat and leave to cool. Just before serving, stir in the rest of the lime juice.

5 To serve, position a brandy snap basket in the middle of each serving plate. Dip the soufflé moulds in a bowl of hot water for a few seconds, then carefully turn out into the brandy snap baskets. Pour the lemon and lime sauce around the baskets. Serve at once.

Kevin Sumner

Brandy Snap Baskets

50 g (2 oz) butter
50 g (2 oz) caster sugar
30 ml (2 tbsp) golden syrup
5 ml (1 tsp) brandy
5 ml (1 tsp) lemon juice
60 ml (4 tbsp) plain flour
5 ml (1 tsp) ground ginger

1 Melt the butter in a saucepan, add the sugar and syrup, and heat gently until dissolved. Remove from the heat and add all the other ingredients. Mix well.

2 For each basket, spread 30 ml (2 tbsp) of the mixture into a round, about 12 cm (5 inches) in diameter on a baking sheet lined with non-stick baking parchment. (Shape and bake 2 baskets at a time.)

3 Cook in a preheated oven at 180°C (350°F) mark 4 for 6-8 minutes. Leave for 20 seconds, then remove the brandy snap using a palette knife and lay over an upturned ramekin. Shape to form a basket, then allow to cool.

Kevin Sumner

Bramble Mousse with Bramble Sauce

675 g (1½ lb) wild blackberries
1 sachet powdered gelatine
150 ml (¼ pint) whipping cream
50 g (2 oz) icing sugar, sifted
2 egg whites (size 1)

Sauce:
120 ml (8 tbsp) reserved blackberry purée (see recipe)
25 g (1 oz) icing sugar, sifted

To Decorate:
borage or other edible flowers
mint leaves

To Serve:
Almond Biscuits (see right)

1 Set aside a few blackberries for decoration. Put the rest into a blender or food processor and work until smooth. Set aside about 120 ml (8 tbsp) blackberry purée for the sauce.

2 Sprinkle the gelatine over 45 ml (3 tbsp) cold water in a small bowl and leave to soak for 2-3 minutes. Stand the bowl over a pan of simmering water until dissolved.

3 Lightly whip the cream until soft peaks form. Stir the icing sugar into the blackberry purée with the dissolved gelatine, then fold in the cream. Whisk the egg whites until stiff and gently fold in the blackberry mousse mixture.

4 Divide the mousse between four 150 ml (¼ pint) ramekins or other individual moulds. Chill the mousses in the refrigerator for at least 1 hour until set.

5 To serve, turn each mousse out on to a dessert plate. For the bramble sauce, stir the icing sugar into the reserved blackberry purée and spoon around the mousse. Decorate with borage or other edible flowers, mint leaves and the reserved blackberries. Serve accompanied by the Almond Biscuits.

Ann Neale

Melt-in-the-Mouth Meringue

5 egg whites
225 g (8 oz) caster sugar
5 ml (1 tsp) wine vinegar
5 ml (1 tsp) vanilla extract
10-15 ml (2-3 tsp) cornflour

To Assemble:
200 ml (7 fl oz) crème fraîche (not low-fat)
15 ml (1 tbsp) toasted flaked almonds
vanilla icing sugar for dusting

Caramel:
60 ml (4 tbsp) caster sugar

To Serve:
Red Berry Compote (see right)
4 mint sprigs

1 Line a 33 x 23 cm (13 x 9 inch) Swiss roll tin with non-stick baking parchment.

2 Whisk the egg whites in a bowl until very stiff. Whisk in the caster sugar 15 ml (1 tbsp) at a time, then whisk in the vinegar, vanilla extract and cornflour.

3 Spread the meringue evenly in the Swiss roll tin. Bake in a preheated oven at 180°C (350°F) mark 4 for 10 minutes. Leave in the tin to cool.

4 When cold, cut the meringue into eight 6 cm (2½ inch) squares. Grease a sheet of foil or a very clean baking sheet with oil. Place 4 meringue squares on the foil and top with the crème fraîche. Place another square of meringue on top at an angle. Sprinkle with a few toasted flaked almonds and dust with vanilla icing sugar.

5 Just before serving make the caramel. Dissolve the sugar in 120 ml (8 tbsp) water in a heavy-based pan over a low heat. Increase the heat and cook, without stirring, to a golden brown caramel. Drizzle the caramel over the top of the meringues, allowing it to run down the sides.

6 Dust each serving plate with vanilla icing sugar and carefully position a meringue on the plate. Place a generous spoonful of fruit compote alongside and decorate with mint. Serve immediately.

Clare Askaroff

Red Berry Compote

450 g (1 lb) mixed soft fruits,
(eg raspberries, redcurrants, blackcurrants, strawberries, stoned cherries, blackberries)
15 ml (1 tbsp) concentrated blackcurrant Ribena
125 g (4 oz) caster sugar
15 ml (1 tbsp) potato flour (approximately)
icing sugar, for dusting

1 Put the fruit in a heavy-based pan and heat very gently for about 1 minute until the juices start to run. Carefully transfer the fruit to a bowl and set aside. Measure the strained juice together with the Ribena. Add the caster sugar.

2 Return the juice to the pan and thicken with the potato flour: use 5 ml (1 tsp) flour per 100 ml (3½ fl oz) juice. Mix the flour with 15 ml (1 tbsp) water, stir into the juice and cook, stirring, for 1-2 minutes. Cool slightly, then pour over the fruit.

3 Sift a little icing sugar over the surface to prevent a skin forming, then cover and chill in the refrigerator until needed. Serve with the Melt-in-the-Mouth Meringue.

Clare Askaroff

Raspberry Pavlovas with a Raspberry and Sloe Gin Coulis

Pavlovas:
2 egg whites
100 g (4 oz) caster sugar

Coulis:
100 g (4 oz) sugar
finely pared rind of 1 orange
1 cinnamon stick
150 ml (¼ pint) water
150 ml (¼ pint) sloe gin
225 g (8 oz) raspberries

Syrup:
finely pared rind of 2 oranges
8 green peppercorns in brine, drained
100 g (4 oz) sugar
150 ml (¼ pint) water

To Serve:
150 ml (¼ pint) double cream, whipped
225 g (8 oz) raspberries

1 To make the pavlovas, whisk the egg whites in a bowl until stiff, then gradually beat in the sugar, 25 g (1 oz) at a time. Spoon the meringue mixture into 8 even-sized mounds on a large baking sheet lined with non-stick baking parchment. Place in a preheated oven at 150°C (300°F) mark 2. Immediately lower the temperature to 140°C (275°F) mark 1 and bake for about 1 hour, then turn off the oven, leaving the pavlovas to cool in the oven.

2 To make the coulis, put the sugar, orange rind and cinnamon in a saucepan with the water and heat gently until the sugar has dissolved. Increase the heat, add the sloe gin and boil rapidly to reduce. Add the raspberries and leave to cool.

3 Discard the orange rind and cinnamon. Purée in a blender or food processor, then pass through a sieve to remove the pips.

4 To make the green peppercorn and orange syrup, cut the orange rind into strips and place in a saucepan with the peppercorns, sugar and water. Slowly bring to the boil, then simmer until reduced to a syrupy consistency.

5 Spread a pool of raspberry coulis on each serving plate and place a meringue on the coulis. Cover the meringue with whipped cream and raspberries. Pour over some of the orange syrup. Place a second meringue on top of the raspberries, setting it at an angle. Decorate the coulis with a splash of cream, feathered with a skewer. Serve immediately.

Joy Skipper

Hazelnut Torte with Mascarpone and Bramble Coulis

Torte:

2 egg whites (size 3)
1.25 ml (¼ tsp) baking powder
125 g (4 oz) caster sugar
125 g (4 oz) hazelnuts, coarsely ground

Filling:

250 g (9 oz) mascarpone cheese
10 ml (2 tsp) icing sugar
22 ml (1½ tbsp) blackberry liqueur or crème de cassis

Bramble Coulis:

175 g (6 oz) blackberries
40 g (1½ oz) icing sugar
7.5 ml (1½ tsp) lemon juice
7.5 ml (1½ tsp) blackberry liqueur

To Decorate:

50 g (2 oz) bitter chocolate, melted
few whole blackberries
mint sprigs

1 To make the torte, whisk the egg whites in a bowl until stiff. Whisk in the baking powder and half of the sugar, then carefully fold in the ground nuts and the rest of the sugar. Spoon onto baking sheets, lined with greaseproof paper or non-stick baking parchment, making two circles about 15 cm (6 inches) in diameter. Bake in a preheated oven at 180°C (350°F) mark 4 for about 30 minutes. Remove from the oven and allow to cool on the paper.

2 To make the bramble coulis, put the blackberries in a blender or food processor with the icing sugar and lemon juice and work to a purée. Pass through a sieve into a bowl to remove the pips, then add the liqueur and keep cool until required.

3 For the torte filling, mix the mascarpone with the icing sugar and liqueur. Invert one torte layer onto a serving plate and carefully spread with the filling. Place the other layer on top. Pipe fine lines of melted chocolate on top to decorate.

4 To serve, cut the torte into wedges and place on individual serving plates. Surround with the blackberry coulis and decorate with chocolate leaves if using, blackberries and mint sprigs.

Marion MacFarlane

Amaretti Chocolate Tortes

4 amaretti biscuits
250 g (9 oz) plain dark chocolate
30 ml (2 tbsp) liquid glucose or glycerine
30 ml (2 tbsp) Amaretto liqueur
300 ml (½ pint) double cream
12-16 blanched almonds
150 ml (¼ pint) single cream
knob of butter

1 Line the bases of 4 ramekin dishes with circles of greaseproof paper. Crush the amaretti biscuits finely and divide evenly between the ramekins.

2 Break 8 oz (225 g) of the chocolate into small pieces and put into a heatproof bowl with the liquid glucose or glycerine and liqueur. Place the bowl over a saucepan of hot water until the chocolate is melted and smooth. Remove the bowl from the pan and leave to cool slightly.

3 Whip the double cream until just thickened, then stir 30 ml (2 tbsp) into the chocolate mixture. Add this chocolate mixture to the remaining cream and stir until well blended. Pour the mixture into the ramekins, dividing it evenly, and tap the ramekins to level the surface of the mixture. Chill in the refrigerator for at least 45 minutes to set firmly.

4 Meanwhile melt the remaining chocolate. Dip each almond into the chocolate to half coat, and place on a foil-lined plate to set. Reserve the remaining chocolate.

5 To serve, re-melt the reserved chocolate and stir in the butter. Spoon into a small greaseproof paper piping bag fitted with a very fine plain nozzle. Run a knife around each ramekin. Place an inverted plate centrally over each ramekin and invert the dish and plate. Carefully remove the ramekins and greaseproof paper.

6 Pour a little cream around each torte, pipe lines of chocolate on the cream and feather with the point of a skewer. Decorate the tortes with the half-coated almonds.

Patti Hall

Chocolate Gâteau

6 eggs, size 3, separated
100 g (3½ oz) caster sugar
100 g (3½ oz) ground almonds
100 g (3½ oz) plain dark chocolate, grated

Topping:
100 g (3½ oz) plain dark chocolate, in pieces
300 ml (½ pint) whipping cream

Chocolate Caraque:
100 g (3½ oz) plain dark chocolate, in pieces

1 Grease a 20 cm (8 inch) loose-bottomed cake tin and line with greaseproof paper.

2 In a bowl, whisk the egg whites until they form firm peaks. Whisk in the sugar, 15 ml (1 tbsp) at a time. In another bowl, lightly beat the egg yolks, then gently fold into the whisked mixture. Add the ground almonds and grated chocolate and fold in lightly until evenly incorporated. Turn the mixture into the prepared cake tin and bake in a preheated oven at 170°C (325°F) mark 3 for 45 minutes. Allow to cool in the tin before turning out.

3 To make the chocolate caraque, melt the chocolate in a heatproof bowl over a pan of hot water, then spread in a thin layer on a marble slab or board. When the chocolate is just set, scrape off long curls by pushing a large knife across the surface of the chocolate.

4 To prepare the topping, melt the chocolate in a heatproof bowl over a pan of hot water. Remove the bowl from the heat and leave to cool slightly. In a bowl, whip the cream until it holds its shape, then fold in the cooled melted chocolate until evenly incorporated.

5 Spread the chocolate cream evenly over the top and sides of the cake. Decorate with the chocolate caraque.

Tony Davis

Blackbottom Cheesecake with Strawberries

Base:
50 g (2 oz) quality dark chocolate
50 g (2 oz) golden granulated sugar
15 ml (1 tbsp) strong black (espresso) coffee
dash of dark rum
50 g (2 oz) unsalted butter
1 egg, size 1

Filling:
125 g (4 oz) cream cheese
150 ml (1/4 pint) soured cream
2 passion fruit
150 ml (1/4 pint) double cream

To Finish:
250 g (8 oz) ripe fragrant strawberries

1 Break up the chocolate and place in a bowl over a pan of hot water, with the sugar, coffee and rum. Warm, stirring, until the chocolate has melted. Remove from the heat. Using a large whisk, beat in the butter in small pieces, a little at a time, until evenly blended. Whisk in the egg.

2 Butter the insides of 4 crumpet rings and stand them on a baking tray lined with non-stick baking parchment. Divide the chocolate mixture evenly between the rings and bake in a preheated oven at 150°C (300°F) mark 2 for about 40 minutes. Allow to cool, then chill.

3 Meanwhile make the filling. Beat the cream cheese and soured cream together in a bowl. Halve the passion fruit and scoop out the pulp and seeds into a sieve over the bowl. Press the fruit through the sieve on to the cream cheese mixture, then beat in. Add the double cream and whip until the mixture is quite stiff.

4 Unmould the chocolate bases on to individual serving plates. Cover with an even thick layer of filling, reserving a little for decoration. Arrange overlapping strawberry slices on top, with their pointed ends radiating out like flower petals.

5 Purée the remaining strawberries in a blender or food processor, then sieve to remove the pips. Spoon a crescent of strawberry purée on to each plate beside the cheesecake, and pipe fine lines of cream cheese filling across it to decorate. Serve immediately.

Sarah Beattie

Individual Chocolate and Rum Bombe with a Rum and Praline Cream

Praline:
50 g (2 oz) unblanched almonds
50 g (2 oz) caster sugar

Chocolate Bombes:
250 g (9 oz) plain chocolate
50 g (2 oz) unsalted butter
60-90 ml (4-6 tbsp) rum, to taste
200 ml (7 fl oz) double cream, lightly whipped

Rum and Praline Cream:
300 ml (½ pint) double cream
25 g (1 oz) praline (see method)
15 ml (1 tbsp) rum, or to taste

To Decorate:
chocolate leaves or curls

1 Place four 150 ml (¼ pint) individual moulds in the refrigerator to chill thoroughly.

2 To make the praline, place the almonds and sugar in a heavy-based pan over a low heat until the sugar melts and turns a nut-brown colour. Immediately remove from the heat and pour into an oiled shallow baking tin. Leave to cool until set hard. When set hard, remove from the dish and grind to a powder in a food processor or blender.

3 For the chocolate bombes, break up the chocolate and put it into a pan with 90 ml (3 fl oz) water. Place over a gentle heat until melted to the consistency of a thick cream. Remove the pan from the heat. Cream the butter in a bowl, then add the melted chocolate and rum to taste. Gradually beat in three quarters of the praline, then fold in the cream. Divide the mixture between the chilled moulds and leave in the refrigerator for approximately 2 hours until set.

4 For the rum and praline cream, whip the cream very lightly, adding the praline and rum.

5 To serve, dip the moulds quickly into hot water and invert on to individual serving plates to release the bombes. Spoon the praline cream around each bombe. Decorate with chocolate leaves or curls and serve immediately.

Jill O'Brien

Lime Sherbet with Hot Cherries

Lime Sherbet:
3 limes
7.5 ml (1½ tsp) lemon juice
85 g (3 oz) caster sugar
20 ml (4 tsp) golden syrup
280 ml (½ pint) milk
140 ml (¼ pint) single cream

Hot Cherries:
680 g (1 lb 8 oz) jar pitted morello cherries in syrup
100 g (3½ oz) sugar
5 ml (1 tsp) lemon juice
30 ml (2 tbsp) kirsch

To Serve:
Pepper Tuile Baskets (see right)
lemon balm or mint sprigs, to decorate

1 Drain the cherries. Purée 225 g (8 oz) of them and pass through a sieve into a small saucepan. Add the sugar, 15 ml (1 tbsp) water and the lemon juice. Bring to the boil, reduce the heat and cook until reduced to approximately 150 ml (¼ pint). Add the rest of the cherries and the kirsch and heat through.

2 To make the lime sherbet, squeeze the juice from the limes and pour it into a shallow freezerproof dish. Add the lemon juice. Place in the freezer for about 30 minutes until frozen to a slushy consistency.

3 Meanwhile, pare the zest from two of the limes in fine shreds and put it in a saucepan. Cover with cold water, bring to the boil and drain. Cover the zest with fresh cold water, bring to the boil and simmer for 20 minutes, then drain.

4 Melt the syrup in a little of the milk. Combine all the ingredients and churn in an ice-cream maker for about 20 minutes. Transfer to the freezer, removing the sherbet 5 minutes before serving.

5 Serve the sherbet in the Pepper Tuile Baskets, decorated with mint sprigs and accompanied by the hot cherries.

Ashley Wilson

Pepper Tuile Baskets

1 egg white (size 3)
50 g (2 oz) caster sugar
pinch of salt
30 g (1 oz) plain flour
30 g (1 oz) unsalted butter, melted
freshly ground black pepper

1 In a bowl, whisk the egg white with the sugar, salt and 10 ml (2 tsp) water until well blended. Stir in the flour and melted butter until smooth. Season generously with black pepper to taste (I use about 5 or 6 turns of the pepper mill).

2 Spread the batter thinly to form 5 circles, each about 12 cm (5 inches) in diameter on a baking tray lined with non-stick baking parchment. (I always make an extra basket in case of a breakage when shaping the biscuits.) Bake in a preheated oven at 200°C (400°F) mark 6 for 5 to 6 minutes until the edges are golden.

3 As soon as the tuiles are removed from the oven, lift from the baking sheet, using a fish slice, and mould each one over an upturned greased teacup to form a basket. If the tuiles become too cool to mould easily, return them to the oven for about 30 seconds to soften.

4 When cool and firm, carefully remove the tuile baskets from the teacups.

Ashley Wilson

Raspberry and Chianti Sorbet

225 g (8 oz) caster sugar
1 bottle of Chianti, or similar red wine
12 mint leaves
300 g (10 oz) frozen raspberries

1 Dissolve the sugar in the wine in a saucepan over a low heat. Increase the heat, add the mint leaves and boil for about 2 minutes. Remove from the heat, add the raspberries and leave to stand for 1 hour.

2 Discard the mint leaves, then purée the raspberries and wine syrup in a blender or food processor. Strain through a nylon sieve to remove pips.

3 Transfer the mixture to an ice-cream machine and churn until frozen, then transfer to the freezer (unless serving imediately). If you do not have an ice-cream maker, freeze the sorbet in a freezerproof container, whisking periodically during freezing to break down the ice crystals and ensure a smooth result.

4 To serve, scoop the sorbet into chilled serving dishes. Serve at once.

Alison Fiander

Cointreau Ice Cream with Blueberry Coulis

Home prepared fruit de bois is used for this recipe (see below), though crème de cassis can be substituted.

Ice Cream:
6 egg yolks
175 g (6 oz) caster sugar
60 ml (4 tbsp) Cointreau
finely grated zest of 2 oranges
600 ml (1 pint) double cream

Blueberry Coulis:
225 g (8 oz) blueberries
15 ml (1 tbsp) crème de fruits de bois (see below), or crème de cassis

Orange Zest Decoration:
knob of unsalted butter
5 ml (1 tsp) icing sugar
zest of 1½ oranges, shredded
splash of Cointreau

To Serve:
kumquat slices, to decorate
Hazelnut Cookies (see right)

1 To make the ice cream, beat the egg yolks and sugar together in a bowl until pale. Add the Cointreau and a quarter of the grated orange zest.

2 In another bowl, lightly whip the cream until thick enough to hold soft peaks. Lightly fold into the whisked egg mixture, with a metal spoon.

3 Transfer to an ice-cream maker and freeze according to the manufacturer's instructions. Alternatively spoon into a freezerproof container and freeze overnight. (Due to the alcohol content this ice cream takes a longtime to freeze.)

4 For the blueberry coulis, purée the blueberries in a blender or food processor, then press the mixture through a fine sieve into a bowl. Add 15 ml (1 tbsp) crème de cassis or crème de fruits de bois.

5 For the decoration, melt the knob of unsalted butter in a small heavy-based pan with the icing sugar. Add the orange zest and Cointreau. Cook until caramelised, then pour onto a heatproof plate and leave to harden. Break into pieces.

6 To serve, scoop the ice cream onto individual plates and surround with the blueberry coulis. Position the caramelised orange zest on top of the ice cream and arrange a few kumquat slices to one side. Serve at once, with the hazelnut cookies.

Charlotte Bircher

Crème de fruits de bois: Soak 900 g (2 lb) mixed soft fruit, such as blackberries, raspberries and blackcurrants, in 1 litre (1¾ pints) red wine for 48 hours, then purée in batches, using a blender or food procesor. Pass through a jelly bag into a preserving pan, pressing the pulp to extract as much juice as possible. Measure the juice and add 900 g (2 lb) sugar to each 1 litre (1¾ pints) liquid. Place the pan over a moderate heat and stir until the sugar has dissolved, then lower the heat and cook below simmering point for 1½-2 hours, until the liquid has reduced by about 5 mm (¼ inch) in depth and looks syrupy. Leave to cool overnight. The following day add approximately 900 ml (1¾ pints) brandy by pouring a tumblerful of brandy into a large bowl, then adding 3 tumblers-ful of syrup, continuing until all of the syrup is used. Pour into sterilised bottles and cork firmly.

Hazelnut Cookies

50 g (2 oz) hazelnuts, skinned
100 g (4 oz) plain flour
pinch of salt
75 g (3 oz) unsalted butter
50 g (2 oz) icing sugar
5 ml (1 tsp) vanilla essence
a little water to mix (if necessary)

1 Spread the hazelnuts out in a shallow baking tin and roast at 180°C (350°F) mark 4 for about 10 minutes until golden. Allow to cool, then finely grind in a food processor. Mix with the flour and salt.

2 Cream the butter and icing sugar together in a bowl, then add the vanilla essence. Stir in the flour and hazelnut mixture to form a smooth, stiff mixture. If it is too dry, mix in a little water.

3 Roll out the dough to a 5 mm (¼ inch) thickness and cut out shapes using a biscuit cutter. Carefully transfer to a baking sheet lined with non-stick baking parchment and cook in a preheated oven at 200°C (400°F) for 10-15 minutes until pale brown.

4 Leave on the baking sheet for a few minutes, then transfer to a wire rack to cool.

Charlotte Bircher

Lemon and Lavender Sorbet

3 lemons
175 g (6 oz) sugar
300 ml (½ pint) water
6 drops of Culpeper's lavender water
1 egg white

To Decorate:
shredded lemon zest
lavender flowers and leaves (optional)

1 Thinly pare the rinds from two of the lemons and place in a saucepan with the sugar and water. Heat gently until the sugar is dissolved, then simmer for 5 minutes. Remove the lemon rind and allow to cool.

2 Squeeze the juice from all 3 lemons and add to the syrup with the lavender water. Transfer to a suitable container and freeze, stirring occasionally. When the mixture is half-frozen, whisk to break down the ice crystals. Whisk the egg white until stiff, then fold into the half-frozen sorbet. Freeze, stirring occasionally, until the sorbet resembles firm snow.

3 Serve scooped into glass dishes, decorated with lemon zest, lavender flowers and leaves if available.

Linda Yewdall

Tart Orange and Lemon Ice Cream with a Bitter Chocolate Sauce

Ice Cream:
4 small mineolas, or other small oranges
2 eggs, separated
75 g (3 oz) caster sugar
finely grated rind and juice of 2 lemons
finely grated rind of 2 oranges
300 ml (½ pint) double cream
juice of 1 lime

Bitter Chocolate Sauce:
200 g (7 oz) bitter chocolate
30 ml (2 tbsp) brandy or Cointreau
60 ml (4 tbsp) double cream
1 small coffee-cup strong black coffee (espresso)

To Decorate:
60 ml (4 tbsp) single cream
shredded lemon zest, blanched
16 raspberries

1 To prepare the mineolas or oranges, slice off their tops and trim their bases to a flat surface. Scoop out as much flesh and pith as possible, then place the orange shells in the freezer.

2 Whisk the egg yolks with the caster sugar until pale and thick. Add the grated lemon and orange rinds. In another bowl, whip the cream until thick, then slowly add the lime juice and nearly all of the lemon juice.

3 Whisk the egg white until soft peaks form. Fold the whipped cream into the egg yolk mixture, then carefully fold in the egg white. Transfer to a freezerproof container and place in the freezer for 30 minutes.

4 Transfer to an ice-cream maker and churn for 15 minutes. Alternatively, whisk by hand. Spoon the ice cream into the mineola or orange shells and place in the freezer until firm.

5 To make the bitter chocolate sauce, combine the chocolate, brandy or Cointreau, cream and half of the coffee in a heavy-based saucepan. Stir over a moderate heat until smooth. Cool, then adjust the consistency as necessary by adding more (cooled) coffee. Leave in the refrigerator until required.

6 To assemble, pour out a little pool of chocolate sauce on to each serving plate and carefully position the ice cream filled oranges in the centre. Spoon 4 drops of cream on the plate (at 12, 3, 6, and 9 o'clock), streak with the tip of a knife, then mount each with a raspberry. Sprinkle with lemon zest to serve.

Roger Ashby

Dark Chocolate Amaretto Ice Cream with White Chocolate Mousse

Ice Cream:
170 g (6 oz) caster sugar
60 ml (4 tbsp) water
100 g (3½ oz) plain chocolate, in pieces
45-60 ml (3-4 tbsp) Amaretto liqueur
600 ml (1 pint) whipping cream

Base:
16 amaretti biscuits
30 ml (2 tbsp) Amaretto liqueur

Mousse:
3 eggs (1 separated)
75 g (3 oz) caster sugar
5 ml (1 tsp) powdered gelatine
100 g (3½ oz) white chocolate, in pieces
140 ml (5 fl oz) double cream

To Decorate:
cocoa powder, for dusting

1 To make the ice cream, put the caster sugar and water in a saucepan and heat gently until the sugar is dissolved. Bring to the boil, lower the heat and cook for about 5 minutes until a syrup is formed, but not until it is caramelised. Leave to cool.

2 Meanwhile melt the chocolate in a heatproof bowl over a pan of simmering water, then slowly add the liqueur to taste. Leave to cool for 10 minutes.

3 Whip the cream in a bowl until soft peaks form, then whisk in the cool sugar syrup. Gradually fold in the melted chocolate.

4 Transfer the mixture to an ice-cream maker and churn until thick. (If you do not have an ice-cream maker, freeze in a suitable container; after 2-4 hours, when partially frozen, whisk thoroughly, then return to the freezer; whisk twice more during freezing.) Once the ice cream is ready, store in the freezer.

5 For the base, crush the amaretti biscuits between 2 sheets of greaseproof paper using a rolling pin. Divide the amaretti crumbs between four 10 cm (4 inch) individual loose-bottomed tins, 2.5 cm (1 inch) in depth. Spread evenly and sprinkle with the liqueur. Press the crumb mixture well down and place the tins in the freezer.

6 To prepare the white chocolate mousse, place the 2 whole eggs, egg yolk and caster sugar in a bowl over a pan of simmering water and whisk until pale and creamy.

7 Meanwhile, sprinkle the gelatine over 15 ml (1 tbsp) water in a small bowl, allow to soften, then stand over a pan of simmering water until dissolved.

8 Melt the white chocolate in a heatproof bowl over a pan of simmering water, then leave to cool for about 10 minutes. Stir the cooled chocolate into the whisked egg, and then add the gelatine and mix thoroughly.

9 In another bowl, whisk the cream until starting to thicken. In a separate bowl, whisk the egg white until it forms soft peaks. Lightly fold the chocolate mixture into the cream until evenly incorporated, then slowly fold this into the whisked egg white.

10 To assemble, remove the tins from the freezer and half-fill with the ice cream. Carefully pour the white chocolate mousse on top until it reaches the top of the tins. Place in the freezer for 1½-2 hours.

11 Remove the desserts from the freezer 10 minutes before serving. Run a knife around the inside of the tins, and carefully transfer the desserts to individual plates. Dust with cocoa powder to serve.

Carolyn Dyer

Cappuccino Ice Cream with Dark Chocolate Sauce

40 g (1½ oz) caster sugar
2 egg yolks
150 ml (¼ pint) cold strong black coffee
150 ml (¼ pint) double cream
150 ml (¼ pint) milk

Dark Chocolate Sauce:
50 g (2 oz) plain chocolate, in pieces
45 ml (3 tbsp) milk

To Serve:
Langue de Chat Biscuits (see right)

1 Dissolve the sugar in 30 ml (2 tbsp) water in a pan over a low heat, then increase the heat and boil for 2-3 minutes. Allow the syrup to cool slightly. Whisk the egg yolks in a bowl until light in colour, then pour in the syrup in a steady stream, whisking continuously.

2 In a large bowl, whisk together the coffee, cream and milk until light and frothy. Gradually add this to the whisked egg mixture, whisking thoroughly.

3 Transfer the mixture to an ice-cream maker and churn for 15-20 minutes until thick and well chilled, but not frozen solid. Transfer to 4 chilled serving dishes and freeze until solid.

4 If you don't have an ice-cream maker, transfer the mixture to a shallow freezer-proof container and freeze for 2-3 hours until mushy. Turn into a bowl and whisk with a fork to break up the ice crystals. Refreeze until half-frozen, then whisk once more. Freeze in the serving dishes.

5 Meanwhile make the chocolate sauce. Melt the chocolate in a heatproof bowl set over a saucepan of hot water or in the microwave on low. Whisk the milk into the melted chocolate until smooth. Leave to cool for about 15 minutes.

6 To serve, transfer the ice cream to the refrigerator about 15 minutes before serving to soften slightly. Pour on the chocolate sauce and serve with Langue de Chat Biscuits.

Kerry Church

Langue de Chat Biscuits

25 g (1 oz) butter
40 g (1½ oz) vanilla sugar
½ egg, size 3, beaten
25 g (1 oz) plain flour, sifted

1 Cream the butter and sugar together in a bowl until soft and light. Beat in the egg a little at a time, then fold in the flour.

2 Transfer the mixture to a piping bag fitted with a 1 cm (½ inch) plain nozzle. Pipe 7.5 cm (3 inch) lengths on a baking sheet lined with non-stick baking parchment, spacing them well apart.

3 Cook in a preheated oven at 220°C (425°F) mark 7 for 6-7 minutes until pale and golden. Leave on the baking sheet for 1 minute then, using a spatula, transfer the biscuits to a wire rack to cool.

Kerry Church

Coconut Ice Cream in Brandy Snap Baskets

For this dessert, it is preferable to make the ice cream a day in advance and leave in the freezer overnight.

150 g (5 oz) coconut powder
300 ml (½ pint) whipping cream
300 ml (½ pint) Greek-style yogurt
15 ml (1 tbsp) sugar
30-45 ml (2-3 tbsp) Malibu

Brandy Snap Baskets:
125 g (4 oz) butter
125 g (4 oz) caster sugar
125 g (4 oz) golden syrup
125 g (4 oz) plain flour
5 ml (1 tsp) ground ginger

To Decorate:
mint sprigs
icing sugar, for dusting

1 Add the coconut powder to the cream, stirring to dissolve. Mix the coconut cream, yogurt, sugar and Malibu together in a bowl.

2 Pour into the ice-cream maker and churn for 20-40 minutes until thick and firm. Transfer to a freezerproof container, cover and freeze until required. (See note.)

3 To make the brandy snap baskets, put the butter, sugar and syrup in a saucepan and heat gently until dissolved and evenly blended. Remove from the heat and stir in the flour and ginger. Beat thoroughly and leave to cool.

4 Place 2 heaped teaspoonfuls of the mixture well apart on a greased baking tray and spread into rounds with the back of a spoon. Bake in a preheated oven at 180°C (350°F) mark 4 for 7-10 minutes until golden brown. Leave on the baking tray for about 1 minute to cool slightly, then carefully lift off with a palette knife and mould each one over a lemon or upturned ramekin to form a basket shape. When set, carefully remove the baskets and set aside. Repeat to make 5 or 6 baskets, to allow for any breakages.

5 To serve, set a brandy snap basket on each serving plate. Dip an ice-cream scoop into hot water, then scoop the ice cream into the brandy snap baskets, placing two scoops in each one. Decorate with sprigs of mint and dust with icing sugar. Serve immediately.

Judith Elliott

Note: If you do not have an ice-cream maker, freeze the ice cream in a shallow container, whisking the semi-frozen mixture several times during freezing to break down the ice crystals and ensure an even-textured result.

If the brandy snaps set firm before you have time to shape them, return the baking tray to the oven for ½-1 minute to soften.

Iced Coffee Amaretti Soufflés

12 amaretti biscuits
2 egg whites
175 g (6 oz) vanilla sugar
90 ml (6 tbsp) water
7.5 ml (1½ tsp) instant coffee dissolved in 7.5 ml (1½ tsp) hot water, or very strong black coffee
15 ml (1 tbsp) Grand Marnier
350 ml (12 fl oz) double cream

To Serve:
4 toasted whole almonds
icing sugar for dusting

1 Prepare 4 ramekins by securing a non-stick baking parchment collar around each one, to stand 5 cm (2 inches) above the rims. Put the amaretti biscuits in a plastic bag and crush with a rolling pin.

2 Whisk the egg whites until stiff. Dissolve the sugar in the water in a heavy-based saucepan over a gentle heat, then bring to the boil and bubble for 3 minutes. Pour the syrup onto the egg whites in a thin stream, whisking constantly at a high speed. Continue whisking until cool, then add the coffee and Grand Marnier.

3 Whip the cream in a separate bowl until thick but not stiff, then lightly fold into the mixture.

4 Spoon the soufflé mixture into the ramekins until they are just over half-full, then sprinkle on a thick layer of crushed biscuits. Cover with the remaining soufflé mixture, until it stands 2.5 cm (1 inch) above the rims.

5 Freeze the soufflés for 1½-2 hours, then carefully remove the paper collars. Coat the sides and tops with the remaining crushed biscuits and place a toasted almond on the top of each one. Dust the tops with sifted icing sugar.

Sarah Marsh

Iced Passion Fruit Soufflé in a Caramel Cage

Soufflé:
2 eggs (size 3), separated
75 g (3 oz) icing sugar
90 ml (3 fl oz) passion fruit juice (see note)
250 ml (8 fl oz) double cream

Caramel Cages:
250 g (9 oz) caster sugar
50 ml (2 fl oz) liquid glucose
a little vegetable oil

To Decorate:
12 small strawberries
½ passion fruit

Strawberry Coulis:
125 g (4 oz) fresh strawberries
icing sugar, to taste

1 Whisk the egg yolks and half of the icing sugar together in a bowl, using an electric whisk if possible, until very pale and foamy. Add the passion fruit juice. In a separate bowl, whisk the egg whites until stiff, then whisk in the rest of the icing sugar. Whip the cream in another bowl until thick. Fold the passion fruit mixture into the whipped cream, then carefully fold in the whisked egg white mixture.

2 Divide the mixture between 4 individual 150 ml (¼ pint) freezerproof moulds. Cover with cling film and freeze until firm.

3 For the caramel, dissolve the sugar in 90 ml (6 tbsp) water in a heavy-based pan over a low heat, then bring to the boil. Add the liquid glucose and cook until the syrup turns a pale caramel colour, ie until it registers 165°C (330°F) on a sugar thermometer. Take off the heat and leave to rest for 2 minutes.

4 Meanwhile with your hand, spread the tiniest amount of oil over the back of a ladle. Dip a spoon into the caramel, let the excess run off then trickle the thread to and fro over the ladle to create a basket. Repeat this procedure if necessary, then gently twist the cage free. Repeat to make a further 3 cages and place into an airtight container. Do not leave them in a humid atmosphere, otherwise they will go sticky and collapse.

5 Dip the strawberries for decoration into the remaining caramel. If the caramel is too thick at this stage, gently reheat. Place the strawberries on non-stick baking parchment and keep in an airtight container.

6 To make the strawberry coulis, purée the strawberries in a blender or food processor, adding icing sugar to taste. Pass through a sieve into a bowl, cover and chill in the refrigerator until required.

7 About 30 minutes before serving, turn out the soufflés onto individual serving plates and place in the refrigerator to soften slightly while still retaining their shape.

8 To serve, spoon the passion fruit pulp on top of the soufflés and cover each soufflé with a caramel cage. Place a spoonful of strawberry coulis to one side of the plate and top with 3 caramel strawberries. Serve immediately.

Gill Tunkle

Note: For the required quantity of juice you will need 8-10 passion fruit. Halve the passion fruit, scoop out the seeds and pulp into a sieve over a bowl and press with the back of a wooden spoon to extract the juice.

Iced Ginger Bombes with Vanilla Stars

2 egg whites
100 g (4 oz) caster sugar

To Assemble:
250 ml (8 fl oz) double cream
grated rind of 1 lemon
30 ml (2 tbsp) kirsch
15 ml (1 tbsp) caster sugar
45 ml (3 tbsp) marinated ginger and crystallised fruits (see note)

Vanilla Stars:
100 g (4 oz) unsalted butter, chilled
50 g (2 oz) icing sugar
75 g (3 oz) plain flour
25 g (1 oz) cornflour
pinch of baking powder
pinch of salt
1 moist vanilla pod, seeds and pulp extracted

To Serve:
few preserved stem ginger slices
kirsch for sprinkling

1 To make the meringues, whisk the egg whites until stiff, then gradually whisk in half of the sugar a spoonful at a time. Fold in the rest of the sugar, using a metal spoon, to yield a firm, glossy meringue. Spoon into small mounds on a baking sheet lined with non-stick baking parchment. Bake in a preheated oven at 95°C (200°F) barely mark ¼ for 2 hours. Transfer to a wire rack to cool.

2 Line 4 individual bombe moulds with cling film. Break up the meringues roughly. Whisk the cream until fairly stiff, then fold in the meringues together with the remaining ingredients. Divide between the moulds; freeze until firm.

3 To make the vanilla stars, cream the butter with the icing sugar in a food processor. Sift the dry ingredients together and add to the creamed mixture with the vanilla pulp and seeds. Work briefly, until the dough begins to hold together. Chill in the refrigerator for about 30 minutes.

4 Carefully roll out the dough to a 5 mm (¼ inch) thickness between sheets of lightly floured non-stick baking parchment. Cut out stars, using a suitable cutter, prick with a fork and place on a baking sheet. Bake in a preheated oven at 180°C (350°F) mark 4 for 15-20 minutes until pale golden brown. Cool on a wire rack.

5 Turn the iced bombes out on to plates and top with a little ginger and kirsch. Serve with the vanilla stars.

Orlando Murrin

Note: Keep a jar of preserved stem ginger, crystallised pineapple and sultanas macerating in brandy.

Index

I

J

K

L

M

N